SECONDARY CERTIFICATE SERIES

Secondary Certificate English

SECONDARY CERTIFICATE SERIES

General Editor:
K. W. WATKINS, B.Sc.(Econ.), Ph.D.

FACING LIFE'S CHALLENGE
A Study of Mark's Gospel for Today
J. HILLS COTTERILL, B.A., Dip.Th.

SECONDARY CERTIFICATE MATHEMATICS
D. T. DANIEL, B.A., Dip.Ed.

SECONDARY CERTIFICATE ENGLISH
P. S. MORRELL, B.A.

COMMERCE AND LIFE
K. LAMBERT, M.A.(Ed.), B.Sc.(Econ.), A.M.B.I.M.

HOUSECRAFT TODAY
G. M. SUTTON

RURAL SCIENCE COURSE
J. A. SHORNEY, M.I.Biol., Dip.R.Ed.

PHYSICS
I. M. L. JENKINS, B.Sc.

BIOLOGY
H. T. PASCOE, B.Sc.

CHEMISTRY
E. J. HANMORE, B.Sc.

LIFE IN OUR SOCIETY
K. LAMBERT, M.A.(Ed.), B.Sc.(Econ.), A.M.B.I.M.

THE WORKING WORLD OF PHYSICS
I. M. L. JENKINS, B.Sc.

Secondary Certificate English

P. S. MORRELL, B.A. Dip. Ed.

Thomas Nelson and Sons Ltd
Nelson House Mayfield Road
Walton-on-Thames Surrey
KT12 5PL UK

Nelson Blackie
Wester Cleddens Road
Bishopbriggs
Glasgow G64 2NZ UK

Thomas Nelson Australia
102 Dodds Street
South Melbourne
Victoria 3205 Australia

Nelson Canada
1120 Birchmount Road
Scarborough Ontario
M1K 5G4 Canada

I(T)P Thomas Nelson is an International
Thomson Publishing Company

I(T)P is used under licence

First published by Thomas Nelson and Sons Ltd 1989

Reprinted 2000

Printed in Singapore

Preface

While others sit deploring poor standards of English, it is the teacher's job to find immediate remedies. Most pupils are on his side, though some might deny it: eventually they see the importance of English and start wanting to improve.

To resolve the confusion of earlier years, however, can be an immense task. English has so many aspects, and a teacher helping boys and girls through the last year or two of their examination course must ensure that all are thoroughly revised. To instil clear understanding and sound methods into his pupils he needs experience, ingenuity, sympathy (in both senses), and a useful textbook.

A book offering "packaged lessons" seems hardly useful at this stage. Successful books of this type provide a lively and well-planned rotation of work, but with older pupils especially, the ever-recurring pattern of exercises becomes tedious, and the piecemeal scattering of material throughout the chapters makes a sustained look at any specific aspect very difficult.

On the whole it seems desirable to collect advice and exercises for children of fourth and fifth year level into clearly defined sections, each dealing with one particular aspect of English. Teachers are then free to organise their own courses, selecting and blending material to suit their own pupils and the needs of any given time. The children may readily consult any section for advice or further practice, and the whole book thus becomes a useful aid to teacher and pupil alike. This method has been adopted here, and the detailed list of contents ensures quick and easy reference to any part of the book. The advice offered to pupils in each section is simply put and fully illustrated, with plenty of exercises to follow.

The general level intended is that of the new C.S.E. examination, but the book will also help children preparing for G.C.E. "O" Level in English. There is ample material to last throughout the fourth year and the first two terms of the fifth year. During the final Summer Term the book's use as a reference guide would be supplemented with practice examination papers.

The aim has not been solely to produce an examination primer. All aspects examined in English have been covered, but so also have many broader issues of taste and appreciation. Artistry in language, as distinct from utility, receives full consideration, and the chapter on

v

literature surveys all that young people need consider when learning to enjoy stories, poems, and plays. The reading lists should help them find plenty of worthwhile reading.

In dealing with spelling, punctuation, vocabulary, and common errors, the intention has been to present essential facts and dangers in simple form, with multiple exercises carefully chosen for timely remedial treatment.

Grateful thanks are due to my colleague, John F. Glass, M.A., for many helpful suggestions; and to Kenneth W. Watkins, Ph.D., for his editorial advice and encouragement.

P. S. Morrell

Harden, 1964

Acknowledgments

For permission to reproduce extracts from copyright material thanks are due to the following:

Edward Arnold (Publishers) Ltd, from *Metalwork* by G. Keeley; B. T. Batsford Ltd, from *A History of Everyday Things in England*, Vol. 4, by M. and C. H. B. Quennell; Basil Blackwell, from *The Nature of the Universe* by Fred Hoyle; G. Bell & Sons Ltd, from *Ski-ing for Beginners* by F. Broderman and G. A. McPartlin; W. Blackwood & Sons Ltd, for "The Shining Streets of London" by A. E. Noyes; The Bodley Head Ltd, from *College Days* by Stephen Leacock; Nigel Calder and Phoenix House Ltd, from *Robots*; Jonathan Cape Ltd and Mrs H. M. Davies, for "The Kingfisher" by W. H. Davies; Jonathan Cape Ltd and the author, for "Now the Full-throated Daffodils" by C. Day Lewis; Cassell & Co Ltd, from *The Cruel Sea* by Nicholas Monsarrat; Chatto & Windus Ltd, from *Tiger in the Smoke* by Margery Allingham; Wm. Collins, Sons & Co Ltd, from *South with Scott* by Admiral Lord Mountevans; Miss D. E. Collins, for an extract from "The Wind in the Trees" from *Tremendous Trifles* by G. K. Chesterton; Curtis Brown Ltd, for "The Zebras" from *Adamastor* by Roy Campbell; J. M. Dent & Sons Ltd, from *Quite Early One Morning* by Dylan Thomas, and *All the Best in France* by Sydney Clark; English Universities Press Ltd, from *Dogs as Pets for Boys and Girls* by Lt.-Col. C. E. G. Hope; Faber & Faber Ltd, for "The Barn" from *Collected Poems* of Stephen Spender, and an extract from "Street Scene" from *Collected Poems* of Louis Macneice; Tony Gibson, from *Jobs and Careers* published by Victor Gollancz Ltd; Rupert Hart-Davis Ltd, from *The Drunken Forest* by Gerald Durrell and *The Golden Honeycomb* by Vincent Cronin; W. Heinemann Ltd, from *The M.C.C. Cricket Coaching Book*; Arnold Haskell and Phoenix House Ltd, from *Going to the Ballet*; Francis Brett Young and W. Heinemann Ltd, from *This Little World*; Longmans Green & Co Ltd, from *Ring of Bright Water* by Gavin Maxwell, and *The Hidden Persuaders* by Vance Packard; Lutterworth Press, from *Understanding Science* by W. H. Crouse and *Quest in Paradise* by David Attenborough; the literary executors of the late Sir Hugh Walpole and Macmillan & Co Ltd, from *Jeremy*; the author's representatives and Macmillan & Co Ltd, for "Worlds" by W. W. Gibson, from *Collected Poems 1905–1925*; Methuen & Co Ltd, from *The Growth of Mechanical Power* by Miles Tomalin; Elizabeth Nicholas, from "Second Sight", published in the *Elizabethan*; Penguin Books and the author, from *Sailing* by Peter Heaton; Routledge & Kegan Paul Ltd and the author, from *The Loch Ness Monster* by Tim Dinsdale; Martin Secker & Warburg Ltd, from *The Misfits* by Arthur Miller; Sidgwick & Jackson Ltd and the author's representatives, for "The Blackbird" from *The Collected Poems of John Drinkwater*; The Royal Society for the Protection of Birds and The Society of Authors, from *Far Away and Long Ago* by W. H. Hudson; The Society of Authors as the literary representatives of the estate of the late Laurence Binyon, for "The Little Dancers"; Ward Lock & Co Ltd, from *A Study in Scarlet* by Sir A. Conan Doyle; Frederick Warne & Co Ltd, from *The Observer's Book of Astronomy* by Patrick Moore, and Norman Nicholson for "Whitehaven" from *Rock Face*.

In some cases it has not been possible to trace the copyright holder. Should any infringement have occurred the publishers tender their apologies.

Contents

Every topic treated in 'this book is listed below, the page-references showing where advice and exercises may be found. Make a habit of re-reading the appropriate advice before tackling any exercise; in this way you will soon learn the methods necessary for successful work.

Contents

Contents

1 Your Writing Purposes

This chapter is really an introduction to Chapters Two, Three, and Four, which explain in detail the various writing tasks you need to master. The tasks are listed here, with a note on "style" or approach to writing, and there are some hints to help you brush up your knowledge of the three basic elements of all writing: words, sentences, and paragraphs.

The tasks considered

Writing is a "do it yourself" job that all must learn, for nobody can conveniently get through life today without it. Letters, notes, reports, instructions all need to be written and are important ways of communicating ideas to other people; we cannot rely on speech alone. Much of your work in English seeks to help you master the art of effective writing, and the main tasks you will meet are as follows:

Group 1	Group 2
Notes or memoranda	Personal diary entries
Telegrams	Notes for talks and speeches
Advertisements	Informal letters
Postcards	Artistic prose descriptions
Brief definitions	Essays
Reports	Magazine articles
Descriptions of objects and processes	
Business letters	

Style—your approach to writing

The writing tasks are grouped as shown because each group demands a special approach, or "style" of writing. In the tasks of Group 1, the essential needs are clarity, simplicity, and conciseness. You cannot waste words on a postcard or in a telegram, and nobody will thank you for a "woolly" or "long-winded" report, an unnecessarily long business letter, or instructions that are not clear. The tasks of Group 2, however, need a different approach. While clarity, the essential feature of all good

1

writing, is certainly needed, there is not now such an urgent need for simplicity or conciseness, for many of these more "artistic" writing jobs will be all the better if you spread yourself in using words: a friend loves to receive a long, newsy letter; many a girl delights in keeping a personal diary, deliciously long and detailed; an essayist or speaker may glory in an elaborate arrangement of cleverly expressed ideas, creating the same effect as an intricate crystal chandelier, or a jewel with many glittering facets.

Whenever you consider your purpose in writing, therefore, decide first what your approach should be: the clear, simple, and concise approach needed for most everyday writing, or the more stylish approach, using words with special regard for their artistic effect. The style of writing you choose must, of course, be suited to the writing job you have to do—it is a matter of commonsense judgment. You would never write applying for a post in the chatty style you use when writing to close friends, nor would you write like a poet when asked for a technical description of how to scrub a floor:

> Come, grasp thy scrubber in a milk-white hand, the while ye scatter droplets, crystal pure, around . . .

Most of your writing for everyday purposes will be of the clear, simple, and concise type, but it is worth considering the other type also: a person who can write (or speak) impressively and persuasively, choosing words for clever effect, will certainly win influence amongst those he meets. In the course of this book all the different elements of style are considered in some detail; look first, however, at the "raw materials" from which you will fashion your writing.

WORDS, WORDS, WORDS

A painter uses colours, arranging them in patterns and shapes, to express his ideas or portray what he sees. In writing, you will use words as your raw material, choosing and arranging them in patterns of sentences and paragraphs, to express your ideas.

Every single word has some sort of mental association for us: biscuit, run, sit, towards, with, through—all conjure up distinct pictures in the mind; it is quite wonderful, really. Through long centuries languages have developed, each containing many words that can be arranged to express quite complicated ideas. Today, as man's knowledge, especially in the newest fields of science, becomes more complex, new words are constantly being invented: it is not long since "sputnik", "telstar", "astronaut" were devised, to mention only three.

One part of growing up is to master as many words as you can: our ability to think clearly and to understand the ideas of others depends on our understanding of words and skill in manipulating them. You already have a large store, for general use, but probably still feel at a loss when reading more complicated ideas expressed in more difficult, "grown up" language. You must tackle the problem systematically; most students give no real attention to enlarging their vocabulary, thinking that words grow naturally in the mind. Nothing ever grows well without some attention. Here are some hints:

How to increase your word power

1 You must read widely, and not always the easiest reading you can find. Any teacher will tell you that a constant reader has a much better grasp of words than others.

2 Keep a special notebook (or fold in half lengthwise the rear pages of your English exercise book; when full, refold and use the other sides—a very useful way). Jot down all new words encountered.

3 Develop the habit of looking up new words in a dictionary: you have to notice and pursue words to learn them.

4 Look out for shades of difference in words of similar meaning: colleague, accomplice, collaborator, associate, etc. We call these similar words *synonyms*. Collect lists of them. Also note *antonyms*—words of opposite meaning.

5 Collect also words formed around various basic root-words: manage, manager, management, managerial, mismanage, unmanageable; practise, practice, practical, unpractical, impracticable, practitioner, etc.

6 Constantly check, revise, and test your new knowledge—and *use* it. Ask about words; and use your dictionary.

7 Notice spelling, as well as word-meanings. Invent little dodges to aid your memory: e.g. sep*arat*e: "*a rat* in it".

8 Work conscientiously through all the vocabulary lists in Chapter Six of this book. These have been chosen with the idea of enlarging your vocabulary to adult proportions.

A warning about words

Supposing you have mastered a vast vocabulary, just to oblige, and now find you often have a choice of several words to express a certain idea. Which to choose? The best guide in practical everyday writing or speech is to be as simple, direct, precise, and as brief as possible. Make sure you are the master over words—never let them master you. Sir Ernest Gowers, a famous civil servant, has given many samples of unnecessary wordiness, a fault in English which he calls "Gobbledygook".

> The position regarding this matter is that owing to the fact that two claims were made by two claimants of the same name some confusion arose.
> (Confusion arose because two people with the same name made a claim.)

The next one defies translation:

> To reduce the risk of war and establish conditions of lasting peace requires the closer co-ordination in the employment of their joint resources to underpin these countries' economies in such a manner as to permit the full maintenance of their social and material standards as well as to adequate development of the necessary measures.

In your more artistic writing, of course, a rich store of words will be very useful, but here again, do not overload things: preserve clarity at all costs, and choose your rich effects with care—too much elaboration will only result in a cluttered, overdone effect.

Sentence and paragraph

Words are the raw material of writing. We must now consider the problem of arranging them. You know, of course, that the two "units" of arrangement are called "sentence" and "paragraph". The whole purpose of arranging words in this way is to help you express ideas clearly, step by step, and to help the reader (or listener) to understand. It will be useful here to revise the main points you need to remember about sentences and paragraphs.

THE SENTENCE

A sentence is an arrangement of words expressing a complete idea:

> He caught the ball neatly.
> I hope to win a prize, if I am lucky.
> My friend will be visiting Paris at Easter.
> I should like to help you, but do not see how I can.

The following are *not* sentences: the ideas are not complete and do not make proper sense when standing alone:

> caught the ball
> if I am lucky
> be visiting Paris
> like to help you

A sentence must contain a *verb* (a "doing" word, suggesting some action or state of being) and a *subject* (the "doer" of the action suggested by the verb):

He lives here.
S V

Alice often visits us at weekends.
S   V

Mrs. Smith discovered the theft.
S   V

My sister has been reading your book.
S   V

Mr. Jones and Miss Phillips will be demonstrating the dance.
S   V

Note that both subject and verb may consist of more than one word. It would be wrong to regard the following as sentences:

> because I like it
> although you saw me

Both contain both a subject and a verb, but neither makes complete sense when standing alone. They are only parts of sentences:

> I should love to buy that blue coat, *because I like it.*
> You did not speak to me, *although you saw me.*

Never try to say too much in any one sentence: all clarity will be lost in a long, rambling state of confusion:

Although I had expected to see him by the river, he wasn't there, nor at the hostel, where we had arranged to meet later, and I didn't know what to do in case he had got lost somewhere or had an accident; if he had and was alone, he would need help, I thought, and so I have come to you to ask whether or not we ought to send out a search party or perhaps just wait a little longer.

5

At the same time, avoid writing always in the shortest of sentences: this results in a jerky, abrupt effect:

I came home early. My mother was out. I didn't know she would be out. It was teatime. I was hungry.

The best way is to vary both the length and structure of your sentences, to avoid monotony:

I came home early, but my mother was out. It had not occurred to me that she would be out, and I was hungry, for it was teatime.

Other faults that may spoil the clarity or effect of your sentences are using unnecessarily long words, more words than are really necessary, vagueness, poor arranging of sentence-parts, faulty grammar. (See Exercise 5.)

Summing up

Always ask yourself these questions:

Does my sentence make complete sense?
Has it a proper verb and subject?
Is it as clearly and simply arranged as possible?
Have I chosen the most suitable words?
Is it too long and rambling?
Is it too short and jerky?
Are there faults of grammar, punctuation, or spelling?

Exercises on sentences

1 Write a single clear sentence on each of the following topics:

Why a coal fire needs a chimney.

The kind of weather we expect in winter.

Furniture usually found in the sitting-room.

What you would like to be, and why.

How a cat differs from a dog.

When and where you went on your last holiday, and for how long.

What to do before crossing a busy road.

What you had for breakfast this morning.

Your name, age, sex, and address.

A teapot: its purpose and general appearance.

6

How to dry a plate when washing up.

What a sandwich consists of.

How summer clothing differs from winter clothing.

Points to look for when buying new shoes.

A bicycle pump: its purpose and general appearance.

How to sweep with a broom.

Your neighbour's hairstyle.

Your favourite television programme, and why you like it.

What you like best to do on Saturdays.

A brief description of an exercise book.

2 Some of the topics in Question 1, you might feel, lend themselves better to *two* or *three* sentences. Rewrite ten of your own choice in this way.

3 Rewrite the following sets of short, jerky sentences in any way you wish, to make in each case two or three longer, more smoothly flowing sentences (you may rearrange, as you wish).

(a) I have seen Charles. It was last night. He was outside the Odeon cinema. He was waiting for a friend. It was about seven. I do not know his friend. It is a boy. He is tall and dark. I think his name is Richard.

(b) There is a dance next week. It should be enjoyable. I am going. I shall have a new dress. Mary is going also. Her mother gave her permission. Are you coming with us? You would enjoy it. I know you would.

(c) We faced our first task. It was to set up our tents. First I unloaded the camping gear. It was very difficult. The wind was blowing hard. It came right across the moor. We thought it would blow us away. The tent canvas billowed like a parachute. We clung on to the ropes. At last we succeeded.

(d) Harry and Joan are my friends. You know them. They have opened a shop. Let me tell you about it. They sell fancy goods. It is near the main shopping centre. They hope to do well. Harry has his paintings on view. He hopes to sell these as well.

(e) I have not been out today. I did not feel like it. Besides, I had plenty to do at home. It is Arthur's birthday tomorrow. He likes to celebrate in style. We are having a party. Will you come? We should like you to come. There will be fifty guests.

4 Rewrite these sentences, which are far too long, dividing them into sets of two or three shorter sentences. Be careful, however, to avoid giving a jerky, abrupt effect:

(*a*) Next Saturday, if it does not rain, I hope to visit my friend Edith, who lives at the other end of our town near the park, and we shall spend a few pleasant hours listening to her favourite records and planning what we shall wear when we go together on the club outing next month, if we go, that is.

(*b*) My uncle is a strange man with a long white moustache that falls into his tea whenever he drinks, and a strange habit of sucking the end of it when he is talking about anything or thinking hard, and a long pointed nose, turned up at the end and bent a little to one side.

(*c*) The reason I have not written to you for so long is that I have had influenza, which left me feeling very tired, and apart from that there was much to do in the shop, with Frank away on holiday and only myself to look after the place in his absence, in addition to my duties about the house and looking after the garden.

(*d*) The wind was howling about the old barn, tearing wisps of straw from the sagging thatched roof and generally making the whole building creak alarmingly, as if it was about to be blown away at any minute across the field in the corner of which it had stood for centuries, at least two, to my certain knowledge.

(*e*) When I reached home I was soaked to the skin and decided that the best thing to do would be to take a hot bath first, which I did, only to hear, as soon as I was sitting in the warm, soapy water, a thunderous knocking on the back door, which turned out to be the local policeman, wondering why our front door had been left wide open, and surprised to see me wrapped only in a towel, dripping my way downstairs to see him.

5 All these sentences are faulty, for the reasons stated. Rewrite each one, in improved form (you may alter the wording).

(*a*) *Badly arranged parts*

An antique table is wanted by a lady with a polished top and four ornamental legs.

8

We were pleased to see Mrs. Dalrymple-Jones at the Show, and First Prize in the class for fat pigs went to her.

A good home is sought for an Alsatian; he will eat anything and is particularly fond of children.

One afternoon between Darley and Hampton during a walk I met my old friend Arthur, after dinner, going home for tea on his horse, after finishing his work at the stables.

My younger brother one afternoon, playing with his bow and arrows, saw some movement in the bushes near by, and fitting an arrow quickly fired it, only to hit my father between the flowering shrubs.

We recognised the man as the one who had fired the shots from the large wart on the end of his nose.

(b) *More words than are really needed*

My failure was owing to the fact that I had omitted to ensure my adequate preparation for the test.

Will you please repair, make good, and otherwise restore to working order this old lawn-mower?

I can neither understand, comprehend, nor make any sense of the piece of writing you have submitted to me for marking purposes.

Insofar as we have hitherto not taken receipt of your letter, I regret not being in a position to take any action with regard to rendering you assistance in the matter to which you referred earlier.

(For many more of these see Chapter Five, Exercises 54–5. For sentences involving common faults of grammar, see Chapter Seven.)

6 These statements should be in one complete sentence. The parts in italic type cannot stand alone. Do the necessary joining.

(a) We went for a long walk yesterday. *A very enjoyable time.*

(b) Three reasons are offered for the popularity of skating. *To keep fit. To learn something difficult. To train for competitions.*

(c) The lights sparkled in a great array of colours. *Red, orange, blue, green, yellow. All colours imaginable.*

(d) I like the chance to relax. *Just sitting, resting after work.*

(e) My sister bought that blue coat. *As it was so nice. Cheap too.*

You should avoid this habit in writing: the parts in italics are *not* sentences, and should not stand alone as they do here.

7 Make proper sentences, incorporating these incomplete statements:

> because I like swimming.
> in the garden.
> on the way to the station.
> to add a little brightness to the party.
> playing with an old piece of carpet and a rubber bone.

8 Write out these sentences and underline the most important statement (or statements) in each:

Example. Although it was quite dark, <u>we managed to find our way.</u>

(a) We like to watch television, if there is a good programme on.

(b) I shall be seeing Harry when he comes here next week.

(c) Did you manage to keep warm this winter, despite the cold?

(d) I shall get the book for you and shall be seeing you soon.

(e) We could not solve the problem, for we did not know how.

(f) The water froze and it burst our pipes.

(g) He took no notice of his father's advice, although it was sound.

(h) Owing to the long delay, we have not yet received his letter.

(i) He managed to build the shed even without my help.

(j) They walked straight past us without speaking, as if they had not seen us.

THE PARAGRAPH

A sentence is an arrangement of ideas clearly expressing a complete idea. A great mass of sentences, however, presenting idea after idea without pause, would be very tiring to read, and so paragraphs are used. A paragraph contains several sentences, grouped together because their ideas all relate to one main theme. In this example the sentences belong together because all deal with the advantages of having a private "den".

> There are real advantages in having one's own "den". We all need to be alone sometimes, to relax, follow hobbies, or do homework without interruption. Sometimes you might wish to entertain a friend away from the family, to talk privately or listen to records. You can also arrange a "den" of your own just as you wish, perhaps even choosing the colour-scheme and equipment, without having to consider anybody else.

You can easily see the value of paragraphing: each paragraph presents a clear-cut set of ideas, all dealing with one main theme. You can focus your attention on these and make sure you understand them, before passing on to the next paragraph, which has a new set of ideas grouped round a new main theme.

When writing your own paragraphs, remember these two rules:

Never introduce more than one main theme into a single paragraph.

Ensure that every sentence you put into a paragraph expresses an idea strictly related to that paragraph's main theme.

The arranging of sentences in a paragraph is important: when you have decided on the ideas you will include, arrange them in the most sensible and effective order. It often helps to make a little plan; this and common sense will soon teach you proper arrangement.

Avoid allowing your paragraphs to become too long and rambling: this will spoil their clarity. If you plan first what is to go into any one paragraph, you can keep its length within manageable limits.

There are two main types of paragraph: some contain what we call a "topic sentence", and others have an "implicit theme".

A topic sentence states clearly the main theme of the paragraph: "These are the main disadvantages of living in the country," or: "I had an unpleasant experience last night."

In the paragraph with implicit theme, there is no direct statement of what the paragraph is about, but this becomes clear as you read:

> After wearing the costume only once, I noticed serious fraying of the shoulder-straps, owing to faulty stitching. More serious was the running of the dyes used in the material. Worst of all, the costume has now shrunk so badly that I can no longer wear it.

. There is no topic sentence here, but it is clear that the paragraph lists faults found in a bathing-costume.

Exercises on writing paragraphs

1 Jot down, in brief note form, five or six random ideas for sentences to be included in each of these paragraph themes, making sure your ideas are fully relevant:

(a) The delights of a hot bath	(b) Tinned food
Plans for spending five pounds	The face of a friend
Father Christmas	Equipment for a picnic
Your present mood	Pleasures of the country

2 Do the same, using these main themes:

  (a) Feelings on getting wet   (b) Crocodiles
      Breaking in new shoes   On staying up late
      Spring cleaning   Sandwiches
      Christmas shopping   On having a bad memory

3 Using the random notes made for Questions 1 and 2, arrange and write a paragraph on each theme, paying special attention to the order of ideas.

4 Plan and write a short paragraph on each of these themes, paying special attention to the order in which you present your ideas:

  (a) A beatnik described   (b) Your life: the first five years
      Casual clothes   Advantages of hovercraft
      Essential drawing equipment   Treating a cold
      Feeding a dog   Habits I dislike

5 Plan and write a short paragraph on each of these themes.

  (a) *To contain a topic sentence*   (b) *To contain an implicit theme*
      Cutting the grass   Polishing metal
      The perfect brother (or sister)   I love receiving letters
      Snow-clearing machines   A man and a mouse
      Schoolchildren need a Union   Old shoes in the rain
      I have blisters   Mail order catalogues

6 Choose any of the paragraphs you have written from Question 5 (a) and rewrite each, deleting the topic sentence and adjusting as necessary to give an implicit theme.

7 Choose any of the paragraphs you have written from Question 5 (b), with implicit theme, and adjust them so that they contain a topic sentence.

8 *Arranging ideas.* Rearrange each of these sets of random ideas into a sensible order, and expand them into sentences, making in each case an effective paragraph of about 100 words. If you include a topic sentence, underline it; if not, label your paragraph "implicit theme":

(*a*) *Wedding*

    parson's name
    place of reception
    bride's outfit
    bridegroom's name
    date and time of
    bride's family
    plans for honeymoon
    bridegroom's family

(*b*) *Accident*

    vehicles involved
    hospital
    names of injured
    date and time
    cause of
    place
    witness said
    police summoned by

9 *Arranging ideas.* These random ideas suggest material for two successive paragraphs. Sort them out and write the paragraphs, each to contain about 60 words, the first with a topic sentence, the second with implicit theme:

Preparing for an interview, and "enduring it" :

manager's greeting	feelings on way there	success
preparing best clothes	upset manager's papers	applying
tongue-tied at first	practising at mirror	confidence
letter of invitation	stark fear	growing

10 *More themes for paragraphs.* Plan and write a paragraph on each of these themes, remembering the need for unity of ideas and sensible arrangement (80–100 words for each paragraph):

Office work	Dirty work	A tiny baby
My tool kit	Jet propulsion	Telegrams
Telephone voices	On being late	Photography
Sunday dinner	Braces are vulgar	My taste in ties

2 Plain Writing for Every Day

After the general advice about writing given in Chapter 1, we shall now look at the tasks of the First Group:

> Notes or memoranda
> Telegrams
> Advertisements
> Postcards
> Brief definitions
> Reports
> Descriptions of objects
>   and processes
> Business letters

In all these tasks your writing must have *clarity, simplicity*, and *conciseness*.

Each task is dealt with in turn, with hints, and exercises for you to try.

NOTES OR MEMORANDA

The purpose of a note or memorandum is to give brief information or instructions to another person, or to act as an aid to memory for yourself.

Hints

1 For brevity, note-form is better than full sentences, providing the notes are clear.

2 Some words may also be abbreviated, but not if clarity is lost.

3 For clarity and simplicity, carefully arrange the ideas in the best order.

Example

To reach 29 Acacia Avenue, N.21, from Kings X

1 By Underground, Picc. Line, direction *Cockfosters*, to *Wood Green*.

2 Leave W.G. Station, cross road to bus-stop (near). Take Nos. 29 or 629; ask for *Winchmore Hill Broadway*.

3 Dismount at B'way, ask for *Station Rd.* (near).

4 Acacia Ave. 2nd left up St. Rd.

Exercises

Write notes on the following:

1 Tasks to do in town next Saturday morning.

2 Directions to a new acquaintance on how to reach your home from a village not far away.

3 Preparations to be made for going away on holiday.

4 Recipes for a friend: biscuits, jam, toffee, etc.

5 A message for someone due to call when you are out.

6 A telephone message received and noted for someone who is out.

7 Hints on a practical task, for a friend.

8 Jobs to be done in arranging a party.

9 Instructions given by mother for housework during her absence.

10 A journey by bus and train: memo of route, times, changes.

11 A shopping list for Christmas.

12 House removal: notes on jobs for day of departure.

13 Notes for friend on feeding your pets while you are away.

14 Notes for a revision programme before term examinations.

15 Others, of your own choosing.

TELEGRAMS

The telegraph service offers a useful way of sending a message quickly. Remember, though, if telephoning is possible, it might be cheaper.

Hints

1 With a charge of so much per word you cannot afford to use words freely: use every means of expressing the essential ideas clearly in as few words as possible. Ingenuity is needed.

2 Abbreviations will not help: even if shortened, a word still counts as a word.

3 You can often save on the name and address of the receiver: the surname only will often do, and the briefest address necessary to ensure arrival.

Examples

WASTEFUL

IMPROVED

Mr. Peter Lane,
The Gables, 39 Essex Road,
Mill Hill, London, N.W.7.
Will meet you tonight outside
Cameo seven o'clock. George.

Lane,
39 Essex Road, N.W.7.

Cameo tonight seven. George.

Tower Estate Agency, Ltd.,
Portland House, 332 Giles' Square,
Bournemouth, Hants.
Request you complete and return
house-conveyance document reference
PP/XY/323 without delay.
Frank Petch

Tower Estates,
332 Giles' Square,
Bournemouth.
Urgently need completed
PP/XY/323. Petch

Exercises

Write telegrams to suit these purposes. Invent the receiver's name and address each time.

1 You are returning home suddenly with a friend as guest. Warn your mother about preparations needed.

2 You are away on holiday and urgently need more money. Ask your unwilling father for a temporary loan. Be tactful!

3 You have forgotten important papers. Ask your brother to send them on, telling him where to find them and where to send them.

4 Ask a friend to reserve seats for a certain theatre for two days ahead, when you will be in town.

5 A taxi firm is to send a car to meet you late at night. State place, time, and destination.

6 Lively and witty wedding congratulations to friends.

7 Send excuses for an appointment missed through forgetfulness.

8 Send birthday greetings to a child. (A day late; you forgot to send a card.)

9 Cancel a hotel reservation, owing to a change of plans.

16

10 Your luggage has been stolen. Send home for essentials.

11 Arrange to meet your best friend at short notice for an important personal discussion. Give a hint of the subject.

12 State your inability to attend an important meeting, owing to a suddenly remembered more important engagement. You must be convincing.

13 Tactfully put off an imminent visit by an awkward relative.

14 A warm-hearted Christmas cable to a close relative abroad.

15 Others, of your own invention.

ADVERTISEMENTS

Preparing advertisements for appearance in newspaper columns is similar to writing telegrams: you pay for the words used, usually at so much per line in "classified" columns, or per square inch in "spaced" advertisements. To save money, you must be as brief as possible.

Hints

1 In classified advertisements, abbreviations will help, if they are recognisable, e.g. Wanted: furn. flat, 2 r'ms & kit. Mod. rent. Careful tenants. Box 0234.

2 For quick contact, use a telephone number if possible; people will not always bother to write to an address or box number.

3 In spaced advertisements you seek to attract attention by the use of larger lettering for some parts, by clever wording, and by effective spacing out. Make sure your wording is attractive and covers all the necessary facts, but do not overcrowd your space.

This   would be better than   *this*

Saturday, July 6th, 1962
GRAND FÊTE
(2.30 – 6 p.m.)
Free admission — Big prizes
PORTLAND SCHOOL — CLARE

A GARDEN FÊTE will be held at the Portland School, Clare, on Saturday, July 6th, 1962, from 2.30 to 6 p.m. Do come and enjoy all the fun of the fair. Lovely prizes and many attractions.

17

Exercises

1 Write classified advertisements on these themes:

(a) A cycle for sale.　　　　　(f) Baby-sitting services offered.
(b) A flat wanted.　　　　　　(g) Seeking part-time employment.
(c) Puppies for sale.　　　　　(h) An offer of gardening services.
(d) A club appeal for funds.　　(i) A wedding notice.
(e) An article lost.　　　　　　(j) Others, of your invention.

2 Write spaced advertisements for the following (useful sizes are 2″ × 1″, 4″ × 2″, but consult a local newspaper to see various other possible sizes):

(a) A church fête.　　　　　　(f) A tennis-club dance.
(b) A jumble sale.　　　　　　(g) An old pupils' reunion dinner.
(c) An amateur play.　　　　　(h) A ladies' hairdresser.
(d) A public meeting.　　　　　(i) A new restaurant.
(e) A shop sale.　　　　　　　(j) Others, of your invention.

POSTCARDS

A postcard is a convenient way of sending a brief message by post. Sizes vary nowadays, but a common size is 5½″ × 3½″. The plain ones, as you know, have one side for the message and on the other side you write the name and address of the receiver, the stamp being affixed in the upper right-hand corner. A picture postcard has its non-picture side divided into halves, one half for the message, and the other for the stamp and name and address of the receiver. On the opposite page you will see samples of both kinds. The top one shows the addressed side of a plain postcard; the lower one shows the back of a picture postcard.

Hints

1 Note, in the examples on the opposite page, the sloping layout of the receiver's name and address. (This layout is also used on envelopes.)

2 You need not start your message with "Dear So-and-So"—the date, followed by the message, and a signature only are customary.

18

POST CARD

Miss Alice Jones,
34 Princess Gardens,
North End,
Sussex.

19/6/63

POSTCARD PICTURE
BY JUDGES' LTD HASTINGS
ENGLAND

I am enjoying
lovely wet weather
here. It is a very
expensive place,
but the hotel is
good.

Harry

GREETINGS AND GOOD WISHES

James Smith Esq,
29 Church Lane,
Hounslow,
Middlesex.

3 Write in proper sentences; your use of words is limited only by the size of the space and of your writing. Some people pack in a great deal, but plan your layout; do not waste space at first and then cramp the last part together.

4 On informal postcards, as distinct from business messages, avoid well-worn comments about weather, "having lovely time", etc.; try to be vivid, amusing, interesting.

5 On picture postcards posted in various Continental countries a five-word greeting goes at a cheaper rate.

Exercises

Write "postcards" to suit the following purposes, in each case ruling a rectangle of $5\frac{1}{2}'' \times 3\frac{1}{2}''$, and using it as a plain or picture postcard, as you think suitable. Invent the receivers' names and addresses (two rectangles will be needed for plain postcards!):

1 To an old friend, suggesting a meeting in the near future.

2 To a business firm, asking them to investigate the delay in dealing with your order.

3 To an elderly aunt, declining an invitation to tea.

4 To a friend, from an English seaside resort.

5 To a plumber, asking him to call and repair slight damage.

6 To your grocer, giving a list of goods and requesting delivery.

7 To a friend, asking him to meet you at the station with his car. You have much luggage.

8 A reply to a friend's long letter, promising a letter very soon.

9 To an hotel, declining an offer of accommodation. (You have found better elsewhere.)

10 To the library, asking for a certain book to be reserved or ordered for you.

11 To a relative, hoping all is well after a long silence.

12 Five-word greetings from abroad.

13 To a taxi-firm, making an advance booking.

14 To a sports-club secretary, requesting a fixture for your team.

15 Others of your own invention.

BRIEF DEFINITIONS

You may often be asked "What is a so-and-so?" You have to state in a few words exactly what you understand by the item or word mentioned. Parents are familiar with this game. ("What is a rickshaw, Daddy?" "Mummy, what are wolves in sheep's clothing?") A few written exercises will help you to develop the art.

Hints

1   If you are defining some object, state briefly:

(*a*) the type or "family" of articles to which it belongs, e.g.:

> An egg-whisk is a *kitchen utensil*.
> A safety-pin is a type of *fastening*.

(*b*) Any special peculiarity of construction or appearance that makes it different from other articles of the same family, e.g.:

> A penknife is a cutting tool *with blades that fold into the handle for easy carrying in the pocket.* . . . .

(*c*) Finally, state the article's special uses, e.g.:

> A penknife is a cutting tool with blades that fold into the handle for easy carrying in the pocket. *It is useful for cutting small items, peeling apples, etc.*

2   If you have to define verbs, or abstract ideas such as "jealousy", "cowardice", "to procrastinate", it is a good idea to give a short example of these in action, e.g.:

> A person who seems unable, through fear, to face up to danger is said to display "cowardice".
> A person who puts off doing something that might easily be done immediately is said to "procrastinate".

N.B. Beware of defining such words in terms of the wrong part of speech, e.g.:

> Cowardice is *to be afraid.*
> To procrastinate is *when you put off doing something.*

(Cowardice is a *feeling*, not "to do something"; to procrastinate is *to do something*, not "when you do something".)

21

Exercises

Define briefly but clearly:

1

a hammer	a cup	a suitcase
a comb	a fork	a trunk
a sponge	a sock	a typewriter
a chair	an exercise book	a newspaper
a table	a carpet	an apron
a ruler	a pair of spectacles	a door
a pen	a potato	an overcoat
a clock	a shoe	a tractor
a watch	an umbrella	a bicycle
a helicopter	a saucepan	a dog-kennel

2

fear	jealousy	to boast
envy	admiration	to conquer
hope	hero-worship	to advertise
despair	complacency	to favour
thought	ignorance	to encourage
speech	education	to persuade
hunger	humility	to loathe
greed	blindness	to underestimate
longing	decay	to sightsee
ambition	growth	to assess

3 Define others of your own choosing: articles, verbs, or abstract qualities.

REPORTS

A report is a detailed statement prepared for someone's information by a person who has carried out a certain test or inquiry, examination or experiment, or who has observed something taking place. A report might be needed, for instance, on the condition of a car, or the police might ask you to give a "statement" of what you saw when an accident took place. A newspaper reporter might write a report on a public meeting and the views expressed there by various people; or you might be asked to give a report of the activities of your club during the past year.

Hints

1   Reports must be simply and clearly expressed; essential information only must be precisely and concisely given.

2   The contents must be arranged in a sensible order, emphasising the most important matters. Section-headings help.

3   Strictly speaking, there is no place in a report for expressing personal opinions; you should confine yourself, unless otherwise invited, to stating what was done, said, seen, or heard. Where personal views are included, a report ceases to be a true report, and becomes a statement coloured by opinion.

4   Sometimes you may be invited to give personal views, comments, or suggestions, but these should always be clearly labelled, and really form no part of the report itself, e.g. "*It seemed* as if the speaker was growing tired of the many questions asked, for after some time he *appeared to* be showing signs of growing impatience . . ." (This may or may not have been true and the reporter's wording clearly suggests that he might have been mistaken.)

Example

Here is a sample report, showing good arrangement, clear and simple statement of facts observed, and ending with a carefully guarded expression of opinions:

A report on the condition of the Hornet De Luxe sports cycle, serial number XP.107653, submitted for examination to Messrs. Hill and West, 3 Borough Road, East Cheam.

Date of examination: 3 April 1962.

Findings

(a) *General mechanical condition:* Good. Ball and roller bearings throughout show no wear or looseness. Frame sound. Wheels unbuckled, but two spokes in front wheel are bent and loose. Chain rather worn. Brakes and cables in good repair, but rear brake-blocks badly worn.

(b) *Accessories:* Dynamo lighting system inefficient, owing to worn brushes in dynamo and worn insulation to wiring. Mudguards both cracked and stays loose, causing rattle. Saddle sound, but seat-cover badly worn.

(c) *Paintwork and plating:* Condition only fair. Frame enamel badly chipped; plating of wheel-rims and handlebars rusted in many places.

Comments and Suggestions

Please note: The management will accept no legal responsibility for the views expressed in this section of the report.

The second-hand market value of this machine is estimated at about £7. Its appearance, however, seems at present unattractive owing to the faults listed in section (c) above. The mechanical and other faults listed in sections (a) and (b) also need urgent attention.

The estimate of cost for new mudguards, chain, rear brake-blocks, dynamo brushes and lighting-set wiring, seat-cover, two spokes, with necessary fitting, is £3. 5s. Re-enamelling of frame would cost an extra £1. 10s., and rubbing-down of rusted parts of plating a further 10s. Perhaps if these improvements were effected, the machine would fetch a good price when offered for sale.

Robert Hill (Proprietor)

This material is organised into clearly headed sections, containing only facts observed; the comments and opinions are reserved until the last section. The style approaches note-form (various "the's" omitted). This is acceptable here, but might not be so in other types of report.

You will get good practice in writing reports in your science lessons: your science teacher has no doubt already shown you how to write accounts of experiments under such headings as: "Apparatus", "Method", "Observations", "Conclusions".

Exercises

Write reports on:

1 The condition of some article you are offering for sale.

2 The state of your garden after a heavy storm.

3 An experiment you have carried out at school.

4 Faults you have observed in something you bought recently.

5 A lesson or talk you attended recently.

6 An accident you have witnessed.

7 An examination of your room after a burglary.

8 The year's activities in a school club.

9 Proceedings at a club's annual general meeting.

10 Your activities last Saturday.

11 Arrangements for a form party; details requested by the Head.

12 Recreational facilities for young people in your locality.

13 What you saw and did when a fire broke out next door.

14 An exhibition or display you have attended.

15 Others of your own choosing.

DESCRIPTIONS

This work involves the describing in detail of some object, or writing clear, step-by-step instructions on how to do something. The task of describing a picture is a variation of the same exercise; all three tasks offer excellent training in straight thinking and proper arrangement of ideas.

Sometimes the job is by no means easy; even a simple article like a deck-chair or a pair of scissors can be very tricky to describe in words and you will need plenty of practice to master the art. At the highest level this is called "technical writing" and some people earn their living by it, preparing handbooks of description and instructions for the working and maintenance of complex machinery. Now for some hints:

Describing objects

1 Your aim is to describe in words, without drawings, the appearance, construction, and use of some object, so that anyone reading your description can easily visualise it. One long-suffering student once described the task as "talking about a pair of scissors to a man from Mars".

2 The best way to start is to write a brief definition (see the hints on "Definitions"), relating the object to its main class or family of similar objects and stating its special features and its uses, e.g.:

> An umbrella is a portable shelter composed of a waterproof cloth canopy which may be tightly stretched in a circular, domed shape or collapsed round a central shaft when not in use. It protects the user from the rain.

3 Next you must give an account of the construction. Plan this carefully, stating the details in a sensible order. Several paragraphs may be needed, each one dealing with one of the main features. You will soon develop an eye for choosing the best order of ideas, and of course each article will present its special problems. The best way to deal with the umbrella is as follows:

(*a*) Central shaft and handle.

(*b*) Flexible steel ribs bearing canopy, and method of hinging to central shaft.

(*c*) Cloth canopy attached to these ribs.

25

(*d*) Rigid struts, hinged to ribs, and to sliding metal collar round central shaft.

(*e*) Spring clips let into shaft to fix collar to open or closed position.

(*f*) What happens when umbrella is opened or closed.

Study this completed account of the umbrella.

An umbrella is a portable shelter, composed of a waterproof cloth canopy which may be tightly stretched in a circular, domed shape, or collapsed round a central shaft when not in use. It protects the user from the rain.

The central shaft is strong, thin rod, circular in section and made of hardwood or steel. Its length may vary between two and three feet. One end carries a handle of convenient shape to allow one hand to hold the shaft upright. The other end is tapered slightly and has a metal cap or "ferrule". A man's umbrella can be used when closed as a walking stick and the ferrule protects the end from wear.

The cloth canopy rests on thin ribs of flexible steel, usually eight in number. These are hinged at one end around a metal collar fastened round the central shaft near the ferrule. The hinging allows the ribs to radiate outwards around the shaft like the spokes of a cartwheel, or lie flat around the shaft and roughly parallel to it. The length of each rib equals approximately the distance between the fixed collar and the commencement of the handle, measured along the central shaft.

The canopy is of waterproofed fabric, cut circular in shape to fit over the ribs when they project radially around the central shaft. It is made from several panels of material stitched together, each panel covering the space between two ribs, like the webbing between a duck's toes. The canopy is stitched firmly to either end of each rib and it fits snugly at the central shaft, leaving no space for rain to seep through. When the ribs lie flat around the central shaft, the canopy lies in neat, loose folds, enclosing both ribs and shaft, and may be furled and fastened tightly.

A second metal collar fits round the central shaft and may slide along it between the handle and fixed collar. Hinged around it are rigid metal struts, one for each umbrella rib. Their outer ends are hinged to the centre of their respective ribs. The length of these rigid struts is carefully calculated, so that when the sliding collar is moved towards the fixed collar, the struts exert a force at the centre of the ribs, making them bend like a bow because of the restricting circular canopy. Thus the canopy is tightly stretched into a circular domed shape.

A spring steel clip is let into the side of the shaft near the handle and another one several inches from the fixed collar. These clips may be pushed into the shaft, letting the sliding collar pass over them, or they may engage in a slit cut in the sliding collar and hold it firmly.

When the umbrella is in the open position the sliding collar is held by the clip nearer the fixed collar. To close the umbrella, release this clip and slide the collar back until it engages in the clip near the handle.

26

Notes

This is a student's effort. Note the care taken to explain everything and the sensible arrangement of ideas; he would have been in real trouble if any other order had been chosen! The account is fairly long and in this case it needs to be. Where size or design varies (lengths, handle patterns) only general information is given. Useful comparisons with familiar things also help one to see what is meant (spokes of a wheel; duck's webbed feet).

Try this description yourself, from memory. See if you can improve it.

Exercises

Write definitions, followed by detailed descriptions, of these items. In each case refer to construction, appearance, and use, and pay special attention to planning the order in which you tackle the various features:

1 comb	6 suitcase	11 canal-lock system
2 gardening spade	7 woollen cardigan	12 gramophone record
3 rake	8 matchbox	13 deck chair
4 dining chair	9 china-cabinet	14 ball-point pen
5 table	10 sock	15 pair of scissors

You can get further practice by describing fully the objects set for defining, in the section entitled "Definitions". Choose other objects yourself.

Describing processes

1 State first the job that has to be done, and list the materials or equipment needed.

2 Next state any preliminary work that has to be done: if it is floor-washing, you would need to sweep, to remove loose dust and dirt.

3 Then give a clear, step-by-step explanation of the method.

How to wash a floor

For floor-washing you need a bucket, hot water, household soap or detergent powder, a scrubbing brush, and several floor-cloths.

First set aside any carpets, rugs, or furniture, and then sweep the floor, to remove loose dirt and dust.

The floor should be washed in successive sections, each of about two square yards, and overlapping slightly. First wet a floor-cloth thoroughly

27

in a bucket of clean hot water, and use this cloth to wet a section of floor. (It may be advisable to work across the floor to end at the door.)

Dip the scrubbing brush in the water, remove it and pass its bristles across the bar of soap; alternatively, put a little soap powder on the bristles. This is more economical than placing soap in the water itself.

Next, scrub the section of floor briskly with the brush, in a circular motion.

To remove soap and dirty water from the floor, dip a cloth in the bucket, wring it out, and then, holding it by two adjacent corners, drag it flat across the floor towards you. This is better than rubbing with a crumpled cloth, though you may have to do it several times, each time rinsing the cloth clean and wringing it out. Eventually, all dirt and surplus water will have been removed.

Repeat this process to clean further sections, changing the water in the bucket when it becomes too dirty. Finally, allow time for the floor to dry, before replacing carpet and furniture.

Exercises

Describe in detail how to do the following, giving materials and equipment, preparation, and step-by-step advice on method:

1 Repainting a kitchen chair.

2 Making a simple wooden article.

3 Washing one's hair.

4 Darning a sock.

5 Baking a cake.

6 Tying a shoelace.

7 Mounting a bicycle and riding off.

8 Making a simple toy for a child.

9 Packing a suitcase.

10 Mending a puncture.

11 Potting spring bulbs (include care in early growth).

12 Making a pot of tea.

13 Washing dishes.

14 Making a bonfire.

15 Others of your own choosing.

28

BUSINESS LETTERS

Everyone has to write business letters and it is important to give a good impression by writing letters which are perfectly correct. Here first are some general hints:

Paper: use unlined white paper, of good quality and size. "Quarto" (8″ × 10″) is very useful. Pale blue or pale grey paper might be used, but is more suitable for informal letters; pink, green, mauve are rather vulgar. Lined paper and small sheets are not recommended.

Envelopes: these should match your paper, though buff-coloured "Manilla" envelopes are much used in business for economy. There are various sizes, but you should avoid the very small, nearly square ones. Practise folding your letters so that they fit into the envelopes with as few folds as possible; there is a correct folding for each size of paper and envelope, which you can easily find by experimenting.

Pen, ink, writing: do not use a ball-point pen; these are good for notes and jottings, but they smudge and make grooves in the paper. A proper fountain pen, with a nib that is not too thick or thin, gives a better effect in letters. Blue-black ink is preferable to other colours, though if your handwriting is of the stylish "italic" kind, black ink is best. Space your writing out well and do not crowd the page. Master the art of writing evenly on unlined paper. You can get a heavily lined backing sheet to put behind your page. Write on both sides if you wish; some people prefer to use one side only. Try to avoid alterations, though an occasional neat correction gives no offence.

Layout: there is an established practice which you must follow exactly. Study the examples:

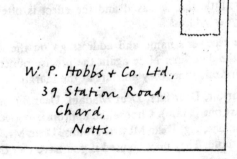

W. P. Hobbs + Co. Ltd.,
39 Station Road,
Chard,
Notts.

Your ref: PC/192.

The Haven,
22 Low Road,
Penfold,
Hants.
23rd. May. 1962.

W. P. Hobbs & Co. Ltd.,
39 Station Road,
Chard,
Notts.

Dear Sirs,

Yours faithfully,
James Smith

Notes

1 The paper should not be overcrowded; leave at least a one-inch margin at either side, and a good border at the top and bottom.

2 Put your own address in the top right-hand corner; successive lines sloping as shown, and punctuate precisely (a comma at the end of each line, with a full stop at the end of the last line: a full stop follows each abbreviated word). Avoid abbreviating such words as Road, Avenue, August: little time is saved and the effect is often ugly. Put the date below your address.

3 The receiver's name and address go on the left side of the page, below the date line. Note again the precise punctuation. The lines do not slope this time; they all start at the margin.

4 Dear Sir, Dear Sirs, Dear Madam, Dear Sir or Madam, Mesdames (this last one is rare). Choose the appropriate greeting. Mentioning the actual name, e.g. Dear Messrs. Hobbs, Dear Mr. Wilson, strikes a less formal note. They may be used if you have met the receiver.

5 The first paragraph begins just below the space between *Dear* and whatever follows (e.g. *Sir*). All other paragraphs begin directly below the start of the first. Thus, each paragraph has its first line "indented", to show that a new paragraph is beginning. Leave a good space between the last line of one paragraph and the first line of the next.

6 The conclusion in business letters is usually *Yours faithfully* with your signature underneath. *Yours faithfully* starts just to the right of the page centre. Sometimes *Yours truly* is used. *Very truly yours* is possible and may strike a rather warmer note. *Yours sincerely* is only used if the receiver is known personally to you and you begin your letter with *Dear* followed by his or her name. You do not use *Yours sincerely* if you begin the letter with *Dear Sir*, etc. To write it to a stranger or a remote superior is not good form. Other conclusions, such as *Yours etc.* should not be used.

7 If you are using a reference number, put *Ref.* in the top left-hand corner of the page, followed by the reference. If you are using the receiver's reference, put *Your ref.*, followed by the reference.

The contents and style of writing

Write as clearly, simply, and concisely as possible; your letter should be courteous but should not waste the reader's time with unnecessary length, wordiness, or muddled ideas. At all costs avoid the needlessly wordy phrases that once passed for "good business style":

I am in receipt of your esteemed communication of the 15th ultimo. . . . (Thank you for your letter of 15th . . .)

I would inform you that . . . (omit these words; just state plainly what has to be stated).

I remain,
      Your obedient servant,   (Yours faithfully,)

The favour of your early reply will oblige. . . . (I look forward to hearing from you soon. . . .)

There are many other such pieces of useless lumber (thanking you in anticipation, with reference to, in respect of, etc.). Use plain words, simply and politely, and arrange your statements sensibly. To achieve the best arrangement, *plan* your business letter before actually writing it. Jot down notes to guide you, and follow this general pattern:

1 State your reason for writing the letter.
2 State any necessary details in connection with this reason.
3 Add a brief conclusion, if necessary, in the interests of courtesy.

31

Examples

25 Oakford Avenue,
Woodmede,
Hampshire.

19th July, 1963.

The Almoner,
Woodmede Cottage Hospital,
Woodmede.

Dear Madam,

I am writing in response to your appeal for voluntary welfare helpers at the Cottage Hospital, and am pleased to offer the services of myself and three of my friends.

We are senior girls at Woodmede School, aged sixteen, and in the second year of our pre-nursing course. We all hope to become nurses one day, and regard this as a wonderful opportunity to see something of hospital life, while at the same time giving a little help to others.

We should all be delighted to spend one evening each week at the Hospital and either Saturday mornings or afternoons. Any kind of work would be acceptable; our only wish is to help wherever you think we might be useful.

No doubt you would want to interview us before deciding whether to accept our offer, and we should be glad to come and see you at any time during next week, when we shall be on holiday.

I look forward to hearing from you and do hope that we shall be able to help in some way.

Yours faithfully,
Lorna Dawson.

19 St Ronan's Road,
Chalk Hill.

15th August, 1963.

St Clare Stamp Mart Ltd.,
43 Hill Street,
London, E.3.

Dear Sirs,

I enclose the wallet of stamps (Serial No: KJ/393), which you kindly sent me under your "Monthly Approvals Scheme" last week.

You will note that I have kept Nos. 7, 9, 14, 26, and 30. A postal order value 7/3 is enclosed in payment for these.

Thank you for your prompt and helpful service.

Yours faithfully,
Alex Robertson.

16 Dixon Street,
Accrington Bridge,
Lincolnshire.

2nd February, 1963.

The Editor,
Accrington Gazette,
14 Connaught Gardens,
Accrington.

Dear Sir,

May I suggest to your correspondent, Mr. J. Boothroyd, that he is perhaps a little unfair in regarding all the young people of Accrington Bridge as "idle, selfish, and thoughtless"?

It does seem to me that Mr. Boothroyd has taken the foolish behaviour of a few as representing the attitude of all of us. I think it is natural when one is young to be high-spirited, but we do not all waste our spare time making nuisances of ourselves. If Mr. Boothroyd would visit the local youth clubs in this town, he would find us working very hard just now on projects to help next week's "Aid to the Elderly" campaign.

Yours faithfully,
R. P. Watson

Exercises

Write these business letters, planning each one carefully beforehand and inventing the necessary names and addresses:

1 To a travel agent, requesting information on camping holidays abroad for youth-club parties.

2 To a bus company, complaining of the poor service in your locality and suggesting possible improvements.

3 To a well-known person, inviting him to address your School Debating Society. You have heard that he dislikes young people.

4 To the secretary of a local sports club, suggesting a fixture.

5 To your local Mayor, offering the services of yourself and friends for part-time voluntary welfare help.

6 To the local Librarian, expressing appreciation of the library services.

7 To a teacher, inviting her to attend a form party.

8 To a newspaper editor, in response to a published letter which criticised local young people as "hooligans".

9 To a firm, requesting information on something you wish to buy.

10 To a museum curator, telling of a mysterious find.

11 To a difficult neighbour, apologising for damage caused to her flowers by your dog.

12 To a sea-captain proposing that your class "adopts" his ship, for the purpose of writing to the crew.

13 To the editor of a local paper, requesting permission for your class to see how the paper is produced.

14 To a local gentleman, requesting permission to use his field for a youth club charity fête.

15 Others of your own choosing.

Applying for a job

This is a type of business letter that you must certainly master. An employer may receive many applications for one post and he will judge which candidates are most worth interviewing from their letters. What you write and the way you present it must be considered most carefully. All the earlier advice about choice of paper, pen, ink, envelopes, folding, layout, style, and arrangement of ideas must be followed, if the reader is to be impressed. Here is a useful plan:

1 State the post for which you wish to be considered.

2 Give a concise but detailed account of yourself, mentioning:

> age
> nationality
> schools attended, with dates
> subjects studied and examinations passed
> posts of responsibility held in school
> previous experience at work, if any
> leisure interests, including special ability at games

To keep your actual letter fairly short, you can list all this information on a separate sheet and state that it is enclosed.

3 Say why you would like to have the post in question, suggesting tactfully why you consider yourself especially suitable.

4 Give the names and addresses and status of two or three people of good standing who would write to support your application, and enclose a copy of at least one testimonial, usually from your headmaster or present employer.

The problem is to give all this information in a sufficiently concise and attractive form to make the reader want to read it and want to see you. Here is a sample:

The Gables,
Summertree Lane,
Boldings,
Kent.

28th July, 1962.

The General Manager,
Peacock Insurance Co. Ltd.,
Chapel Road,
Blightstone.

Dear Sir,

I should like to be considered for the post of Junior Clerk, as advertised in the "Blightstone Courier" of 25th July.

Full details of my personal history are enclosed, and you will see that I have the educational attainments needed for this post. My two years' experience of general office work should also be of value.

My reason for wishing to change my present employment is that I am now seeking work with a larger organisation, where hard work, reliability, and initiative might (one day) win me promotion to greater responsibility. In particular I should like to help with the interviewing of clients, for I feel I have a friendly and tactful personality that might prove useful in such work.

I enclose the names and addresses of two persons who would write on my behalf, and a copy of a testimonial from my present employer.

Yours faithfully,
Janet Leaver (Miss)

Notes

This writer does not waste the reader's time. She clearly shows where the necessary personal details may be found, and tactfully suggests that her qualifications are satisfactory. She hints, without boasting or fuss, that she has useful experience and useful qualities of personality. She obviously wants to work hard and get on, and she has a clear idea of what she would like to do.

Exercises

1 Plan a sheet of personal history, listing in order all the essential items and giving the names and addresses of two people who would write on your behalf. (Invent details if you wish, as this is for practice only.)

2 Write a letter of application for a post offered in a current newspaper. Cut out the advertisement and paste it in your book alongside your work.

Note: You can do Exercise 2 many times, choosing different advertisements. An interesting variation is to prepare a complete application, letter, personal history sheet, and testimonial (invented), for a given post. Use suitable stationery and submit the application to your teacher. If the class works in groups, several people "applying" for one post, your teacher can select the ones worth "interviewing", and you can discuss why they are the best. A mock interview will follow and your teacher will advise on how to behave at such times. Remember, though, that you are not advised to invent anything when making real applications!

3 Imagination in Writing

In the last chapter we looked at all the workaday writing tasks. The clear, simple, and concise way of writing is best for such everyday jobs —plain words for plain purposes. Some writing tasks, however, give you much more chance to enjoy yourself. Your own viewpoints and experiences, special knowledge of hobbies and interests, pet "hates", moods, and fancies all offer material for lively writing. Your efforts will still need to be clear, of course, but they need not always be as severely simple and concise as a business letter or a report. You can give your imagination more freedom, to experiment with ideas and different touches of style. Here are the writing tasks we shall now consider:

> Keeping a diary (with a difference!)
> Planning talks and speeches
> Writing to friends or relatives
> Imaginative prose descriptions

A DIARY WITH A DIFFERENCE

Pocket diaries give only a little space each day in which to write; most people only use them for noting appointments. A few buy the "page-a-day" kind, or even bigger "five year" diaries, and enjoy keeping a secret record of daily thoughts and experiences, but most of us are too busy, or see no need for this.

Here is an idea, however, which might lead to a big improvement in your English. Many students, lively as they are, seem short of interesting ideas to write about. If you are one of these, start keeping a "Writer's Diary"—just as an artist keeps a sketchbook for setting down impressions of things seen or imagined, so you can jot down notes on unusual things seen and done, interesting people encountered, ideas that come your way, amusing stories or experiences, fleeting impressions. Many of these are often quickly forgotten, but if you note them down you will get useful practice in writing, and at the same time a wealth of material to help you in English, especially when writing essays.

Get an exercise book and try it out. This list of suggestions should be entered on the first page, to guide you:

Ideas for my Writer's Diary

Descriptions of things seen: nature, weather, animals, articles, people; faces, places, scenes, incidents, street, country, home, garden, shop. . . .

Personal experiences and feelings: amusing, sad, thought-provoking, moods, wishes, ambitions, disappointments, relations with other people, dreams, fears, mistakes. . . .

Ideas and points of view: read, heard (books, magazines, newspapers, radio, film, television), modern problems, religion, politics, people's behaviour, science, new fashions and "crazes", criticisms of stories read, films and television programmes seen. . . .

Colourful language: read, heard, invented. . . .

Anything else I fancy writing about . . . ?

Here now are some extracts from a boy's "Writer's Diary":

. . . Why do I play rugger?—score this season: one try, three torn shirts, one broken thumb. Does it build character to be sat on, face ground in mud?

Men in bowler hats: stupid, like black melons with brims.

Real dogs—and pampered lapdogs: women spending pounds, having poodles shampooed, scented, manicured, even dyed to match their hair. Best steak to eat—criminal!

Puddles, rippling with ridges, like the wash from a paddling duck; miniature oceans.

Why do some people have so much and others nothing? Starving Africans. How can we help? Are you a better person if you have to struggle for what you get?

My dog's tail: whisk, twist, twirl, wag with pleasure, droop with woe. What if people's noses were the same? Does your nose wag?

Exercises

To get you started on your own "Writer's Diary" here are some exercises to discuss and write in class:

1 Describe, vividly but briefly, the face of a person you saw recently.

2 Describe a pet animal: playing, sleeping, eating, moving.

3 Do the same for a wild animal.

4 Describe vividly in a few sentences something recently seen: an article, incident, or scene.

5 Describe, each in a few lines, what you think about: shy people, people who are always talking, people who show off, people who live dangerously, old people.

6 Do the same, for: lonely people, people who are especially good-looking, snobs, spoilt children, lazy people.

7 Describe a striking scene: sunset, gathering storm, windy day, market-place, or something of your own choice.

8 Write some brief thoughts about each of these topics: greed, anger, being ill, work, a personal fear.

9 Do the same about: war, religion, music, a picture you like, eating too much at a party.

10 Collect ten short pieces of description (sentence or phrase) which seem to you to show a striking use of words.

11 Briefly describe: a personal memory, a dream or ambition, a gay experience, a sad discovery, an unkind action.

12 Do the same for: a moment of fear, a new thought, a curious find, an amusing idea, a feeling of envy.

13 Make short collections of words and phrases that would vividly describe: a deserted beach, a sad old man, cooking smells, a fat man laughing, the charm of flowers.

14 Do the same for: an old steam engine, a factory conveyor-belt, poverty, the parched desert, a boasting person.

15 Briefly say what it is in life that makes you: embarrassed, impatient, curious, despairing, afraid.

PLANNING TALKS AND SPEECHES

No-one can escape making a speech at some time or another—at weddings, birthday parties, club-suppers, or even on those lesser occasions when everybody's attention somehow turns to you, and it's *your* turn to speak! Most people feel a little nervous until they have had a little practice at speech-making, but confidence soon grows.

The main rules have been summarised as: "Stand up, speak up, shut up". Certainly you must stand erect, look at your audience, and avoid nervous "fiddling". You must also speak clearly, so that all can understand, and you must not bore the listeners by rambling on too long. But there is more to consider. A skilled speaker is a pleasure to hear: his manner relaxed, his voice pleasing and clear, he holds the audience spellbound by a clever blend of what he says and the way he says it. All seems natural and even unprepared, but most good speakers do some serious planning beforehand, and so must you. This is how to set about it:

39

1   Consider your subject and the time allowed for your talk, and briefly note down some ideas, in any order, trying to choose those that seem most interesting and thought-provoking.

2   Now review these ideas, rejecting or developing some in your mind, and organise them into a sensible order: to do this, divide your page down the centre and note your main themes down the left-hand side. The right-hand column is for more detailed notes to help you when talking about each main theme. A note or two on particular little touches of style in presentation will also be helpful here:

Subject: What You Can Do With Eggs (3 minutes)

Opening remarks	Humorous: What you cannot do: throw at speaker. Speak mock-seriously as expert: considerable research done.
Familiar uses: England	Boiled, fried, poached, scrambled, plain omelette; used for cooking also. Rather dull range of uses, reflects dullness of English cooking.
Fancy uses: foreign	Egg romantic: *hundreds* of egg-dishes: describe a few "mouth-waterers" (get from cookery book). Many Continental "crimes" concealed this way. Hamlet/omelette joke.
Non-eating uses	For sticking-power: painters of old. Collectors: blow and keep only shells (demonstrate?). Beauty-treatment: women rub on skin; babies on face, at breakfast.
Chinese custom	Brisk trade in eggs, aged and rotten—great delicacy.
Conclusion	Nature note—all a "yolk": The common cormorant or shag lays eggs inside a paper bag. The reason, I am told, is plain: It's to protect them from the rain.

40

Note the attempts planned here to amuse and entertain: a lively beginning and ending and a variety of ideas throughout; mouth-watering examples and a demonstration of egg-blowing; each main theme amply but not too lengthily developed.

Here is one last piece of advice: once you have prepared your notes, learn and practise them before you give the talk. When you are actually speaking, you must avoid constantly dipping into your notes. Nothing depresses an audience more than a speaker who is constantly pausing to consult his notes, like a horse dipping into his nose-bag. An occasional short glance may be permitted, but not more. And never *read* a speech: this is a real insult to your listeners.

Exercises

Prepare notes for a talk on each of these topics. Each talk should last for 3–5 minutes. Consider carefully the quality and arrangement of ideas, start, and finish, and the need for effective touches of style.

1. People's faces.
2. An unusual hobby.
3. In praise of teacher.
4. On getting wet.
5. The pleasures of not walking.
6. I often lose my temper.
7. Reading in bed.
8. A favourite book.
9. Spiders.
10. Spring-cleaning.
11. A welcome to a school guest.
12. A bridegroom's (or bride's) speech.
13. Comedians.
14. My bad habits.
15. Thanks to a visiting speaker.
16. A 21st birthday speech.
17. A speech to the family on Christmas Day.
18. Money.
19. Myself when very young.
20. My favourite foods.

Others, of your own choosing.

WRITING TO FRIENDS OR RELATIVES

When you write to friends or relatives, your approach is much more relaxed than in a business letter; you are using your pen to talk to people of whom you are fond, and your letters will probably be fairly long and full of little personal items: amusing experiences, news of yourself and friends, or members of the family, secrets, plans for the future, things seen, done, bought, and thought.

A letter of this kind is fairly easy to write, for you know you have a willing and eager reader. It is a pity, therefore, that some people write rather dull letters: "Is there anything in Mabel's letter?" "Oh, nothing much. The same old dreary stuff. Here, you'd better read it." Never let this be said about your letters; here are some hints to help you write in a lively and interesting way:

Layout

19 Smith Street,
Hampton,
Derbyshire.

17th March, 1963.

Dear Charles,

Sincerely yours,
Fred

Notes

1 Put your own address, with date beneath it, in the top right-hand corner.

2 There is no need to write the name and address of the receiver above the greeting, as was necessary with business letters.

3 Dear Charles, or My dear Alice, are the best forms of greeting.

4 Paragraphing and envelope layout are the same as for the business letter.

5 Suitable leave-takings are: Yours sincerely, Sincerely yours, Yours, Yours ever, With love from, followed by your Christian name, or Christian name with surname if you are writing to a person who is as yet only an acquaintance.

6 Remember the advice given in connection with business letters about choice of paper, pen, and ink.

Style

(*a*) You may be rather more conversational than in business letters, using such shortened forms as I'll, won't, isn't, and a lively approach that would seem out of place in more formal letters: "I'd love you to drop in and see me just as soon as you can . . ." has a warmth you would reserve for a friend; it would hardly be correct to write to the local chimney-sweep in this way.

(*b*) Although you are writing in a conversational style, do avoid using too much slang; this would make your letter seem too vulgar:

> "Tee-hee," I chortled. "I bet he'll not stick his long nose in my affairs again. That's settled his hash, not 'alf, eh? But nuff said about him, the stinker. Must ring off now, old fruit, and away to the grub department to rustle up some din. Bye-bye, old pal. . . ."

(*c*) Try to put your ideas clearly, avoiding over-lengthy or involved sentences and vague language like ". . . a sort of a thing, you know. . . ."

(*d*) Try to select your words for good descriptive effect: some people's letters give pleasure in this way, with vivid little accounts of things bought, places visited, new decorations at home, amusing events, etc. A plain, simple statement often fails to give any idea of your real feelings. Compare:

> ". . . I have a bad cold and headache and so cannot come on Saturday. . . ."

43

". . . Imagine me just now, with a huge, ruby-red nose, like a circus-clown; a perpetual tear sparkling on its end; a million multi-coloured cold-germs fighting for possession of my system, and you will understand why we ought not to meet this Saturday. . . ."

Contents

Most of your letters to friends and relatives will be of the "newsy" type, and so often these are only a dreary catalogue of unimportant everyday matters. To help improve the news value of your letters, choose topics from the list that follows; any of these items can be treated in a lively way, and any three or four combined would make an interesting letter:

Brief but vivid descriptions of places or things seen
Amusing or unusual experiences, of yourself or others
Delicious "scandal" (not harmful, though)
Happy memories shared
Plans for future meetings or activities
Accounts of interesting people met
Ambitions
New clothes
Interesting news of family or mutual friends
Funny stories (if really good)
Thoughts and viewpoints on interesting topics
Good films seen or books read (but do not bore with long descriptions)
An account of progress in your hobbies
Home and garden: new features, or plans for improvement
Health of self or others (but do not harp on it)

Include a variety of topics in your letter; you risk boring the reader if you dwell heavily on only one or two matters. Try also to avoid seeming too wrapped up in your own affairs: much will be about yourself, of course, but you can also show a keen interest in your reader's activities and interests. Ask questions about them, and pass on anything you may have seen or heard that might help or interest him in his hobbies.

Exercises

1 Write a newsy letter to a close friend of your own age, treating the following matters:

An amusing personal experience
News of mutual friends
Some thoughts on an interesting topic
A good film seen recently

2 As above, but treating these matters:

> Some delicious scandal (not harmful)
> Plans for a future meeting
> Happy memories shared
> Progress in hobbies

3 Write to an elderly relative, of whom you are really fond, including these topics:

> News of your family
> An interesting place you have just visited
> Your ambitions for the future, asking for advice
> Improvements to house and garden

4 Write to a favourite cousin, treating the following matters:

> Your new clothes
> An unusual person you have met
> The problem of how to handle parents
> A book you can recommend

5 Write to your family, while you are staying with friends on holiday, mentioning these topics:

> What you have done and seen
> Your hosts' home described
> An unusual and pleasant experience
> Asking about life at home in your absence

(You can write other letters along similar lines, selecting three or four main topics to write about. In every case remember the need to study your reader's interests as well as your own.)

Social letters with a special purpose

Apart from the ordinary "newsy" letter, we all have to write "thank you" letters, letters of apology, requests for advice or help (or letters offering the same), expressions of sympathy, letters accepting or declining invitations.

In some of these the lively, "chatty" approach will be out of place: you need simple, clear language, with proper regard for tact, sincerity, and human warmth. We shall now consider each of these special purposes:

(*a*) A letter thanking someone for a gift, or accepting an invitation should not be a dull, brief acknowledgment that makes the reader feel you are only writing because you have to. Say first how much you appreciate the gift, or invitation, and why. Then include some "newsy" writing, to show the reader that you enjoy writing to him anyway, and end by expressing your thanks once more.

(*b*) If you write to decline an invitation, you need a good reason. State it simply and clearly, without lengthy details which might make the reader think you have invented an excuse. Stress that you would very much like to accept, if it were possible. End with some general news, to show that you are happy to be writing, even though you cannot accept the invitation.

(*c*) Letters of apology should get straight to the point. If you admit your fault and show that it was really not intended, you will probably be forgiven. A long-winded excuse that tries to save you from blame will seem insincere; be simple and direct in apology.

(*d*) Requests for help or advice should also get straight to the point: convince your reader simply, without "gushing", that you value his friendship and good sense, state your problem, and ask for what you want. Beware of offering a reward: a good friend will want to help and you might offend him by suggesting he might want payment.

(*e*) Offers of help or advice must be extremely tactful in approach; many people are sensitive or proud about accepting help. Show that your offer is made because of your fondness for the person concerned, and make it possible for your reader to refuse gracefully if he prefers to do so.

(*f*) Expressions of sympathy, especially where death or sad misfortune is concerned, should be very short and simple. Long letters dwelling on grief will only make the reader more unhappy. Just say how sorry you are, stress that you are thinking of the person concerned, and offer to help in any way you can. If the matter is less serious, a temporary illness or a minor stroke of bad luck, for instance, your letter could be longer, and without overdoing it you could include some more general news designed to cheer up your reader.

Ask your teacher to work through each of these types with you, and to give you useful models for your notebook.

Exercises

6 Write a letter thanking a close friend for a gift, and include some other news.

7 Write a letter thanking an elderly relative for a gift (which was quite unsuitable for you) and include some other suitable news.

8 Write a letter to a friend who is in hospital after losing the sight of one eye in a serious accident.

9 Write to a small child who is ill in hospital with measles.

10 Write to cheer up a friend who has just failed an important examination, which you have passed.

11 Write an apology to an old lady you know well who was severely shaken when you knocked her down with your bicycle.

12 Write an amusing letter inviting your best friend to your fancy-dress party.

13 Write a letter rebuking in a kindly way a friend who has embarrassed you by talking to others about your private affairs.

14 Write a tactful letter offering advice to a friend who is about to do something you consider unwise.

15 Write to an awkward neighbour, tactfully declining her invitation to tea.

16 Write to ask advice from an influential uncle about your choice of career, without suggesting that you want him to give you a job.

17 Write to an aunt, sympathising with her over the death of her small son.

18 Write to an elderly relative, apologising for having forgotten to visit her for tea, as you had arranged.

19 Write to ask a close friend for advice on an important problem that is troubling you.

20 Write to an older relative, asking him to do something for you that you know will involve him in considerable inconvenience.

IMAGINATIVE PROSE DESCRIPTIONS

We all enjoy reading a good story, but it must be well told, so as to grip our imagination and hold us captive to the end. A clever writer can do this: his words create an atmosphere so vivid and compelling that you can see clearly in your mind's eye the scenes or people described; you feel real emotions with the characters, sharing their fears, joys, and sorrows; you almost smell the scents and hear the sounds that are suggested, so strong is the power of imagination:

> August Bank Holiday. A tune on an ice-cream cornet. A slap of sea and a tickle of sand. A fanfare of sunshades opening. A wince and whinny of bathers dancing into deceptive water. A tuck of dresses. A rolling of trousers. A compromise of paddlers. A sunburn of girls and a lark of boys. A silent hullabaloo of balloons. . . .
>
> From *Quite Early One Morning*, by Dylan Thomas

In this snatch of writing, the jolly, carefree atmosphere of a seaside town in high summer is cleverly suggested—surprisingly enough, for there is not a proper sentence in the piece! It is an array of fragments —but what fragments! Each is rich in suggestion and our imagination does the rest. Ice-cream cornet, slap and tickle, tucked-up dresses, rolled-up trousers for paddling, larking boys, bathing-beauties, balloons —all convey the breezy mood of "I do like to be beside the seaside" Tune and fanfare, even from such unlikely instruments as ice-cream cornet and sunshades, remind us that somewhere will be "the brass band playing 'Tiddley-om-pom-pom'". There is no need to mention whelks, wet seaweed, or the sand in your sandwiches—we're down on the beach already.

People who write like this try to convey a definite mood or atmosphere, and they choose ideas and words deliberately to stimulate your imagination:

> Little naked navvies dug canals; children with spades and no ambition built fleeting castles; wispy young men, outside the bathing huts, whistled at substantial young women and dogs who desired thrown stones more than the bones of elephants. Recalcitrant uncles huddled over lukewarm ale in the tiger-striped marquees. Mothers in black, like wobbling mountains, gasped under the discarded dresses of daughters who shrilly braved the goblin waves. . . .

Exercises

Study these descriptions, and write a short appreciation of each, saying what mood each writer is trying to convey and showing how the choice of ideas and descriptive words helps to strengthen the atmosphere:

1 I saw something—a fin moving stealthily through the water, slipping along like a black dhow sail, making scarcely a ripple. It was a killer whale. As though attracted by my gaze it turned quickly and came straight towards our floe. The high dorsal fin passed out of my view and a moment later I

heard the great beast snorting on the other side. . . . It was an ugly, pig-like sound—and deadly sinister. I waited, scarcely daring to breathe. The floe trembled as the monster skimmed beneath it.

From *The White South*, by Hammond Innes

2 The sky was cloudless, the sun shone out bright and warm, the songs of birds, and hum of myriads of summer insects, filled the air; and the cottage gardens, crowded with flowers of every rich and beautiful tint, sparkled in the heavy dew, like beds of glittering jewels. Everything bore the stamp of summer, and none of its beautiful colours had yet faded from the dye.

From *The Pickwick Papers*, by Charles Dickens

3 We worked out of the Thames under canvas, with a North Sea pilot on board. His name was Jermyn, and he dodged all day long about the galley drying his handkerchief before the stove. Apparently he never slept. He was a dismal man, with a perpetual tear sparkling at the end of his nose, who either had been in trouble, or was in trouble, or expected to be in trouble—couldn't be happy unless something went wrong.

From *Youth*, by Joseph Conrad

4 Over the meadow a mist was moving, white and silent as the fringe of down on the owl's feathers. Since the fading of shadows it had been straying from the wood beyond the mill-leat, bearing in its breath the scents of the day, when bees had bended bluebell and primrose. Now the bees slept, and mice were running through the flowers. Over the old year's leaves the vapour moved, silent and wan, the wraith of waters once filling the ancient wide river-bed—men say that the sea's tides covered all this land, when the Roman galleys drifted up under the hills.

From *Tarka the Otter*, by Henry Williamson

5 Mrs. Cash came in. . . . She was a sturdy little person, nearer sixty than fifty, very solid on her feet, very tidy. Her very good black coat was buttoned up to her throat and finished with a tippet of very good brown fur. Her massive face and the thick coils of wonderfully arranged iron-grey hair, together with the sleek flat hat which sat upon it, seemed so much all of one piece that the notion of them ever coming apart was slightly shocking. She carried a large black bag, holding it squarely on her stomach with both neatly gloved hands, and her eyes were round and bright and knowing.

From *Tiger in the Smoke*, by Margery Allingham

6 The two big boilers stood side by side, separated by a few feet and a protective railing. Their massive round iron sides were rusted brown and then greyed over with dust, but the railings encircling them had been painted bright green, so that in their roughcast heavy skins the two boilers looked like huge dormant pachyderms enclosed by a bright fence, truncated featureless monsters, but alive. They never moved, never quivered, made no sound. Yet they seemed to live. Of huge weight, they enclosed within

their bellies a tremendous sleeping power, hundreds of compressed degrees of heat, piled-up energy bursting to split free.

From *The Boiler Room*, by William Sansom

7   He was a little man, with a dusty puckered face and an immense upper lip so that he looked like a wise old monkey; and he had spent all his long life among stones. There were bits of stone all over him. He handled the stones about him, some of which he showed to us, at once easily and lovingly, as women handle their babies. He was like a being that had been created out of stone, a quarry gnome.

From *An English Journey*, by J. B. Priestley

8   One went up three steps to the glass-panelled door and peeped into a broad, low room with a bar and a beer-engine, behind which were many bright and helpful-looking bottles against mirrors, and great and little pewter measures, and bottles fastened with brass wire upside down, with their corks replaced by taps, and a white china cask labelled "Shrub", and cigar boxes, and boxes of cigarettes, and a couple of Toby jugs and a beautifully coloured hunting scene framed and glazed, showing the most elegant people taking Piper's Cherry Brandy.

From *The History of Mr. Polly*, by H. G. Wells

Hints for writing artistic prose descriptions

(a) There are four main types, and you should practise them all:

Object	Windmill.	Juke Box.
Scene	Snowy Landscape.	Coal Mine.
Person or Animal	Circus Clown.	Tiger.
Action or Event	Boxing Match.	Fire Fighting.

(b) Keep your first attempts to one paragraph (50–100 words) on each topic.

(c) First decide which mood or atmosphere you will convey. This governs your whole approach, for all your descriptive details will be chosen to contribute to that atmosphere. Examples: *Nature:* youthful spring—boisterous autumn—brooding heat—raging storm—crisp frost? *A Person:* jolly—sinister—pathetic—ugly?

(d) Briefly note some random ideas, all suggested by your chosen mood. Seek fairly unusual effects and picturesque words and phrases—don't just choose the obvious. Colours, shapes, sounds, smells, movements, comparisons with other things—any of these might be chosen for inclusion. The descriptive pieces given above suggest the sort of artistic effects you might aim at; you should also consult the chapter "Picturesque Language".

50

(*e*) Now organise your ideas into an effective order. Perhaps you will reject some at this stage, or add others as your imagination works. Concentrate on bold, broad effects, and do not let your sentences become too long and rambling: a confused clutter of too many details or too many elaborate words will only produce a muddled or dazzling effect, like this:

> Winged hosts of minute, multi-plumaged oriental birds cried hysterically, breathlessly, against the pitiless, onrushing, cruel might of the engulfing, threatening storm, barging and thrusting delicate winged bodies through the spiky, tangled mass of interwoven branches which formed the denseness of the mango forest, from which, emerging, the deep mauve peaks of towering hills stood, silent, bare and expectant, battered slopes resistant, mutely facing the onslaught of the dull, monotonous, icy sheets of softly gliding rain. . . .

This young writer has vivid ideas and a wealth of words, but she should use her effects much more sparingly, and in shorter sentences:

> A host of tiny birds fled hysterically before the oncoming storm, to seek a refuge in the spiky mango-forest. Towering hills stood mauve and bleak, as the gliding rain came down. . . .

Exercises

9 Choose a descriptive poem that you like, and borrow its mood and some of its most effective words and phrases, adding other touches of your own, to make an effective piece of prose description. This can be done many times with different poems.

10 Choose, from your reading of prose or verse, a short passage of description that appeals to you, write it out and add a short appreciation, mentioning the mood conveyed and how it is achieved.

11 Write a descriptive paragraph on each of these topics:

A wrecked ship beneath the waves	Yacht under sail
A tumbledown barn	A woodland pool
Across the rooftops	A fat woman laughing
Junk-shop window	A chimney sweep
Traffic jam	A flower stall

12 Write a descriptive paragraph on each of these "action" topics. Try to ensure a good "pace"—a swift-moving description of events:

An express train passing	A highwayman pursued
Smash and grab	A craftsman at work

Kitten at play	A ski-jumper
A giant machine in motion	A footballer scores
Fight with an octopus	Bats in flight

13 Here are ten more topics for descriptive paragraphs:

Fish on a slab	Space-rocket taking off
A caged lion	A curious relative
An old lady's sitting-room	Puppy in trouble
A newspaper seller	A weeping child
Fish and chip shop	Museum display cabinet

14 Describe, in a pair of contrasting paragraphs, each of the following topics:

(a) Your small brother, grubby from the garden, and emerging later, pink and clean from his bath.

(b) Your sitting-room, ready for a party, and afterwards, when the guests have departed.

(c) Yourself on your best behaviour, and later, when letting off steam.

(d) View of the city on a business day, and on Sunday.

(e) A ruined castle, and as it appeared centuries ago.

(f) A cat in smug, purring mood, and later, when annoyed.

(g) The scene from your window, in two different seasons.

(h) A garden scene, with sky overcast, and later, when the sun comes out.

(i) Your kitchen or workshop before a "do it yourself" session, and after.

(j) A village during a flood, and after the water has subsided.

4 Essays and Magazine Articles

WRITING ESSAYS

How many compositions have you written already? You can probably look back over at least seven years of them: "A Day by the Sea", "My Hobbies", "A Favourite Uncle". Some, no doubt, have been praised, perhaps for reasons you were not sure about; others will have limped home in a sorry state, bleeding red ink from a mass of teacher-inflicted wounds. It seems a mysterious business, ruled by chance, needing a touch of genius that few seem to possess.

At this stage it will be worthwhile to take a close look at essay writing. You can improve your efforts a great deal if you understand the problems involved, and this chapter covers all you need to know.

What is an essay?

"Composition" is a better word than "essay", for the task is to compose an interesting piece of writing by carefully choosing and arranging ideas on a chosen topic, and expressing them in an effective way. The result is fairly short—your essays will comprise about 250–300 words[1]—and within these limits you must capture your reader's interest, keep him entertained throughout, and send him away feeling that he has read something really worth while. Clearly, then, your ideas must be well chosen, well arranged, and well expressed—remember these three key words: *choice*, *arrangement*, and *expression* of ideas.

Choosing your topic

It is very pleasant to have a completely free choice of title, for this means you can write about something that really interests you, something about which you have special knowledge. Anything written from first-hand knowledge or special interest is almost sure to be lively and entertaining, providing you do not bore your reader with too much commonplace detail or dull ideas.

Usually, however, you have to choose from a list of six or seven titles, and you need practice to help you choose the subject on which you will be able to write best. Again, look first for a title which offers scope for

Suggested length for C.S.E. G.C.E. "O" level requires 450–500.

your personal interests or special knowledge; there is usually something for most people. Beware, however, of a title that might interest you but about which you cannot say much.

Before making your choice, moreover, you need to know from experience which type of essay you can handle best. Titles generally suggest one or other of the following main approaches:

Factual: Giving detailed information or advice:

How to keep fit	Sir Francis Drake
Starting a stamp collection	Some modern inventions

Argumentative: Stating your own views or considering various points of view:

Should we abolish fox-hunting?	Modern traffic problems
What I dislike about people	Should we have to work?

Descriptive: Describing in an artistic or imaginative way a place or person, scene or event:

A snowy landscape	Busy market scene
My favourite relative	The school play

Narrative: Writing a short story:

Holiday adventure	Crime on the moor
I could not sleep that night	An explosion rent the air

Reflective: An imaginative collection of your own thoughts, impressions, personal memories, artistic descriptions, all inspired by the title:

Castles in the air	Childhood fancies
A sky full of stars	On being an invalid

When you know which of these approaches you can handle best, you will be able to choose your title accordingly. Sometimes, of course, you can blend several of these approaches into one essay. An argument against fox-hunting will be strengthened by a vivid description of the chase; a story needs the support of clever descriptive touches, for "atmosphere"; even a factual essay can be enriched by a personal memory or a lively piece of argument. Experiment with them all, but remember that your main aim is to interest and entertain your reader;

54

to do this, you must choose a topic well suited to your knowledge and interests and involving the approaches you can handle best.

Exercises

1 Say which of these titles you would choose, and why, outlining the general approach or blend of approaches you would select:

Triumphs of engineering	The opposite sex
It was a narrow escape	Precious stones
Madame Tussaud's waxworks	A green and pleasant land
Is war inevitable?	Holiday beach scene

2 Do the same as in Question 1, choosing from these titles:

Vintage cars	Hairdresser's shop
Useless inventions	Hats and their wearers
School games	Caught in the act
The romance of maps	I hate experts

3 Do the same as in Questions 1 and 2:

Useful tools which I need	Look before you leap
Old coins	Dentist's waiting-room
Carnival procession	The best things in life are free
The common cold	An absorbing hobby

4 Write down three titles on which you would choose to write if you had a completely free choice In each case outline your approach, and say why you have chosen both title and approach.

5 Write down three of the titles given above which you would *not* on any account choose to write about, and explain in some detail why you would not choose each of them.

6 Explain briefly which approach or blend of approaches you would choose for each of these titles, saying why you think your choice would be effective:

Looking at the stars
Shipwreck
Wedding reception

7 Do the same as in Question 6, using these titles:

Workshop scene
Rivers
I cleaned the old lamp

55

8 Write brief notes suggesting main ideas for each of these titles, showing how you would produce the blend of approaches suggested:

It was touch and go   (Narrative, with vivid description)
The Olympic Games   (Facts, argument, description)
British seaside resorts   (Description, argument, reflection)
Holidays abroad   (Argument, description, narrative)

Choosing your ideas

Your task is to *interest* your reader, by offering him worthwhile information, thought-provoking argument, an entertaining story, some imaginative description, or a blend of some of these. Whatever your approach, choose ideas with a high "interest-value"; nothing is more boring than a dull recital of the familiar and obvious:

> There are many kinds of clocks: big ones, small ones; some with alarms to wake us up, some with chimes to mark the hours; electric and winding clocks; wrist and pocket watches. . . .

What a tedious catalogue—we *know* all this! A far better choice would be: how earliest man became aware of time passing—by moving shadows, night and day; early methods of measuring time: sundial, hourglass, graduated candle; early mechanical clocks, powered by dripping water; the moving pendulum idea, and so on. There is much more interest in these ideas, even before you mention the modern marvels of precision engineering—clocks with multiple dials to tell the time simultaneously all over the world, tiny watches no bigger than a match-head, etc.

Think hard, then, about your chosen title. How can you include some really interesting or unusual ideas? Here is an example or two:

Workshop scene: Briefly describe the room: benches, tools, shavings, clippings, etc., then focus on weird product: like an octopus dressed in tartan—fanciful description to lead reader on, then announce: it is a workshop producing bagpipes! Scope now for explaining unusual tools, processes, materials, noises, etc.

The school play: After the usual description of feverish preparation backstage, in various departments, include the "secret" thoughts of several beholders: a small boy, his sister, a father who didn't want to come, the headmaster, the harassed producer.

Should we have to work? Describe our world as it might be if nobody worked; consider the delights of idling, but stress the decay of character resulting from idling as a permanent habit; include brief imagined interviews with a champion idler and a hard-pressed worker (plumber after a frosty winter?).

Exercises

9 For each of these titles jot down ten ideas at random, in brief note form, striving for good "interest-value":

Motor-cycling   Breakfast-time moods
Modern homes   Shopping

10 As Question 9, using these titles:

Painting and decorating A rock-pool
Power   Shopping for other people

11 As Questions 9 and 10, using these titles:

Dress design   Mountaineering
Roses   Christmas Day

12 Suggest in brief outline some ideas for an entertaining essay on each of these "old favourite" topics:

A day by the sea   The countryside in Spring
My summer holiday   My pet

13 As Question 12, using these titles:

Down on the farm   My own room
The season I like best   My plans for the future

14 Write down in brief note form some interesting ideas on each of these titles for "argumentative" essays:

The colour-bar   Can we have too much money?
Should gambling be banned? Are cats worth keeping?

15 Do the same as in Question 14 for these essay titles, which are suitable for the "reflective" approach:

On making a wish   Lost opportunities
Youth and old age   Pictures in the fire

Keeping to the point

It is usually at the early stage of "idea-choosing" that many people commit the grave blunder of straying from the point. "Fogbound Seashore," you say. "A nice chance for a lively tale of Cornish smugglers, or spy-catching." The ideas begin to flow and all starts well—on the seashore and in the fog. Very soon, however, your characters put to sea and the shore is left behind. Then the fog lifts—and you're off the point! Be constantly on your guard against this fault, which is always heavily penalised. It can so easily happen that "A holiday adventure" becomes an account of an entire holiday, and not an adventure that you had while on holiday; "Professional sport" can easily be narrowed down to football only, or even to a glowing account of Tottenham Hotspurs, by a keen 'Spurs supporter. "Lopsided planning" is another fault to avoid: dealing with only one side of an argument, for instance, when the title calls for several viewpoints, or giving too much attention to one aspect and not enough to others.

Exercise

16 Discuss any of the titles in the "Choosing ideas" exercises (9–15), showing how it might be possible to write off the point, or in a "lopsided" way.

Planning your approach in more detail

Once you have decided your main approach to a title, you need to plan in greater detail. The table on the next page suggests some useful essay patterns. It by no means exhausts the possibilities, and is intended only to start you experimenting.

Some well-worn themes to avoid: (a) The "cops and robbers" theme, with trivial adventures, leading to arrest for the "baddies" and reward for the "goodies". (b) The dreary "catalogue": "There are many kinds of bridges . . ." (c) The "dream adventure", from which you awake being called by Mum, and realise "it was all a dream". (d) The "story of a stray dog or piece of coal" type, where you imagine yourself the item concerned, suffering strange adventures.

Arranging your ideas

Nobody enjoys reading a confused muddle. Once you have chosen your title, therefore, and the ideas have come into your mind, you must organise them into a clear and sensible order, to give your essay a

58

Type of Essay	Sample Titles	Possible Scheme
People's lives Developments	Lord Nelson History of flight	Treat events in order of occurrence (with descriptive or argumentative touches)
Hobbies, interests	Sailing for fun	Pleasures; beginner's basic equipment; simple methods; more advanced aspects; costs
Argument: various sides considered	Are parents useful?	Outline advantages and disadvantages, or various viewpoints, with lively illustrations. Draw conclusions?
Argument: putting your own views	I hate noise	Lively argument to persuade reader, with vivid descriptions to support your views
Considering problems	The colour bar	State problem, examine its causes, illustrate its effects, suggest possible solutions
Story	A stranger came	1 Events in order of occurrence, including vivid description of scenes, thoughts, and action. Unexpected end? 2 "Flashback" method: open with awkward situation, add "flashback" review of events which led to it; return to present and describe action-packed conclusion
Description	Fairground scene	1 "Roving report" method: constant shift of interest, describing general scene and special details; sounds, sights, colours, smells, movements 2 "Contrast" method: fair in full swing; fair after closing. Many variations possible: new/old, day/night, actual/ideal, changing seasons, etc. 3 "Unusual or fantastic" stressed: startling, unusual, unexpected. Beauty in common things, strange qualities in scene, person, or place, weird atmosphere of dream-world. Useful in stories also
Reflections	Firelight shadows	Blend of fanciful description, interesting thoughts, feelings, and memories, possibly also a brief anecdote, all suggested by title

pattern that can be easily followed by the reader. You may be tempted, when short of time, to write an essay without making any proper plan beforehand. Guard against this; if you have no plan to guide you while writing, you will be asking your mind to do too much at once and the result will be jumbled ideas, repetition, a long-winded style, and poor balance—some ideas given too much attention and others not enough. It is much easier to have a fairly detailed working plan, showing all the main ideas in their proper order, with suggestions for development; your mind can then concentrate on expressing the ideas effectively in sentences.

Constructing a working plan

So far we have considered mainly your choice of title and various general approaches to essay writing. Before you write any essay, however, you must prepare a detailed plan, showing all your main ideas properly arranged. Once you have this, you can devote all your attention to the actual job of writing, without having to worry about what idea you should introduce next, or whether you are putting the ideas in the best order.

Train yourself to write essays of five to seven paragraphs, 250–300 words in all for C.S.E., 450–500 for G.C.E. You w ll usually have one hour for the task; spend the first fifteen minutes planning and the rest on the final writing, allowing if possible about five minutes at the end for reading through and improving. Here is a useful method for planning:

Think hard about your chosen title and jot down your main lines of approach:

Memories of Late Summer

Approach: mainly descriptive, based on country walk; some comments on town versus country living; reflections on approaching rest-season of nature; own feelings. . . .

As you are doing this, randon. ideas will be entering your mind. Now make a list of these, in brief notes. Some may already be grouping themselves in your mind under certain main themes, but do not worry too much just now about the order:

Ideas: Myself, a town-dweller on country walk; contrast town and country; Sussex Downs (I know well); route?; weather; changing scene: hilltop, wood, country lane, pool; creatures: snake startled, birds (their song), insects; things seen: pack-bridge, old mill, ruined cottage; mood of approaching autumn: colours, smells, life slowing down for winter, squirrel storing nuts.

The next task is to arrange your ideas carefully, still in brief notes. Study your random list, trying to group the ideas round several main headings. Some people like to write out the main themes, deciding on the best order for them, and then they write the ideas that bear upon each main theme opposite. This is a good method, because you end with a complete plan that is easy to follow. It would look like this:

Memories of Late Summer

Main paragraph themes	*Ideas for development*
1 Town-dweller takes walk in country.	Fresh air of Downs, trees, colours of Nature, contrasted with smoky grime, mildewed brick of city. Outline of route: past mill, down lane, over common, through wood. Mild, mellow warmth.
2 Old mill	Decaying, suggesting decline of year; broken millwheel contrasts with surging stream water: life still in nature. Birds, insects, haunt mill: also still active—summer not yet over.
3 Lane to the common	Tree-shaded, like tunnel; green, but first leaves turning red, some falling. Wild flowers, still enjoying sun's warmth. Old pack-bridge—seen many years and seasons pass, like this one now.
4 The common	Bracken browning. Derelict hut—further signs of decay. Charcoal-burning: sharp tang of smoke—an autumn smell. Coloured snake crosses path.
5 The wood	Haunt of birdsong—sounds still gay, heedless of dying year. Squirrel thoughtful—gathering nuts for winter. Rotting leaves from past autumns—soon to be added to.
6 My favourite season	Season of mists and mellow fruitfulness; richness of summer, but tinged with approaching winter. All these clear memories—but happened many years ago. Now *I* am in autumn years of life.

61

Exercises

17 Prepare a working plan for writing a single paragraph on each of
these themes. Pay special attention to the order of ideas, and make
sure that each idea you present bears directly on the main theme:

> Reasons for keeping (or for not keeping) a dog
> Some unusual ideas for tasty breakfasts
> The pains of washing up
> Basic equipment for your hobbies workroom

18 As Question 17, using these titles:

> The unfriendliness of cats
> First thoughts on camping in winter
> The advantages of being clever with your hands
> The contents of a pocket

19 Prepare a working plan for a series of two paragraphs on each of
these themes:

> Getting up early and lying late in bed
> On losing and keeping your temper
> The joys and sorrows of your pet hobby
> Setting out for school, and going home in the evening

20 As Question 19, using these themes:

> On having too much money, and too little
> Your newest and oldest clothing
> Churchyard scene, by night and by day
> How to make friends, and how to lose them

21 Prepare a plan for an essay, choosing your own title, and showing:

(*a*) random ideas.

(*b*) arrangement of ideas into 5–7 paragraphs, main themes and
ideas for development to be shown for each paragraph.

22 Plan an essay as for Question 21, but choosing from these titles:

> Fire Learning to be practical
> The dangers of gossip Drawing, pleasures and pains
> Music and me How to be happy though poor

23 Choose your own title and prepare an essay plan for each of the following:

(*a*) An argumentative essay, presenting your own views.

(*b*) The same, considering several viewpoints.

(*c*) A short story with an unusual ending.

(*d*) A factual essay, treating one of your own interests.

EXPRESSING YOUR IDEAS

The need for clarity

You have chosen an essay-title and worked out a plan. Now you can concentrate on writing the essay itself.

The first need in all writing, remember, is clarity. Your plan already provides for a clear, step-by-step unfolding of ideas: the paragraph themes are arranged in order, with ideas for developing each theme arranged alongside. You must now keep the following points in mind while writing your essay:

1 Each sentence must express its idea clearly. Do not try to crowd too much into any sentence; the effect will be too long and rambling, and clarity will suffer.

2 Avoid letting your paragraphs become too long and rambling, also.

3 Avoid unnecessary wordiness and long-winded phrases:

In consequence of his inability to . . . (Because he could not . . .)
And thus we see why it is that . . . (Clearly, then, . . .)

4 In descriptive writing, use the effects sparingly. Clarity will suffer if you overload with riches:

The warm splendour of golden-yellow summer sunlight slanted down from the amber orb floating enskied in a sea of cloud-littered blue, ploughing a merry path of bright beams down my uncle's rosy face.

(The warm sun came out and sent a golden beam slanting down my uncle's face.)

5 Check that each sentence is fully relevant to its paragraph theme.

6 Check grammar, spelling, punctuation, and ensure that each sentence is a complete sentence. Avoid faults like these:

What did I see at the fair? *A mass of multi-coloured roundabouts. A dazzle of side-shows. A motley throng of people. A whirl of merry movement.*

63

These are effective phrases, but they cannot stand as sentences. Join them up:

> What did I see at the fair? A mass of multi-coloured roundabouts whirled amidst a dazzle of side-shows. Merrily they moved, and a motley throng of people rode with them, or watched, or tried their skill.

7 Help your reader by providing a few "stepping-stones" or aids to clear understanding:

(*a*) Sum up parts of a long argument at intervals, before introducing more ideas:

> Gardening is, then, an absorbing hobby, offering plenty of exercise, delight for the lover of flowers, produce for the larder, and all at little cost.

(*b*) Let the last sentence of one paragraph lead on to the theme of the next, hinting at what will follow:

> Having considered the pleasures of gardening, we must now review its pains and disappointments. . . .

(*c*) Use linking phrases or short sentences, to connect your last idea with the next:

> Another advantage is that . . .
> Because of this difficulty we had to . . .
> Apart from this one must remember to . . .
> This plan failed, for the following reasons . . .
> The long climb was over, and now the valley lay . . .

Exercises

24 Plan and write a paragraph of 60–80 words on each of these topics, paying special attention to clarity of expression. Ideas must be well arranged and relevant; sentences clear, correct, and of reasonable length:

The advantages of hire-purchase	The dangers of smoking
The difficulties of being shy	How to spend money wisely

25 As Question 24, using these topics:

How to avoid sunburn	A practical job you enjoy
A useful gadget	Mending something

26 As Questions 24 and 25, using these descriptive topics, but being careful not to spoil the clarity by too much richness of effect:

Sunset	A runaway horse
A busy machine-shop	A self-service store

27 Plan and write twin paragraphs, using each of these topics, providing
a link between first and second paragraphs:

Swimming, in the sea and at the baths
Buying something you have longed for, and losing it next day
In praise of hot meals, and cold meals considered
Saturday night and Monday morning

Expressing ideas—plain or elaborate style?

You have practised both main styles—the plain, simple, and concise, for
everyday purposes, and the more elaborate, imaginative approach used
for special artistic effects. Probably you feel more at home with the plain
style; most people do, for the other can be tricky. Never think, though,
that the plain approach is unsuitable for essays: if you have interesting
ideas and can express them in good, lively, plain English, then you can
write good essays. This piece from a boy's essay on fishing proves the
point: there is nothing fancy about the style; it is plain English, but full
of action and tense excitement:

> My float bobs, then glides beneath the surface. This time I have hooked a
> monster! After his first plunge, I gain control. I wind in, but off he goes
> again. The line tears out against the screeching check of reel, cracking my
> knuckles against the reel handles. I feel him tire after that long swift dive,
> but still he races to the far bank, thrusting up-river, smashing through
> clumps of weed. He turns again downstream, in a last frantic dash for
> freedom. Out of the water he bursts, in a high leap, and I glimpse his long
> curved body, the sculptured head and ringed spots on a tawny ground. It
> is a huge rainbow trout.

The next piece, about model-making, is also in plain English, but the
writer's obvious enthusiasm for his hobby makes for good reading:

> My best model is of Nelson's famous flagship, H.M.S. Victory. I made it
> from a plastic kit, quite dear, but beautifully moulded in precise detail. I
> often wonder who makes the moulds for these models—the tiniest detail
> shows. I say "shows", but a part of the model-maker's strange pleasure is
> in making parts that do not show. H.M.S. Victory has a fully-detailed main
> gun-deck, with thirty tiny cannon ranged to port and starboard. I waited
> weeks before shutting all this from view by placing the upper deck on top,
> but knowing that it is there gives me an added, secret pleasure. . . .

The best advice you can have is to practise expressing interesting
ideas in good, clear, accurate English. Once you can do this, by all
means experiment with more elaborate styles, and you will probably
master those as well. Here are two samples which show imaginative
touches used to advantage, in a description and an argument:

65

Soon the rain streams heavily down. The sky changes from amber to a dull brown, and the pool grows dark with mud. The wind shrieks with wicked delight and hurls itself against the cliffs. Trees bow and sway in their bewilderment.

She thinks of the poem, "The Pied Piper of Hamelin", and, ". . . as the mumbling grows to a mighty rumbling . . ." she stands flushed and excited, watching the storm rise to a crescendo. The wind draws breath, then, rushing in, clutches the birch-trees' graceful pride of leaves and flings it far into the sea. Here waits a frothing, heaving mass of white horses who, with wild eyes and tangled manes, plunge their hooves like knives against the cliff and roll madly in the surf. . . .

To be a perfect visitor, you must of course be quite insane. In quick succession, simultaneously even, you must chat, watch television, eat to capacity and far beyond, admire the decorations, fend off the cat stalking your new nylons, play at dolls, trains and Davy Crockett, and show no pain when little Charlie scalps you with his rubber hatchet. I know you need to be insane. I experienced all this yesterday. I am. . . .

Exercises

28 Write a short paragraph in plain style on each of these topics, then rewrite it, attempting a more imaginative, elaborate style:

A huge machine in action	On falling downstairs
Coffee-bar scene	An aircraft taking off

29 As Question 28, using these topics:

An awkward customer	An animal in distress
A fool I have known	The pains of not winning

30 State in plain English your point of view on each of these topics, and add a short imaginative illustration for each one:

Small children should live in cages
Woman's place is in the home
Family teas on Sunday (with relatives) should be illegal
Can it be pleasant to be famous?

Beginning and ending an essay

Give plenty of thought to both ends of your essay—the start and the finish. With your opening sentences you must arrest the reader's attention and make him want to read on. A witty remark, a startling idea, a quotation, a little anecdote, a striking description—all are possibilities. As you approach the end, provide a sentence or two that

66

will round the essay off neatly; never let it tail off drearily. A short summing up, a final thought-provoking statement, a witty comment, or final touch of description is needed. Study these beginnings and endings, taken from students' essays:

My Plans for the Future

I am only fifteen, but already I am working on plans for my retirement. . . .

. . . And there, amidst my treasures, one day I shall die—but not from overwork.

A Nursery for a Small Child

My brother Mark, aged four, is a shocking child, and I plan for him a playroom in the form of a padded cell, with black, dirt-concealing walls and bars at the window. . . .

. . . There is one last item, which we all regard as essential: a heavy mallet beside his little cot, to help us get him to sleep.

The New Year

Ring out, wild bells, to the wild sky,
The flying cloud, the frosty light:
The year is dying in the night;
Ring out, wild bells, and let him die. . . .

. . . Ring out the old, ring in the new,
Ring, happy bells, across the snow:
The year is going, let him go;
Ring out the false, ring in the true.

How to Become a Millionaire

To make a million, they say, is easy; the problem is how to get your first thousand. . . .

. . . Well, now you know how to do it. Can anyone lend me a thousand pounds?

Exercises

31 Write an effective beginning and ending for each of these essays:

Spiders	Building your own boat
A dangerous occupation	Training for my future career

32 As Question 31, using these titles:

Highwaymen	What makes us laugh?
Father "does it himself"	There is nothing left to explore

33 As Questions 31 and 32, using these titles:

I shall never be rich   Pop singers
Some people do talk   The loneliness of old people

A touch of humour

Your essays should be lively, and a light-hearted, amusing touch will certainly help, unless of course you are writing on such very serious topics as "Keep death off the roads". Experiment with humour, but gradually at first. What may seem funny to you will not necessarily amuse others, and so it is safer to try little incidental touches first and see how these are received. To write a whole essay along humorous lines is not easy, unless you have a real talent for amusing writing.

Here are examples of the main possibilities. Note that the humour is rarely "broad": jokes that raise a loud guffaw are for red-nosed comedians, not essay-writers. Aim for light, smile-provoking effects. Be fairly brief also, yet vivid, choosing quaint or unexpected features:

(a) *Describing appearances—people, animals, scenes, or things:*

He had a nutcracker face—chin and nose trying to come together over a sunken mouth—and it was framed in iron-grey fluffy hair, that looked like a chin-strap of cotton-wool sprinkled with coal-dust.

Joseph Conrad

She was the youngest chimp I had ever seen: she could not walk, and was the proud possessor of four teeth only. She arrived in a basket out of which she peered with wide-eyed interest, sucking her left foot.

Gerald Durrell

On one corner stood two men, one carrying a big easy chair, the other a bouquet of pink and white tulips stuck in mimosa. They waited for the traffic to pass; and when this got tiresome, one put down the chair and the other sat down on it and smelled his bouquet.

Ludwig Bemelmans

Who would be an ornament? For ninety years my porcelain angel has been sitting on a cold porcelain slab, wings folded and nothing to do but gaze at his shiny white porcelain feet. You cannot even wiggle porcelain toes.

(b) *Looking at people's strange habits, failings, and mannerisms:*

My father never throws anything away. "Waste not, want not" is his favourite motto, and so we shall be slowly engulfed in a sea of miscellaneous junk. It will be a sad and needless death for whenever he does want something he always goes out and buys it. . . .

68

(c) Treating normally serious ideas in a light-hearted way:

The desire to collect things goes back to the dawn of man, when our ancestors shambled forth with stone axe or club, to bring back a sabre-toothed tiger, a mammoth—or a mate. Can you not feel the stirrings of blood-lust as you hunt through your latest packet of assorted used stamps? . . .

(d) Seeing the funny side of an awkward situation:

"Keep quite still, old boy, the Gaboon Viper is under your chair."

My remark had an extraordinary and arresting effect on my companion. He left the chair with a speed and suddenness that was startling, and suggestive of the better examples of levitation. The tin can, the hammer and the tin cutters went flying in various parts of the hut, and the supper table was all but overturned.

Gerald Durrell

(e) Making a witty comment:

Yet breakfast in bed is not the joy some persons would have us think of it. There are crumbs. . . .

E. V. Lucas

The first thing a small boy learns when he is given a drum is that he will never—ever—get another.

(f) Presenting quaint, whimsical ideas:

"Do you need bed-knobs, scissors . . . ?" I forget how the rest of the notice ran—I saw it only for an instant above a shop from the top of a bus in Camden Town. Scissors, of course, everybody needs, but . . . the question, "Do you need bed-knobs?" seems curiously inviting.

Robert Lynd

(g) Amusing personal memories:

It is strange to find oneself suddenly a thief. In a café once, I stayed behind to pay for our tea. As I left, I saw that Sheila had left her blue coat hanging by the door. It was a warm day and she must have forgotten it. Taking it down I wandered out. There stood Sheila, at the corner—wearing her blue coat.

Exercises

34 Write a short, amusing paragraph on each of these themes:

An old traction engine	I lost my train ticket
A tame duck	Unexpected visitors

35 As Question 34, using these titles:

Back wheels stuck in a ditch	Mending one's first puncture
He leapt before he looked	Gypsy fortune-teller

36 As Questions 34 and 35, using these themes:

My funniest experience   She is a peculiar person
Weird fashions in clothes   How to fall off a horse

Faults of style to avoid

1 *Monotony of sentence construction:*

I do not believe in the Loch Ness monster. I think the idea is silly. I have read the evidence. People invent stories about the monster. They want to become famous, perhaps. Maybe they want to get money from newspapers. They are wrong to mislead us. I think they should be prosecuted. They spread such silly ideas.

Each of these sentences is correct, but the total effect is very tedious because all are constructed in the same way: I do . . ., I think . . ., I have . . ., People invent . . ., etc. They are all very short, moreover, giving a jerky, abrupt effect. Always try to vary the pattern of your sentences, and their length, to avoid these faults.

Do you believe in the Loch Ness monster? After reading the evidence, I have concluded that the idea is silly. People who wish to become famous or earn money from the newspapers have probably invented stories telling of a monster, and I think it is very wrong to mislead us like this. Should they not be prosecuted for spreading such silly ideas?

2 *The wasteful "conversational" approach:* Avoid writing long passages of imagined conversation. This is useful in a novel but very wasteful of time and space in a short essay. In "Unexpected Guests", for instance, a few lines vividly condemning the "doorstep lingerer" are better than a whole page of conversation revealing her in action:

Next on my list for execution is the "doorstep-lingerer". There are those who won't come in and those who do, but linger while departing. Both transform your house into an arctic outpost and you to a shivering icicle, for they never call in warm weather.

3 *Slang, well-worn phrases, and over-enthusiastic language:*

I got a good ticking-off from my boss. . . .
We had a smashing session at the hop, my mates and I. . . .
Far be it from me to criticise, but . . .
She's got a super new skirt with oodles of frilly lace. It's ravishing, a dream, simply gorgeous. . . .

Language like this is often picturesque and lively when spoken, but you should not write it, for it only seems silly and vulgar on paper. Aim to use a rather more elegant style for essays, and avoid also abbreviations such as: wouldn't, shan't, I'll, won't.

Exercises

Your guide to essay writing is now complete. Most of the preliminary exercises involved the writing of paragraphs, and this is a useful approach, for if you can write a good paragraph you can learn to write a good essay. Here now are enough essay titles to last you for quite some time. Each essay should be about 5–7 paragraphs, 250–300 words if you are writing for C.S.E. (450–500 for G.C.E. "O" level). Look regularly at all the advice given in this chapter and do your best to apply it. Read and criticise one another's essays also, after they have been marked. You can learn much from comparing efforts in this way. Get your teacher to read and discuss some of the best of modern essays with you also.

ESSAY TITLES

1 Monsters
  What is wrong with schools?
  Riding on a bus
  It was a very strange holiday
  Winter seashore

2 The house of the future
  Human qualities I admire
  The romance of machines
  Modern traffic problems
  Looking through a telescope

3 Ships and the sea
  Should people keep pets?
  Mountains
  Good taste in clothes
  My ideal magazine

4 Myself in twenty years' time
  Some unpleasant animals
  Favourite meals, and others
  Moon landscape
  Lost in a fog

5 The charm of gardens
  Amateur actors
  A lost city
  Must we play games?
  Going to the pictures

6 Just daydreaming
  Collecting things
  I have some bad habits
  What I like about foreigners
  Alone in a deserted city

7 Is it wise to make plans?
  A pleasant hobby
  A room of one's own
  Must we tolerate our parents?
  The old museum

8 What makes us laugh?
  This house is haunted
  Memories, pleasant and un-
    pleasant?
  September
  An ideal schoolteacher

9 Modern furniture
  The old and the new
  Jungle scene
  My best friend
  Growing up is so painful

10 A shepherd's life
   Making things
   Can we improve youth clubs?
   The people next door
   First day of the sales

11 Three months' holiday
 Money and me ✓
 Villages today
 My favourite place
 Dark-night scare

12 The personality of dogs
 Troubles never come singly ✓
 Looking at the moon
 What can we look forward to? ✓
 My favourite reading ✓

13 House on fire
 How to make friends ✓
 Music and me ✓
 Tramping for fun
 I lost my way

14 It's time to get up again ⌐
 What to do with £30,000 ✓
 Seen at the zoo
 Helping at home
 Is ambition worth having?

15 Old people
 Nobody understands me ✓
 Beauty in unusual places ✓
 What are the English like?
 I did not like his face ✓

16 Ideas for a film or play
 Noises
 The colour of one's skin
 An old antique shop
 Men's clothes are out of date

17 Are you emigrating?
 Is it good to be young? ✓
 On being a tourist ✓
 Lakeland scene
 Tense moments I have known ✓

18 Brothers and sisters ✓
 Newspapers
 The Olympic Games
 The rain came down
 Dancing

19 Speed and speed-fiends
 Planning a road-safety week
 At the jumble sale
 Detective stories ✓
 Punctuality is over-rated

20 How to become a millionaire
 Novel suggestions for school clubs
 Dangerous professions ✓
 On wearing a hat ✓
 View of a port

21 Shipwreck
 Escaping from one's problems ✓
 Overheard in the bus ✓
 It was a curious shop
 Is co-education wise?

22 Things I hate doing ✓
 Advertising today
 Island in the tropics
 This house has seen much ✓
 Peace in our time

23 Television and education
 An old shopkeeper
 A journey that is different
 What I want to be ✓
 Modern art

24 Autumn colours
 In defence of wasting time
 Politics and ordinary people
 Poetry and poets
 Ships in bottles

25 Camouflage in nature
 How to be happy though poor
 Spare-time jobs
 The Loch Ness monster
 My earliest memories

26 Flying
 Can we improve examinations?
 Sometimes I hate people ✓
 The cathedral
 View from a hilltop

27 On giving a party
  Flowers
  Pleasures of doing nothing
  Walking in the rain
  I received a strange parcel

28 Highwaymen
  Going to the theatre
  Every man is an artist
  Fishing-boats
  Qualities we need today

29 My library
  Fancy-dress ball
  Mathematics and me
  Snow in the city
  Is it best to be ignorant?

30 The scrap-yard
  Pockets
  An ideal school magazine
  And then I broke the vase
  I have thrown away my television
    set

31 On lending a hand
  Are the railways out of date?
  School uniforms
  At the flower show
  Smugglers old and new

32 Motor-cycling
  Living in the space-age
  Politicians
  Old-fashioned rooms
  It looked like a good car

33 Doing it yourself
  Modern exploration
  Do you believe in ghosts
  My first and last television ap-
    pearance
  People's names

34 Beauty in young animals
  A test-pilot's life
  Machinery has stifled craftsman-
    ship
  Canal boats
  I could not sleep that night

35 Skyscrapers
  Home sweet home
  Why do people climb mountains?
  At the circus
  How to keep fit

36 Gold
  The pleasures and pains of singing
  On feeling shy
  If I were a Member of Parliament
  Television advertising

37 A policeman's lot is not a happy
    one
  Birthdays
  Is civilisation progressing?
  Funny episodes in my life
  The art of idling

38 My first bathe of the season
  Holidays at home
  Boy-and-girl friendships
  Car assembly line
  Some strange inventions

39 Christmas cards
  The lifeboat service
  Problems of being an only child
  Evening at the youth club
  Captive beasts and birds

40 Park scene in winter
  Women's clothes
  The end of the world
  Quaint superstitions
  Week-end shopping

41 Meanness
  Bonfire night
  Looking after a horrible child
  On having one's fortune told
  Why are some people so boring?

42 Do girls have a better time than
    boys?
  Clever people
  I decided to do something crazy
  What I most fear about the future
  Funny stories

73

43 The form photograph
   Gossiping
   Do faces reveal character?
   A spell in hospital
   Witches

44 Going to a party
   Bathing dresses, old and new
   An unfortunate birthday
   Pirates
   A sky full of stars

45 It is good to be silly at times
   A secret garden
   Spending money wisely
   A night spent out of doors
   Peculiar animals

46 I shall never go fishing again
   We can never really know people
   Breakfast time at my house
   Scene in a chocolate factory
   Forgetfulness

47 Some people are so rude
   An underground waterway
   Plastics today
   At the football match
   Keeping fish

48 The volcano erupted
   Ideas for a mobile shop
   The romance of airports
   Comedians
   Family tea-parties

49 Crooked old streets
   Preparing for my future job
   I suddenly became famous
   Should we enjoy having more
      leisure?
   Energy

50 Patent medicines
   Young people are not what they
      were
   Garden cities
   Railway-station platforms
   A knock came at the door

MAGAZINE ARTICLES

All you have learnt from your essay-writing comes into play here; a
magazine article is, of course, an essay. Some may be shorter than the
compositions which you write for homework and examinations, but you
can easily adjust the length without forgetting the need for good ideas
and arrangement, and care in all those aspects of English usage that
make for effective writing.

The shorter the article, the more effective must be your work: you
have to make a real impact in limited space. Your readers will be stern
critics—your own school-fellows. This need not put you off; use a vivid,
lively approach; feature unusual events or interests; bring in humour;
in reports set out your facts clearly and concisely, and avoid like the
plague a dreary recital of information everybody knows already.

Exercises

Here are some topics to practise; your classwork on these themes should
provide a host of good articles to delight your harassed school-magazine
editor.

74

(*a*) *Reports on School Affairs during the Year*

 1 The school play

 2 Open day

 3 The carol service

 4 The School fashion show

 5 Christmas socials

 6 Talks by visiting speakers

 7 School outings and visits

 8 Sports day

 9 Money collected for charities

10 Bring-and-buy sales

11 School debates

12 The school garden fête

13 Prize-award day

14 Harvest festival

15 Sports fixtures

16 Musical concerts

17 Foreign journeys

18 Film-shows

19 Speech contest

20 The library

21 Parent-Teacher Association

22 House notes

23 After-school clubs

24 Exhibitions

25 Duke of Edinburgh's Award

26 Ship-Adoption activities

27 New school projects

28 The year in Science, Art, Music, Rural Studies, or other suitable departments

(*b*) *Accounts of Personal Hobbies, Interests, and Experiences*

29 Unusual holidays

30 Keeping various pets

31 Youth-club activities

32 Making something (pottery, woodwork, metalwork, etc.)

33 Cycling or walking excursions

34 Books read and enjoyed

35 Learning something new and different (e.g. water ski-ing, formation dancing, etc.)

36 Various hobbies, if possible of unusual appeal, such as bell-ringing, keeping pet snakes, collecting unusual things, etc.

37 Amusing experiences

38 Points of view, on subjects of special interest to young people: pet "hates", ambitions

(c) *Fanciful Writing*

39 Short stories

40 Descriptions of people, places, or things, in one or two paragraphs

41 Conversations overheard

42 Poems

43 Essays on fanciful, imaginative themes

These suggestions by no means exhaust the possibilities; you can easily think of other lively and original contributions.

5 Understanding

COMPREHENSION

A good deal of your work in English involves what we call "comprehension". It is just as necessary to understand ideas expressed by others as to express your own ideas well. To develop your understanding, therefore, you are asked to read chosen passages carefully and then answer questions on them. In this way you learn to read with real attention, and by degrees you find yourself able to understand quite difficult ideas—a fairly useful accomplishment, you will agree.

Before looking at the advice on comprehension work, however, consider your own reading and thinking. What holds many young people back is their failure ever to read or listen to anything but the simplest of ideas, in the simplest of language. Just as a lack of proper food hinders your growth, so will your thinking and understanding be hampered if you never nourish your mind with "food for thought". As you grow up, therefore, look for more grown-up reading, of all kinds—not just the "comics" and picture-papers that really cater for grown-ups without much intelligence. There is plenty to read nowadays that will interest you, and which is in no way "stuffy". A later chapter in this book contains many suggestions, and your teacher can give you further advice, so please do not spend all your reading time insulting your intelligence with rubbish.

What is a comprehension exercise?

Having suggested that "going into training" for comprehension really involves choosing your general reading wisely, let us look at a typical comprehension exercise. It usually contains several paragraphs, amounting to 500 or 600 words in all. It may be an extract from a longer article, or from a book. Prose description or narrative is sometimes offered; even a poem; but a piece of argument, with closely reasoned ideas, is the most popular choice. The questions seek to find out whether you understand the ideas presented and the words and phrases used; sometimes you may also have to comment on the writer's style, pointing out examples of humour, for instance, or figures of speech and other effective details. You may have to write a short summary, in simple terms, of the ideas presented. It all adds up to understanding the piece set before you.

The method for comprehension

1 Read the whole passage slowly and carefully, ignoring the questions at first. In this reading you must aim to understand:

(a) the subject of the passage as a whole
(b) the main theme of each paragraph in turn

2 Re-read each paragraph in closer detail—perhaps several times, considering the various ideas which elaborate each main theme.

A few brief pencilled notes may help you fix the train of ideas clearly in your mind during these early readings.

3 Only after this careful preliminary reading should you look at the questions; these are numbered and lettered, and there should be no objection to your answering them in any order, providing you clearly number or letter each answer to match its question. Try the easier, shorter ones first; in the case of those questions needing a longer answer, rough out an answer first in pencil, and only write it in fair copy when you are satisfied with it. Your final copy should have its answers clearly set out and well spaced in relation one to another. You need not waste time writing out the questions themselves; just put the number or letter, and your answer alongside. If you do give a brief heading to an answer, to aid the marker, underline it neatly.

A short-worked example of comprehension

The passage

As soon as afternoon school was over and the children had burst out into the street with their jackdaw babble, volunteers, directed by Mr. Winter, began to strip the schoolroom. Police-constable Page, regarding this as a semi-official occasion, and having discarded his tunic and rolled up his shirt-sleeves, was only recognisable by his uniform trousers and boots, above which and a mufti waistcoat his big, honest face, well-nourished on plain country fare, had the look of a healthy schoolboy's. Joe Atkins, the blacksmith, also brought his huge strength to the job, moving ponderously, like one of the plough-horses he spent his days in shoeing. When he saw Morgan Jones, his pale brow beaded with sweat and his thin chest pumping, pushing this way and that at the desk which was his seat of authority, Joe Atkins's horny hands descended on it like steel grapples; they hove it aloft and swung the whole massive weight over his shoulder.

"You leave him to me, Mr. Jones," he said. "It be knack as does it."

From *This Little World*, by F. Brett Young

The questions

1 Give a word or phrase of the same meaning as the following words used in this passage:

> discarded   ponderously   pumping

2 Explain, briefly but clearly, the meaning of each of these phrases, as used in this passage:

> jackdaw babble   a semi-official occasion
> horny hands   beaded with sweat

3 What was Morgan Jones's profession? Explain in your own words how this is made clear in the passage.

4 Comment briefly on the two similes used here, explaining why they are effective.

5 State briefly but clearly how Mr. Jones is shown to have little strength, in contrast to the blacksmith.

Model answers

1 *discarded:* taken off.
ponderously: with slow, deliberate movements.
pumping: heaving up and down, from the exertion.

2 *jackdaw babble:* This phrase suggests the noisy chatter of the children, not unlike that of jackdaws.
a semi-official occasion: While the event was not strictly speaking part of the policeman's duties, he felt it was important enough to merit police help in an informal capacity.
horny hands: The word "horny" describes hands made hard and "leathery" by much manual work.
beaded with sweat: The perspiration on Mr. Jones's brow stood out in little drops, like beads.

3 It is clear that Mr. Jones was the schoolmaster, for his desk is referred to as "the seat of his authority"—the place at which he sat when in charge of the schoolroom.

4 (a) The blacksmith is described as ". . . moving ponderously, like one of the plough-horses. . . ." His great strength is thus well emphasised: one can imagine him moving slowly, with firm, heavy steps and the muscular bulk of a plough-horse

(b) Later, his "horny hands descended . . . like steel grapples". This simile again stresses the blacksmith's great strength: one thinks of the great steel jaws of a crane's grappling hooks, closing on some object it is going to lift.

5 The schoolmaster is described as pale-faced and thin-chested, tugging breathlessly at the desk and unable to move it. In contrast, the black-smith has "huge strength", like a plough-horse, and "horny", work-toughened hands, "like steel grapples". He lifts the desk effortlessly over his shoulder.

Comprehension dangers and difficulties

1 An exact understanding of the ideas is looked for; vague statements, or those worded in a "woolly", confused fashion, will not score much.

2 Always read the questions with great care, and try to appreciate the form in which you are to present your answer: in some cases a single word or short phrase will be enough; in others, however, a complete sentence or several sentences may be needed. Do not waste words, but put clearly and concisely all that is needed to answer the question fully.

3 When asked to explain words or phrases used in the passage, always locate them first, reading before and after the place where they occur, until you see what they mean as used in that particular passage. Then explain accordingly.

4 It is very important, when explaining words or phrases, to explain them *in terms of the right part of speech*: it would be quite wrong, for instance, when explaining "semi-official occasion", to write:

> *semi-official occasion:* this means *to look upon* the event as something not in the ordinary line of duty.

The word "occasion" is a noun, and must be explained in terms of a noun. Failure to do this is a very common error, and you must avoid it. Ask yourself whether the word is a noun, verb, or adjective, and explain accordingly. If it is a verb, explain in terms of the form of the verb used, for example:

> *pumping:* heav*ing* up and down (not "to heave" or "when he heaves", etc.).

Phrases amount essentially to noun, verb, or adjective also, and must be explained as such:

> *with their jackdaw babble:* i.e. with *something* ("babble" is a noun).

It would be wrong to put:

"This means *to make* a noise like jackdaws."

5   Never miss out questions by mistake—especially if you alter the order of answering. Do not leave blank spaces either; these can earn you nothing; write something, as sensible as you can make it, even if you are not sure of the right answer.

6   Beware of over-hasty thinking, resulting in answers wide of the mark. This is a test in straight thinking, not hasty guess-work.

7   If you quote words or phrases from the passage in your answer, enclose them in the usual quotation marks. Remember also the need to punctuate marginal numbers and letters, short headings, etc.

SUMMARISING

Writing a summary is another test, and a severe one, of your ability to understand ideas. You have to reduce a piece of writing to about one-third of its original length, preserving only the most important ideas, and expressing them in clear and simple language. All the long words, fancy style, and elaborate illustrations in the original passage must be swept aside, leaving only the main thoughts.

Summarising, then, involves careful reading, deciding which are the main ideas, making sure you understand them fully, and re-expressing them in simple English. When you think about it, something very similar goes on in your mind whenever you read, or listen to someone speaking. You could never remember all the words actually used, and so your mind constantly sifts the information selecting and rephrasing the essential ideas in simple form. Summarising is only doing in a formal way, on paper, what your mind does all the time. For sharpening the wits, and training you to grasp essential points, there is no finer exercise.

The method for summarising

1   As with comprehension work, first read the whole piece several times, slowly and carefully, trying to understand:

(a) the subject of the passage as a whole
(b) the main theme of each paragraph

2   Now study each paragraph in turn, and, in brief note form and simple wording, write a numbered list of the chief ideas.

3 Check and re-check this list, to ensure that your numbered main points do represent the main ideas of the original.

4 Next, use these notes to prepare a first connected draft of your summary, or "précis". If the notes were carefully done, it is easy to expand them into proper sentences. Your style must be simple and concise, and you must use approximately the number of words allowed. It is best to keep to the paragraphing of the original; this is easy if you draw lines amongst your numbered list of points, to show the original paragraph divisions. Sometimes, however, as in the example below, you might be able to improve the paragraphing slightly.

5 Check and adjust your first draft where necessary; never be afraid to alter it; and then write up your summary in completed form.

Here is a short sample, showing the method in action:

The piece

It was not so much his uncommon bulk that so much distinguished him from other sperm-whales, but a peculiar snow-white wrinkled forehead, and a high, pyramidical white hump. These were his prominent features; the tokens whereby he revealed his identity, at a long distance, to those who knew him.

The rest of his body was so streaked, and spotted, and marbled with the same shrouded hue, that, in the end, he had gained his distinctive appellation of the White Whale; a name, indeed, literally justified by his vivid aspect, when seen gliding at high noon through a dark blue sea, leaving a milky wake of creamy foam, all spangled with golden gleamings. Nor was it his unwonted magnitude, nor his remarkable hue, nor yet his deformed lower jaw, that so much invested the whale with natural terror, as that unexampled, intelligent malignity which, according to specific accounts, he had over and over again evinced in his assaults. More than all, his treacherous retreats struck more of dismay than perhaps aught else. For, when swimming before his exulting pursuers, with every apparent symptom of alarm, he had several times been known to turn round suddenly, and bearing down on them, either stave their boats to splinters, or drive them back in consternation to their ship.   (213 words)

From *Moby Dick*, by Herman Melville

Reduce this passage to a summary of 60–80 words.

Numbered list of main points

1 Recognisable far off by wrinkled forehead, great hump—both white.
2 Whole body mottled white, hence name "White Whale".
3 Striking sight: moving, white against blue sea, sun on wake.

New para.

4   Evil cunning more feared than size, colour, or misshapen jaw.

5   Would turn unexpectedly on boats, to scatter or destroy.

First draft	*Finished summary*
The great whale was recognisable by his wrinkled forehead and huge hump, both white. His whole body was in fact mottled with white, and so men called him "The White Whale". He was a striking sight, as he moved along, white against a blue background of sea, the sunlight glistening on his wake. (53)	One could recognise the huge whale by his wrinkled forehead and huge hump, both white. Indeed, his whole body was mottled with white, and men called him "The White Whale". He looked most striking, moving white against a blue sea, with sunlight glistening on his wake. (46)
Men feared his evil cunning, however, more than his size or colour or misshapen jaw. One of his tricks was to turn unexpectedly to attack the boats chasing him, aiming either to scatter or destroy them. (89)	Men feared his evil cunning far more than his great size, or colour, or misshapen jaw. Sometimes, when swimming away, he would turn unexpectedly and attack the whalers' boats, to destroy or scatter them. (80)

Some more hints about summarising

1   Ensure, by frequent checking, that your summary's main points really represent the main ideas of the original.

2   Break down the elaborate language and style of the original into plain, concise English; summarise in *your own* words, not those of the original. Be precise: vague, confused statements have no place in a summary. Avoid using figures of speech.

3   Work within the word-limits allowed, and always count and state the number of words you have used. A few adjustments in the wording of your first draft will usually suffice (compare the two sample versions in the example worked above). If you are very wide of the mark, your selecting of main points may have been faulty, and you should look again.

4   Develop an eye for balance and proportion of ideas. Summarising involves an even "shrinking" of the original passage, and each main idea in your summary must retain the same degree of prominence and importance as it had in the original. A common error amongst beginners is to use too many words to express the first idea or so, leaving too few words to express ideas that follow. The last part then becomes cramped and the original balance of ideas is lost.

5 Details of dates, names, and numbers in an original passage are generally important items, and you should normally retain them in your summary.

6 If the original passage contains direct (or "quoted") speech, or if the writer has written in the first person (the "I" or "We" approach), you must convert the passage into *indirect* speech in your summary. Thus: Jenny said, "I shall soon be ready" becomes: Jenny said she would soon be ready.

It is easy to convert direct speech into indirect: just think of yourself as a reporter, reporting what has been said. Imagine that your summary is to begin with the words: "He (or she) said that . . ." It need not begin in this way, but to think of it in these terms gives you the right approach for using indirect speech throughout.

COMPREHENSION EXERCISES

Thirty-five prose passages for comprehension now follow, and ten poems. All are graded approximately in order of difficulty.

Most of the prose passages are also suitable for summarising. Wherever this is so, one of the questions invites you to write a summary, and states the number of words allowed. While you still lack experience in summarising, you should do the comprehension exercises first, and only attempt the summary afterwards: the comprehension work will help you to understand the passage, and you will then be well on the way to making a good summary. Later, as your skill improves, try doing the summary first and the comprehension exercises afterwards. In the exercises the numbers in brackets are the line numbers of the passage.

Prose passages Nos. 3, 4, 7, 11, 13, 14, 16, 17, 18, 22, 25, 27, 29, 32, and 33 contain direct speech which must be converted into indirect. To accustom yourself to the idea of indirect speech, work through some of these pieces orally, doing the necessary conversion without any shortening at first. Later, when you summarise, you can re-express the same ideas, still in indirect speech, but more briefly.

1 THE BIG FEET OF EGGBERT, THE SCREAMER BIRD

Eggbert's feet were the bane of his life. There was so much of them, and they would get tangled together when he walked. Then there was the danger that he would tread on his own toes and fall down and make an exhibition of himself, as he had done on the first day. So he kept a very
5 close watch on his feet for any signs of insubordination. He would sometimes stand for as long as ten minutes with bent head, gravely staring at his toes as they wiggled gently in the grass, spread out like the arms of a starfish. Eggbert's whole desire, obviously, was to be dis-associated from these outsize feet. He felt irritated by them. Without
10 them, he was sure, he could gambol about the lawn with the airy grace of a dried thistle-head. Occasionally, having watched his feet for some time, he would decide that he had lulled them into a sense of false security. Then, when they least suspected it, he would launch his body forward in an effort to speed across the lawn and leave these hateful
15 extremities behind. But although he tried this trick many times, it never succeeded. The feet were always too quick for him, and as soon as he moved they would deliberately and maliciously twist themselves into a knot, and Eggbert would fall head first into the daisies.

His feet were continually letting him down, in more ways than one.
20 Eggbert had a deep ambition to capture a butterfly. Why this was we could not find out, for Eggbert could not tell us. All we knew was that screamers were supposed to be entirely vegetarian, but whenever a butterfly hovered within six feet of Eggbert his whole being seemed to be filled with blood-lust, his eyes would take on a fanatical and most
25 un-vegetarian-like gleam, and he would endeavour to stalk it. However, in order to stalk a butterfly with any hope of success one has to keep one's eyes firmly fixed on it. This Eggbert knew, but the trouble was that as soon as he watched the butterfly with quivering concentration, his feet, left to their own devices, would start to play up, treading on each
30 other's toes, crossing over each other, and sometimes even trying to walk in the wrong directions. As soon as Eggbert dragged his eyes away from the quarry, his feet would start to behave, but by the time he looked back again the butterfly would have disappeared.

From *The Drunken Forest*, by Gerald Durrell

1   Give a word or short phrase that means the same as the following:

>   bane   (1)
>   insubordination   (5)
>   disassociated   (8–9)
>   maliciously   (17)
>   blood-lust   (24)

2   Explain each of the following phrases:

>   these hateful extremities   (14–15)
>   with quivering concentration   (28)
>   left to their own devices   (29)

3   What is meant by the words "he would decide that he had lulled them into a sense of false security . . ."?   (12–13)

4   Comment on the effectiveness of the words "with the airy grace of a dried thistle-head. . . ."   (10–11)

5   In what ways are we persuaded that Eggbert looked on his feet as not really belonging to him at all?

6   Briefly explain the phrase "make an exhibition of himself. . . ."   (3–4)

7   Explain the meaning of "his eyes would take on a fanatical and most un-vegetarian-like gleam . . ."   (24–5)

8   Write an amusing paragraph, describing Eggbert's examination of a sleeping crocodile.

9   What do we learn from this piece of writing about Gerald Durrel himself?

2 SEA BATHING—VICTORIAN STYLE

Sea bathing, in Victorian times, was not quite the light-hearted amusement that it is today. There was no running down from hotel to beach in a bath robe, no sunbathing, or lying about on the sands in bathing-dresses after the dip. Everything had to be done in an orderly and
5 extremely decorous manner. Mixed bathing was not allowed anywhere. Men and women each had their separate part of the beach, and they were not supposed to meet in the water.

Bathing clothes were also carefully regulated. Men usually wore simple bathing-drawers and no more, but women were obliged to wear
10 thick, cumbersome serge garments that covered them completely from head to foot. These satisfied the demands of modesty, but they must have been extremely uncomfortable for swimming.

Even thus decently covered, women were not supposed to show themselves on the beach whilst in bathing-attire. They had to wait their
15 turn for a bathing-machine, a sort of wooden cabin on wheels which was drawn right down to the water's edge by horses. On its seaward side a sort of hood or canopy projected outwards and downwards over the water, completely screening the bather until she was actually in the sea. There was a bathing-woman in attendance, part of whose duty was to
20 dip—in other words, to seize the bather as soon as she emerged and dip her forcibly under water two or three times. This was supposed to be for the benefit of her health, and no doubt it was all right in the hands of the gentle. But most bathing-women were the reverse of gentle, and to be dipped by them must have been a decidedly strenuous form of
25 exercise.

In course of time, however, those ideas changed. The hood disappeared when it was no longer thought shocking for a girl to be seen on the steps of the machine in bathing-dress. Then towards the end of the century some daring individual conceived the idea of using small
30 coloured tents which could be easily set up and taken down, and which also did away with wearisome waits because they were not hired but were the property of the user.

From *A History of Everyday Things in England*,
by Marjorie and C. H. B. Quennell

1 Briefly explain the meaning of each of the following:

> an orderly and extremely decorous manner   (4–5)
> carefully regulated   (8)
> cumbersome serge garments   (10)
> seaward side   (16)
> the demands of modesty   (11)

2 What peril awaited the Victorian bathing "belle" when she stepped from her bathing-machine into the sea?

3 What was the main reason for having bathing-machines on Victorian beaches?

4 Briefly list *five* reasons which must have made bathing unpleasant for a Victorian girl.

5 What do the phrases "decently covered" (13) and "daring individual" (29) suggest to you about the writers' attitude to what they are describing?

6 What was the principal drawback of the bathing-machine, which eventually led to its disappearance?

7 Write a summary of this passage, in 100–20 words.

8 What do you learn from this passage about people who lived in Queen Victoria's day?

9 Write an amusing paragraph in which a Victorian bathing-machine and a pretty young lady meet for the first time.

3   SHERLOCK HOLMES VISITS THE SCENE OF THE CRIME

Number 3, Lauriston Gardens, wore an ill-omened look. It was one of
four which stood back some little way from the street, two being
occupied and two empty. The latter looked out with three tiers of vacant
melancholy windows, which were blank and dreary, save that here and
5 there a "To Let" card had developed into a cataract upon the bleared
panes. A small garden sprinkled over with a scattered eruption of sickly
plants separated each of these houses from the street, and was traversed
by a narrow pathway, yellowish in colour, and consisting apparently of
a mixture of clay and of gravel. The whole place was very sloppy from
10 the rain which had fallen through the night. The garden was bounded
by a three-foot brick wall with a fringe of wood rails upon the top, and
against this wall was leaning a stalwart police-constable, surrounded by
a small knot of loafers, who craned their necks and strained their eyes
in the vain hope of catching some glimpse of the proceedings within.
15   I had imagined that Sherlock Holmes would at once have hurried
into the house and plunged into a study of the mystery. Nothing
appeared to be further from his intention. With an air of nonchalance
which, under the circumstances, seemed to me to border upon affectation, he lounged up and down the pavement, and gazed vacantly at the
20 ground, the sky, the opposite houses and the line of railings. Having
finished his scrutiny, he proceeded slowly down the path, or rather down
the fringe of grass which flanked the path, keeping his eyes riveted upon
the ground. Twice he stopped, and once I saw him smile, and heard him
utter an exclamation of satisfaction. There were many marks of foot-
25 steps upon the wet clayey soil, but since the police had been coming and
going over it, I was unable to see how my companion could hope to
learn anything from it. Still I had had such extraordinary evidence of the
quickness of his perceptive faculties, that I had no doubt that he could
see a great deal which was hidden from me.

From *A Study in Scarlet*, by Sir Arthur Conan Doyle

1   Briefly explain the following phrases; refer especially to the adjectives used:

> an ill-omened look   (1)
> melancholy windows   (4)
> bleared panes   (5-6)
> a stalwart police-constable   (12)
> the vain hope   (14)

2   Comment, in about 25 words, on the way in which the writer conveys an impression of wretchedness and drabness in his first paragraph.

3   Explain the meaning of each of the following:

an air of nonchalance which, under the circumstances, seemed to me to border upon affectation   (17-19)

I had had such extraordinary evidence of the quickness of his perceptive faculties   (27-8)

4   Give a word or short phrase that might be used here in place of the following:

> cataract   (5)
> eruption   (6)
> knot   (13)
> craned   (13)
> lounged   (19)
> vacantly   (19)
> scrutiny   (21)

5   Write a short but vivid character sketch of the great detective, Sherlock Holmes.

6   Add another paragraph to this extract from *A Study in Scarlet*, in which Holmes enters the house and makes an astonishing discovery.

7   Sherlock Holmes's friend, Dr. Watson, is telling this story. What sort of man do you imagine him to be, judging from the way he speaks?

4 MR. WINKLE PREPARES FOR SKATING

Old Wardle led the way to a pretty large sheet of ice and the fat boy and Mr. Weller, having shovelled and swept away the snow which had fallen on it during the night, Mr. Bob Sawyer adjusted his skates with a dexterity which to Mr. Winkle was perfectly marvellous, and described
5 circles with his left leg and cut figures of eight, and inscribed upon the ice, without once stopping for breath, a great many other pleasant and astonishing devices, to the excessive satisfaction of Mr. Pickwick, Mr. Tupman and the ladies. . . .

All this time, Mr. Winkle, with his face and hands blue with cold,
10 had been forcing a gimlet into the soles of his feet, and putting his skates on, with the points behind, and getting the straps into a very complicated and entangled state, with the assistance of Mr. Snodgrass, who knew rather less about skates than a Hindoo. At length, however, with the assistance of Mr. Weller, the unfortunate skates were firmly screwed and
15 buckled on, and Mr. Winkle was raised to his feet.

"Now, then, sir," said Sam, in an encouraging tone; "off vith you, and show 'em how to do it."

"Stop, Sam, stop!" said Mr. Winkle, trembling violently, and clutching hold of Sam's arms with the grasp of a drowning man. "How
20 slippery it is, Sam!"

"Not an uncommon thing upon ice, sir," replied Mr. Weller. "Hold up, sir!"

This last observation of Mr. Weller's bore reference to a demonstration Mr. Winkle made at the instant, of a frantic desire to throw his feet
25 in the air, and dash the back of his head on the ice. . . .

"Now, Winkle," cried Mr. Pickwick, quite unconscious that there was anything the matter. "Come; the ladies are all anxiety."

"Yes, yes," replied Mr. Winkle, with a ghastly smile. "I'm coming."

From *The Pickwick Papers*, by Charles Dickens

1   Turn the second half of this account into indirect speech (beginning at line 16); you may adjust the wording to give a rather more modern effect if you wish.

2   Give a word or short phrase that could be used here in place of each of the following:

> dexterity   (4)
> inscribed   (5)
> devices   (7)
> observation   (23)
> unconscious   (26)

3   Explain why Mr. Snodgrass's knowledge of skates should be compared with that of a Hindoo.

4   Give a word or phrase explaining the force of the adjective in each of the following:

> *excessive* satisfaction   (7)
> *unfortunate* skates   (14)
> *ghastly* smile   (28)

5   Rewrite lines 23–5 in simple modern English.

6   Explain briefly what Mr. Pickwick meant when he said: ". . . the ladies are all anxiety" (27).

7   State simply, in about 25 words, what you consider makes us smile at this description of Mr. Winkle's preparations for skating.

8   Invent another paragraph, to continue this account of Mr. Winkle's skating adventure, in which he unexpectedly performs a miracle of skating, purely by accident.

9   Turn to the *Pickwick Papers* and see how Charles Dickens continued the episode.

5 A FLYING ROBOT

The automatic pilot can fly a big air-liner for hours without attention. First think of what the human Captain has to do. He knows which course he has to follow by his compass, and he must remain at a constant height shown on his altimeter. He watches these instruments
5 as he flies, adjusting his rudder to keep the compass needle steady and his elevators to control his height. At the same time he has to keep the aircraft upright, and he must manipulate his ailerons to do so. Air pockets and gusts of wind may be repeatedly throwing the aircraft about. Yet all these things the automatic pilot looks after while the
10 Captain sits back and drinks his coffee.

It works directly from the special instruments by which it can compare what the plane ought to be doing with what it actually is doing. At the heart of it is a gyroscope, a spinning top loosely held so that it will always point in the same direction, whatever the plane may do.
15 Against it the robot can judge the movements of the aircraft and so decide what adjustments it must make to correct them. Each part of the automatic pilot imitates one part or another of the Captain's actions.

In many ways the robot is a better pilot than the human being, because it can act more quickly. For instance it can use an instrument
20 which measures what the air is doing several feet ahead of the aircraft, and in the split second which it has to spare before the aircraft covers the intervening space it can begin to adjust the controls so that it is not taken unawares by a gust of wind or an "air pocket". When this "gust alleviator" is working, the aircraft travels as smoothly as can be.

25 You can imagine that if a robot pilot goes wrong the consequences can be very frightening to anyone travelling in the aircraft. To guard against this there are now robot "monitors"—extra robots which keep an eye on the automatic pilot and watch for the first indication that it is going "haywire".

From *Robots*, by Nigel Calder

1   Write a definition of the word "robot".

2   Briefly state the two main tasks mentioned in the first paragraph which can be performed by the automatic pilot.

3   For what main reason is an automatic pilot more reliable than a human pilot?

4   Explain in your own words what a "gust alleviator" (23–4) does.

5   Briefly explain the meaning of each of the following:

> altimeter (4)
> air pockets (7–8)
> intervening space (22)
> monitors (27)
> haywire (29)

6   List the three main "control surfaces" of an aircraft, and state briefly what each one does.

7   Write a summary of this passage, in 120–40 words.

8   Write a paragraph outlining what other uses you foresee for robot devices, in particular to help our modern road-traffic problems.

9   Write an amusing paragraph entitled "I made a robot to help in the home".

6 COUNTRY FAIR

It was the moment when the sun, sinking behind the woods and hills,
leaves a faint white crystal sky and a world transformed in an instant
from sharp outlines and material form into coloured mist and rising
vapour. The Fair also was transformed, putting forward all its lights
5 and becoming, after the glaring tawdriness of the day, a place of shadow
and sudden circles of flame and dim obscurity.

Lights, even as Jeremy watched, sprang into the air, wavered, fal-
tered, hesitated, then rocked into a steady glow, only shifting a little
with the haze. On either side of him were rough, wooden stalls, and
10 these were illuminated with gas, which sizzled and hissed like angry
snakes. The stalls were covered with everything invented by man; here
a sweet stall, with thick, sticky lumps of white and green and red, glass
bottles of bulls' eyes and peppermints, thick slabs of almond toffee and
pink coconut icing, boxes of round chocolate creams and sticks of
15 liquorice, lumps of gingerbread, with coloured pictures stuck on them,
saffron buns, plum cakes in glass jars, and chains of little sugary biscuits
hanging on long red strings. There was the old-clothes stall with trousers
and coats and waistcoats, all shabby and lanky, swinging beneath the
gas, and piles of clothes on the boards, all nondescript and unhappy and
20 faded; there was the stall with the farm implements, and the medicine
stall, and the flower stall, and the vegetable stall, and many, many
another. Each place had his or her guardian, vociferous, red-faced,
screaming out the wares, lowering the voice to cajole, raising it again to
draw back a retreating customer, carrying on suddenly an intimate
25 conversation with the next-door shopkeeper, laughing, quarrelling,
arguing.

To Jeremy it was a world of giant heights and depths. Behind the
stalls, beyond the lane down which he moved, was an uncertain glory,
a threatening peril. He fancied that strange animals moved there; he
30 thought he heard a lion roar and an elephant bellow. The din of the
sellers all about him made it impossible to tell what was happening
beyond there; only the lights and bells, shouts and cries, confusing
smells, and a great roar of distant voices.

From *Jeremy*, by Sir Hugh Walpole

1 Briefly explain the following phrases:

> the glaring tawdriness of the day (5)
> all nondescript and unhappy and faded (19–20)
> lowering the voice to cajole (23)
> an intimate conversation (24–5)
> confusing smells (32–3)

2 What do the phrases "a world of giant heights and depths" and "an uncertain glory, a threatening peril" tell you about the small boy's state of mind as he walked through the fairground? Give your answer in about thirty words.

3 Discuss the writer's use of *either* colour, *or* sounds, to enliven his description of the scene.

4 Give a word or short phrase of the same meaning as each of the following:

> dim obscurity (6)
> faltered (7–8)
> lanky (18)
> vociferous (22)

5 Is there anything especially significant about this passage of description, bearing in mind that a small boy is involved?

6 Rewrite the first sentence in your own words, so as to describe quite clearly the moment of sunset that the writer has in mind.

7 Write a plain summary of this passage, in about 100 words. Compare it with the original. Which do you prefer, and why?

7 STARTING THE HORSELESS CARRIAGE

"Oh, Arthur," said Sophia, "you must be very clever."

The viscount, his eyes nearly shut, sat quite still on his horse. He looked down his nose at them, at Arthur standing beside the machine, at Arthur's hands splayed on the carriage seat's back, broken-nailed,
5 square, streaked with oil; at Sophia in her clean, dark-green habit standing obstinately beside Arthur; at the hideous naked parts of the engine, oily, metallic, clumsily beaten out of pieces salvaged from scrap-heaps. His lip curled, thought Sophia, who liked to read the works of lady novelists. She said to Arthur, with an oblique look, "Shall I get in
10 now? Is she ready to go?"

"Near enough," said Arthur. He frowned in concentration at the end of the sashcord, which he held in his hand. Sophia hitched up her riding habit and clambered into the seat, realising, with faint surprise, that it was rather pleasant not to be helped along by a gentlemanly hand
15 holding her elbow or clasping her fingers. It gave her a feeling of freedom and progress. She sat up very straight and flashed at the viscount a sideways glance of malice, defiance and complacency.

"Sophia," said the viscount in a private voice, ignoring Arthur who was anyway lost in a trance, "everyone is looking. Think twice before
20 you make yourself a laughing-stock in front of the whole village."

"Thank you; I have," said Sophia. "Twice at least. People always laugh at pioneers, don't they? Good-bye, Francis—I don't suppose we shall go far."

. . . There was a prodigious explosion of sound; the machine rocked
25 like a touched-off cannon, roared and popped, vomited great billows of bluish smoke. From the duck pond into which his horse had flung him, through the mud that plastered his features and clotted on his lashes, the viscount saw Arthur and Sophia, sitting stiffly upright side by side, grinding and jerking away in slow motion across the green. They did
30 not look back. The set of their shoulders, the rigidity of their heads, told him they had seen his fall. Between the lodge gates and up the distant drive shot a whitish blur: that was his horse.

From *The Fall*, by Margaret Bonham

1   What signs are there in this passage that Sophia's proposal to ride in Arthur's car is disapproved of by the viscount?

2   Briefly explain the following words and phrases from the passage:

> splayed   (4)
> complacency   (17)
> lost in a trance   (19)
> a laughing-stock   (20)
> people always laugh at pioneers   (21–2)

3   What hint of Sophia's character is given in lines 8–9: ". . . His lips curled, thought Sophia, who liked to read the works of lady novelists. . . ."?

4   What do we learn in the passage about her attitude to the Viscount?

5   Comment, in about forty words, on the ways in which the writer achieves a humorous effect in the last paragraph.

6   Explain the meaning of the sentence: "The set of their shoulders, the rigidity of their heads, told him they had seen his fall."   (30–31)

7   Give a word or phrase of the same meaning as the following:

> salvaged   (7)
> with an oblique look   (9)
> a prodigious explosion of sound   (24)
> vomited great billows of bluish smoke   (25-6)
> clotted   (27)

8   Write a short newspaper account of this sad accident, such as might have appeared in the local paper in the early days of motor-cars.

9   Write a paragraph continuing the episode, as the car careers over the village green.

8 SKI-ING

If you can do the turns and downhill runs on the nursery slopes with moderate success you will find an ever growing desire to try your skill on more varied terrain farther afield. What greater satisfaction is there than to tour in the hills and mountains? Whether you tour on your own or in the company of congenial friends, your discovery of ski-ing as a sport and a means of locomotion will give you a feeling of well-being such as you can seldom experience in any other sport. The wide open spaces, sunshine, the scenery and the feeling of being in the best of company on top of the world are exhilarating and the inevitable thirst, appetite and even the weariness at the end of the day are by no means the least agreeable aspects of touring.

Almost every tour begins with a climb. It may be a long or it may be merely a short one to begin with but vary the method of climbing. Use the herringbone, traversing and side-stepping methods as and when best suited to the terrain and you will conserve much of your energy. Do not rest too frequently until you have reached the top or whatever other goal you have set yourself. Keep up a steady and rhythmical pace all the time. Now you will know how fit you are but beware of taking on more than you can manage. Remember you require strength and endurance for the downhill run also. If you have practised conscientiously on the nursery slopes, you will discover that you have acquired a state of fitness that you have never expected. When you have reached a height on your first tour, you will be amazed at what you have achieved with comparatively little effort. Unless you are an active sportsman and are really in good physical condition, you cannot expect to climb for any length of time without feeling the effects of it. Therefore, do not attempt too large a tour within the first few days of your ski-ing holiday even if you are no longer a novice. Do not over-tax yourself because, if you do, there is a danger of falls through lack of control during your descent when you need just as much fitness and strength as you do in climbing. . . .

If you go on a long tour, remember the following:

1. Never go alone. You may need help or you may have to assist someone else.

2. Always inform someone responsible where you are going and when you estimate to return.

3. Check the weather conditions carefully. When in doubt ask some knowledgeable local person for advice.

4. Always carry the essential equipment with you.

40   5. Never overestimate your strength, fitness or prowess.

From *Ski-ing for Beginners*, by F. Broderman and G. A. McPartlin

1 Express in your own words the principal pleasures of ski-ing that are mentioned in this passage.

2 In what way can a skier save strength and energy while climbing uphill?

3 What can happen to a skier who overtaxes his strength?

4 Explain the following phrases:

    nursery slopes   (1)
    more varied terrain   (3)
    a means of locomotion   (6)
    some knowledgeable local person   (37-8)

5 Briefly state the possible dangers the writers have in mind when they offer hints Nos. 3, 4, and 5.

6 What is the wisdom behind the precaution advised in hint No. 2?

7 Write a summary of this passage, in 140-60 words.

8 Would this form of winter sport attract you or not? Give your reasons.

9 Imagine yourself ski-ing down a ski-jump, shortly before you launch yourself out into mid-air. Write a vivid paragraph describing your feelings.

9 A Dog's Intelligence

You must not overrate your dog's intelligence. Basically, he is like all animals a creature of instinct, without reasoning power. He cannot think things out or make a plan. Watch a dog trying to get a large stick through a small hole in a fence. To you or me it would, I am sure, be
5 the simplest thing to go through and pull it through after by one end. If the dog does that it will be by accident, and the test is to see whether, presented with the same problem a little while afterwards, he solves it at once. That is his limitation, and you must always keep that in mind in your dealings with him.

10   On his own he acts by instinct, or at the call of his natural desires, to eat, drink, sleep, and so on. The little business he goes through when settling down to sleep, attempting to dig himself in as it were, and curling round and round, is pure instinct, inherited from ancient ancestors sleeping in the open. With human beings he also acts under
15 instruction, according to what and how he has been taught; again, working dogs, such as gun dogs and sheepdogs, also have the power of heredity behind them, which inclines them to act in the way they are being taught.

Still, within his limits, the dog is one of the most intelligent of
20 animals, having a receptive mind, a good memory and usually a willingness to learn. He also has, as we know, great power of affection, and also a sense of sin; he knows very quickly when he has done wrong. See his guilty look when presented with the evidence of crime; though that may also sometimes be merely fear. We must always be careful not
25 to endow our dogs with human traits and feelings. All the same, he is extremely sensitive to atmosphere, and can differentiate between people. A puppy soon learns to know his master or mistress, usually, I think, by his sense of smell and hearing. Both are extremely acute. The range of human hearing is from 20 to 20,000 vibrations a second; that of the
30 dog is up to 70,000 or 100,000; so he can hear sounds that are inaudible to us, and at the same time is very sensitive to tone—and to the state of mind behind a tone of voice.

From *Dogs as Pets for Boys and Girls*, by Lt.-Col. C. E. G. Hope

1 Briefly explain the meaning of each of the following phrases:

> a creature of instinct (2)
> the power of heredity (16–17)
> a receptive mind (20)
> a sense of sin (22)
> extremely sensitive to atmosphere (26)

2 What does the writer mean when he warns us against "endowing our dogs with human traits and feelings"? (25)

3 Read the second paragraph carefully, and then write a clear definition of the word "instinct".

4 Briefly explain, in your own words, the main quality that is missing from a dog's intelligence.

6 Give a word or phrase that means the same as each of the following:

> Basically (1)
> limitation (8)
> differentiate (26)
> acute (28)
> inaudible (30)

What feature makes it easier to train a sheepdog or a gundog to do his work?

7 Summarise the last paragraph of this passage (starting at line 19), stating clearly in about 50 words the main features of a dog's intelligence and other useful qualities.

8 Do you think these facts about the intelligence of dogs might also apply to cats in some respects, or do you regard cats as more intelligent?

9 Write a short character sketch of a St. Bernard.

10 BE SENSIBLE WITH MACHINES

The worker controls hand tools at will and is exercising thought in doing so; if not, he soon becomes aware of the fact either by injuring himself or by ruining his work. Carelessness breaks drills, hits fingers, cuts to wrong measure; in fact very many things go wrong for lack of concen-
5 tration. With electrically driven machines continual intense concentration is absolutely necessary to maintain complete control of the machine. Remember that *you* have the brains and not the machine. The machine is your servant and working to your will; your will is mechanically transferred to the machine by various controls; you must fully under-
10 stand the controls and what they control. Machines are meant to produce work by processes which if done by hand would be long and tedious, and machines are made capable of doing work which cannot be done by hand. They have been made to the most accurate measurements and great engineering skill has been exercised to get such an
15 accuracy which can be ruined by one thoughtless worker. Through lack of concentration he can wreck a most expensive machine. A jammed drill on work not properly fixed down may put the spindle out on a drilling machine; this can be serious when the makers have made the spindle true to a matter of a thousandth of an inch. If one's attention is
20 diverted when using a lathe, as an example, the traverse may go too far and hit the chuck jaws, or a travelling tool jam into a shoulder of turned work. If you use machine tools treat them with the respect they deserve. Do not interfere with handles or levers on any machines, even if stationary. Do not leave any machines running unattended. Never
25 interfere with gear levers when a machine is in motion.

Many machines run from 400 volts power, so always remember not to interfere with switches or supply; report anything you consider wrong after switching off the isolating switch. Never wait for something to happen. Do not interfere with speed levers or gears may be damaged;
30 know the machine before using it; find out the levers that can be used when the machine is in motion (usually only those on the saddle, apron and tailstock on a lathe). To operate on any machine you should be fully conversant with the operation of all controls. Never experiment.

From *Metalwork*, by G. Keeley

1   Explain in about 25 words why you think this extract ends with the words "Never experiment".

2   Briefly explain the meaning of the following phrases:

> continual intense concentration   (5–6)
> your will is mechanically transferred   (8–9)
> if one's attention is diverted   (19–20)
> treat them with the respect they deserve   (22)

3   What is the key sentence in the first paragraph that sums up the attitude you should have towards any machine you might operate? Write out this sentence, and then explain in your own words exactly what it means.

4   What principal failure on the part of a machine-operator might lead to trouble?

5   Give another word or short phrase for each of the following:

> exercising   (1)
> tedious   (12)
> chuck jaws   (21)
> isolating switch   (28)

6   Why should you "never wait for something to happen"?   (28–9)

7   What is the difference, if any, between controlling hand tools and machines?

8   Write a paragraph explaining the difficulties you experienced when first learning to use any particular hand tool or machine.

9   Briefly outline the qualities you think are essential in a person wishing to become a skilled craftsman working with powerful and expensive machines.

10   Summarise this passage, in 140–60 words.

11 THE DANCE OF A BIRD OF PARADISE

His calls began to increase in frequency, and I carefully adjusted the
position of the parabolic reflector until they produced the highest
response on the meter of the recorder. Charles crouched behind his
camera, his eye to the viewfinder, his finger on the starting button.

5   With electrifying suddenness, the bird ducked his head and throwing
his magnificent plumes over his back, he scuttled down his branch, a
tremulous fountain of colour, shrieking passionately. Up and down the
branch he danced in a frenzy. After half a minute he seemed to get out
of breath, for his shrieks ceased and he danced in silence.

10   As we watched, enthralled, I remembered that Fred had told us that,
according to the local people, the birds sometimes become so over-
wrought that they fall off their branches exhausted and can be picked
up from the ground before they recover. Now, watching the dance, I was
well able to believe that this might indeed happen.

15   Abruptly the tension snapped and the bird stopped dancing. Uncon-
cernedly he resumed his preening; but after a few minutes he began his
dance again. Three times he performed this ecstatic display and twice we
were able to change our position in the banana grove to get another view
of him. Then, as the rays of the rising sun flooded the tree, his passions
20 seemed to subside and his shrieks changed to a growling bubble. This
lasted for a few seconds. Then he opened his wings and glided down to
the valley from where he had come. The hens flew after him. The dance
was over.

Exultantly, we packed up our equipment. It was the climax of our
25 expedition; at last we had witnessed the whole of the magical, fabled
dance of a wild Count Raggi's Bird of Paradise.

From *Quest in Paradise*, by David Attenborough

1   Briefly state *three* reasons why David Attenborough and his companions went in search of the Bird of Paradise.

2   Explain the meaning of each of the following phrases:

> with electrifying suddenness   (5)
> a tremulous fountain of colour   (7)
> in a frenzy   (8)
> the tension snapped   (15)

3   How might it be possible sometimes to catch one of these birds in a very simple way?

4   Give a word or phrase that might be used here in place of each of the following:

> frequency   (1)
> scuttled   (6)
> overwrought   (11–12)
> preening   (16)
> ecstatic   (17)
> subside   (20)
> exultantly   (24)
> climax   (24)

5   What exactly does David Attenborough mean when he describes this bird's dance as "fabled"?   (25)

6   Write a plain and concise outline, suitable for an entry in a small handbook of tropical birds, describing the dance of a Bird of Paradise. (40–50 words)

7   Write a summary of this passage, in 100–20 words, remembering the need for indirect speech.

8   What do you imagine might be the difficulties and disappointments in David Attenborough's life as a naturalist?

9   Write a paragraph describing vividly the scene in the banana grove after the human visitors had gone.

12 YOUTH LEADER

There is one snag in this job which very soon presents itself. A school-teacher has a certain right to be heeded, and his class knows it. A youth leader has no rights whatever. Nor has he a "captive audience". He is a friendly intruder upon young people's spare time. He may be brimming
5 over with constructive ideas and stimulating advice, but his time will be wasted if he once forgets that he is making suggestions which no-one is obliged to accept.

When the "youth movement" first took shape towards the end of the last century, no-one needed to worry about offering his help in the
10 wrong way. The men and women who started organisations like the Boy Scouts and the Boys Brigade, lads' clubs and girls' clubs, were entering a field where young people were under-privileged and deprived. The leaders were benefactors, and like the soup-kitchens which other charitable people established, there was no need to worry about the
15 demand for the goods supplied. Young people in the slums of the East End of Liverpool, in the Tiger Bay of the Cardiff Docks, in the Gorbals, were starving for warmth, light, clean surroundings and the companion-ship of dedicated Christian workers who made them feel they mattered, and who brought discipline and order which gave them self-respect.

20 The pioneers did a first-class job for the young people of their own day, and we owe them a lot. But times have changed: the needs of young people have changed, and so the job of the youth leader must change too. He cannot expect people to queue quietly for what he chooses to dish out. Youth work is now a service, not a charity.

25 What is a modern youth leader up against?

There are three white elephants that most youth organisations inherit from the past, as you may have noticed yourself. First, make-do premises, frequently schoolrooms or church halls borrowed for the evening—along with the idea that such makeshifts are quite good
30 enough for youth. Second, the mistaken belief that the Programme of Activities is the sole responsibility of an adult leader. This means that instead of being the steward or secretary of the kind of Club to which adults belong, he is just another Headmaster, arranging a curriculum. The third white elephant that burdens modern youth organisations is
35 the well-intentioned but hopelessly negative attitude—that the be-all and end-all of clubs is "to keep the youngsters off the streets".

From *Jobs and Careers*, by Tony Gibson

1   Briefly explain the following phrases, used in the passage:

captive audience   (3)
constructive ideas   (5)
under-privileged and deprived   (12)
white elephants   (26)
the well-intentioned but hopelessly negative attitude   (35)

2   Why, and in what ways, was the early youth movement a charity? (24)

3   Explain the idea of the youth leader as "a friendly intruder upon young people's spare time".   (4)

4   State in your own words the principal idea which no youth leader should overlook.

5   Why do you think the writer opposes the idea of a youth leader as taking the lead in planning the club's activities?   (30–1)

6   Explain why the idea of "keeping the youngsters off the streets" (36) has been a hindrance to the youth clubs.

7   Write a summary of this passage, in 140–60 words.

8   What do you think are the main difficulties which a youth leader might encounter?

9   Write a paragraph of lively description entitled: "At the Youth Club".

13 OTTER IN FLIGHT

I was on tenterhooks to see what manner of passenger would be my immediate neighbour. I had a moment of real dismay when I saw her to be an elegantly dressed and soignée American woman in early middle age. Such a one, I thought, would have little sympathy or tolerance for
5 the draggled and dirty otter cub that would so soon and so inevitably be in her midst. For a moment the lid held, and as I sat down and fastened my safety belt there seemed to be a temporary silence from within. . . .

I had brought a brief-case full of old newspapers and a parcel of fish,
10 and with these scant resources I prepared myself to withstand a siege. I arranged newspapers to cover all the floor around my feet, rang for the air hostess, and asked her to keep the fish in a cool place. I have retained the most profound admiration for that air hostess, and in subsequent sieges and skirmishes with otters in public places I have
15 found my thoughts turning towards her as a man's mind turns to water in desert wastes. She was the very queen of her kind. I took her into my confidence; the events of the last half hour together with the prospect of the next twenty-four had shaken my equilibrium a little, and I daresay I was not too coherent, but she took it all in her graceful sheer nylon
20 stride, and she received the ill-wrapped fish into her shapely hands as though I were travelling royalty depositing a jewel case with her for safe keeping. Then she turned and spoke with her country-woman on my left. Would I not prefer, she then enquired, to have my pet on my knee? The animal would surely feel happier there, and my neighbour had no
25 objection. I could have kissed her hand in the depth of my gratitude. But, not knowing otters, I was quite unprepared for what followed.

I unlocked the padlock and opened the lid, and Mij was out like a flash. He dodged my fumbling hands with an eel-like wriggle and disappeared at high speed down the fuselage of the aircraft. As I tried to
30 get into the gangway I could follow his progress among the passengers by a wave of disturbance among them not unlike that caused by the passage of a stoat through a hen run. There were squawks and shrieks and a flapping of travelling-coats, and half-way down the fuselage a woman stood up on her seat screaming out, "A rat! A rat!" Then the
35 air hostess reached her, and within a matter of seconds she was seated again and smiling benignly. That goddess, I believe, could have controlled a panic-stricken crowd single-handed.

From *Ring of Bright Water*, by Gavin Maxwell

1 Explain the meaning of each of the following phrases:

> on tenterhooks   (1)
> I took her into my confidence   (16–17)
> had shaken my equilibrium   (18)
> in the depth of my gratitude   (25)
> my fumbling hands   (28)

2 Describe in your own words the qualities revealed here as being necessary in air hostesses.

3 Why did the writer fear that his American neighbour on the plane would hardly appreciate his otter?

4 Give a word or short phrase which means the same as each of the following:

> soignée   (3)
> resources   (10)
> profound   (13)
> subsequent   (14)
> coherent   (19)
> benignly   (36)

5 What exactly had the writer in mind when he wrote of "withstanding a siege"?   (10)

6 Quote an amusing example of the writer's humorous style from the second paragraph, and comment briefly on its effectiveness.

7 Write a summary of this passage, in 140–60 words, remembering the need for indirect speech.

8 Write an amusing paragraph of advice on "How to keep a chimpanzee happy while flying".

9 Write a paragraph revealing what the air-hostess *really* thought about this episode.

14 CAPTAIN SCOTT'S LAST ANTARCTIC EXPEDITION

I am the last living man to have seen Captain Scott far away in the uttermost South, when half a lifetime ago I turned Northward in charge of the last supporting party in Latitude 87° 35′ S.

The main object of our expedition was to reach the South Pole and
5 secure for the British nation the honour of that achievement, but the attainment of the Pole was far from being the only object in view, for Scott intended to extend his former discoveries and bring back a rich harvest of scientific results. Certainly no expedition up to 1910 had ever left our shores with a more ambitious scientific programme, nor was any
10 enterprise of this description hitherto undertaken by a more enthusiastic and determined personnel. We should never have collected our expeditionary funds merely from the scientific point of view; in fact, many of our larger supporters cared not one iota for science, but the idea of the Polar adventure captured their interest. On the other hand, a number
15 of our supporters affected a contempt for the Polar dash and only interested themselves in the question of advanced scientific study in the Antarctic. As the expedition progressed, however, the most unenthusiastic member of the company developed the serious taste, and in no case did we ever hear from the scientific staff complaints that the Naval
20 members failed to help them in their work with a zeal that was quite unexpected. This applies more particularly to the seamen and stokers.

Captain Scott originally intended to make his winter quarters in King Edward VII Land, but altered the arrangements after the fullest discussion with his scientific friends and advisers, and planned that a
25 small party of six should examine this part of the Antarctic and follow the coast southward from its junction with the Great Ice Barrier, penetrating as far south as they were able, surveying geographically and geologically. This part of the programme was never carried out, owing to the ice conditions thereabouts preventing a landing either on the
30 Barrier or in King Edward VII Land itself.

From *South with Scott*, by Admiral Lord Mountevans

1   Briefly outline the two main interests which led people to support Captain Scott's expedition.

2   Give a word or phrase of the same meaning as each of the following:

> attainment   (6)
> ambitious   (9)
> enterprise   (10)
> contempt   (15)
> zeal   (20)

3   Explain clearly what is meant by "surveying geographically and geologically".   (27–8)

4   Briefly explain the following phrases:

> expeditionary funds   (11–12)
> Polar dash   (15)
> the serious taste   (18)

5   State in your own words what other purpose Captain Scott had in mind, apart from reaching the South Pole.

6   What did Lord Mountevans evidently feel was the most helpful quality in those who went on the expedition?

7   Write a summary of this extract, in 120–40 words, remembering the need for indirect speech.

8   How would you select men to take part in an expedition of this kind?

9   Why do you suppose people willingly take such great risks as did Captain Scott and his companions?

15   MAN-MADE MOONS

Until 1957 the Earth had only one satellite—the Moon. Of course there is still only one natural attendant, but in recent years the Moon has been joined by various other bodies made on Earth and launched into space by means of rocket power.

5   After the war, rocket vehicles powered by liquid propellants were used to send instruments into the upper atmosphere. Valuable results were obtained, but it became clear that the ordinary rocket is limited in scope. It could remain aloft for only a few minutes at best, and then fell back to the ground, destroying itself and often destroying its instruments
10   as well—despite various refinements such as the breaking away and parachuting down of the instrument containers.

The American research workers therefore determined to launch an artificial satellite, but were forestalled by the Russians. On October 4 1957 Soviet scientists launched Sputnik I, a sphere weighing 184 lb.,
15   which entered an orbit round the Earth, and at once began to transmit radio signals which were heard by operators all over the world. Since then many other satellites have been similarly launched. The American vehicles are very small, but the Russian techniques are much better, so that relatively massive vehicles have been sent up.

20   Once an artificial satellite has been launched by rocket power, and has begun journeying round the Earth, it will move according to the same laws as those which govern a natural body such as the Moon. If it remains beyond the atmosphere it will be permanent. If however it enters the upper air at any point in its orbit, it will eventually descend
25   into the denser regions, and will be destroyed in the same fashion as a meteor.

Ultimately, of course, our aim is to achieve true space-travel, and to send men to the Moon and planets. Before the war such ideas were generally dismissed as science fiction, but there is nothing fantastic about
30   them now. Rockets have been sent to the Moon and beyond the Moon; men have travelled round the Earth in free fall; few scientists doubt that manned interplanetary flight will become possible within the next few decades.

From *The Observer's Book of Astronomy*, by Patrick Moore

1 Briefly explain the following phrases used in this passage:

> natural attendant (2)
> limited in scope (7–8)
> an artificial satellite (13)
> relatively massive vehicles (19)
> manned interplanetary flight (32)

2 What is the essential difference between an "ordinary rocket" (7) and an "artificial satellite"? (13)

3 In what two ways have Russian space ventures been more successful than the American?

4 Write a word or short phrase that might be used here in place of the following:

> propellant (5)
> forestalled (13)
> orbit (15)
> techniques (18)
> decades (33)

5 Why is the word "satellite", usually reserved for actual planets, given also to the objects sent into orbit by man?

6 What principal danger faces an artificial satellite as it journeys round the earth in orbit?

7 Write a summary of this passage, in 120–40 words.

8 What qualities would you consider essential in a man chosen to pilot a space-rocket?

9 Why do you imagine scientists devote all their lives to such problems as space-research, which seem to be hardly of much immediate practical value?

16   SCHOOLMASTERS AND PARENTS

The parents of the boys at school naturally fill a broad page in the schoolmaster's life and are responsible for many of his sorrows. There are all kinds and classes of them. Most acceptable to the schoolmaster is the old-fashioned type of British father who enters his boy at the
5 school and says:

"Now I want this boy well thrashed if he doesn't behave himself. If you have any trouble with him let me know and I'll come and thrash him myself. He's to have a shilling a week pocket money and if he spends more than that let me know and I'll stop his money altogether." Brutal
10 though his speech sounds, the real effect of it is to create a strong prejudice in the little boy's favour, and when his father curtly says, "Goodbye, Jack," and he answers, "Goodbye, father," in a trembling voice, the schoolmaster would be a hound indeed who could be unkind to him.

15   But very different is the case of the up-to-date parent.

"Now I've just given Jimmy fifty dollars," he says to the schoolmaster in the same tone as he would use to an inferior clerk in his office, "and I've explained to him that when he wants any more he's to tell you to go to the bank and draw for him what he needs." After which he goes
20 on to explain that Jimmy is a boy of very peculiar disposition, requiring the greatest nicety of treatment; that they find if he gets in tempers the best way is to humour him and presently he'll come round. Jimmy, it appears, can be led, if gently led, but never driven. During all of which time the schoolmaster, insulted by being treated as an underling—for
25 the iron bites deeply into the soul of every one of them—has already fixed his eye on the undisciplined young pup called Jimmy with a view to trying out the problem of seeing whether he can't be driven after all.

But the greatest nuisance of all to the schoolmaster is the parent who does his boy's home exercises and works his boy's sums. I suppose they
30 mean well by it. But it is a disastrous thing to do for any child. . . .

I remember one case in particular of a parent who did not do the boy's exercise but, after letting the boy do it himself, wrote across the face of it a withering comment addressed to me and reading: "From this exercise you can see that my boy, after six months of your teaching,
35 is completely ignorant. How do you account for it?"

I sent the exercise back to him with the added note: "I think it must be hereditary."

From *College Days*, by STEPHEN LEACOCK

1   Briefly describe the three types of parent mentioned by the writer of this passage.

2   What evidence is there here that the writer's sympathy was with the boys rather than with their parents?

3   Explain the following phrases:

> of very peculiar disposition   (20)
> the greatest nicety of treatment   (21)
> treated as an underling   (24)
> a withering comment   (33)

4   What does the writer mean when he says: ". . . the iron bites deeply into the soul of every one of them . . ."?   (25)

5   Briefly explain the following:

> a strong prejudice in the little boy's favour   (10–11)
> curtly   (11)
> the best way is to humour him   (22)
> hereditary   (37)

6   What qualities do you look for in a teacher? Do you think Stephen Leacock had the right qualities?

7   Write an amusing paragraph entitled "The worst thing that ever happened to me in school".

17 WINDY DAY

I am sitting under tall trees, with a great wind boiling like surf about the
tops of them, so that their living load of leaves rocks and roars in
something that is at once exultation and agony. I feel, in fact, as if I
were actually sitting at the bottom of the sea among mere anchors and
5 ropes, while over my head and over the green twilight of water sounded
the everlasting rush of waves and the toil and crash of shipwreck of
tremendous ships. The wind tugs at the trees as if it might pluck them
root and all out of the earth like tufts of grass. Or, to try another
desperate figure of speech for this unspeakable energy, the trees are
10 straining and tearing and lashing as if they were a tribe of dragons each
tied by the tail.

As I look at these top-heavy giants tortured by an invisible and
violent witchcraft, a phrase comes back into my mind. I remember a
little boy of my acquaintance who was once walking in Battersea Park
15 under just such torn skies and tossing trees. He did not like the wind at
all; it blew in his face too much; it made him shut his eyes; and it blew
off his hat, of which he was very proud. He was, as far as I remember,
about four. After complaining repeatedly of the atmospheric unrest, he
said at last to his mother, "Well, why don't you take away the trees, and
20 then it wouldn't wind."

Nothing could be more intelligent or natural than this mistake.
Anyone looking for the first time at the trees might fancy that they were
indeed vast and titanic fans, which by their mere waving agitated the air
around them for miles. Nothing, I say, could be more human and
25 excusable than the belief that it is the trees which make the wind.

From *The Wind and the Trees*, by G. K. Chesterton

1 Write out and comment on the effectiveness of *two* similes used in this passage.

2 Why does the writer think that the little boy's quaint idea about the trees was not so silly after all? (21)

3 Briefly explain the meaning of each of the following words and phrases used here:

> exultation (3)
> unspeakable energy (9)
> top-heavy giants (12)
> torn skies (15)
> atmospheric unrest (18)
> intelligent (21)
> titanic fans (23)

4 For what reasons did the writer imagine himself to be beneath the sea as he sat under the trees?

5 Why should he think of the trees as being "tortured by an invisible and violent witchcraft"? (12–13)

6 Comment on the writer's use of the *sounds* of words to help get his effects in the first paragraph.

7 Why does he talk of "another *desperate* figure of speech"? (8–9)

8 Write a vivid paragraph entitled "The wind in the trees".

9 Explain a mistaken idea which you had when you were still very young.

18   IN SEARCH OF THE LOCH NESS MONSTER

A hunter who follows the trail of an animal he has seen for a few brief moments in the open (with the sunlight shining on it perhaps) knows very well that if the spoor peters out, he must cast about and find it once again if he is to continue in pursuit.

5   This is the position in which I found myself after the second expedition to the loch in July of 1960. I had seen the Monster, and had met others who had watched it at much closer range, and with all the accumulated bits of information I knew quite a lot about it—but here the trail ended, leaving me with two alternatives. Either I could give up
10 the chase in search of the creature's identity and accept one of the dozen or so established theories about it, or I could cast about in search of other information which might ultimately lead again towards the quarry.

It was not a difficult decision to make, because there is nothing so dreadfully dull as accepting other people's theories at face value; and if
15 one is to be proven wrong it is better to be able to recognise and admit to one's own mistakes rather than to someone else's.

Thinking about the Monster, the one thing that seemed obvious about it was the fact that it could hardly be the last surviving remnant of an otherwise extinct species. This was much too romantic, because I
20 had learned that for all its legendary background and other incredible features the facts about it dovetailed well together in a logical sensible manner, and besides there was ample written evidence to suggest that similar creatures existed in the sea and in other lakes about the world....

After some consideration I decided to repeat again what I had done
25 with the Monster evidence—collect it, every bit I could find, analyse and classify it and then pursue the trail that seemed most promising, searching out the clues which seemed to point a way towards the truth.

From *Loch Ness Monster*, by Tim Dinsdale

1   Briefly explain each of the following phrases, as used in this passage:

established theories   (11)
at face value   (14)
extinct species   (19)
the facts about it dovetailed well together   (21)

2   State simply, in your own words, the two possible courses of action which faced Mr. Dinsdale in 1960.

3   Why did he decide to go on with his inquiries?

4   What do you learn from the last paragraph about the methods of working used by true explorers or researchers?

5   Give a single word which means the same as each of the following:

spoor   (3)
accumulated   (8)
ultimately   (12)
logical   (21)
ample   (22)

6   .What rather startling fact about this "monster" is revealed in this passage?

7   Write a summary in about 100–20 words of this passage, remembering the need for indirect speech.

8   Write a pen-portrait of the Monster, as you imagine he might look.

9   Do you agree that it would be a pity if all the stories about monsters and strange happenings were to be silenced, or would you welcome a world without mysteries? Give your reasons.

19 CORVETTE CAPTAIN, 1940

The Captain carried them all.

For him there was no fixed watch, no time set aside when he was free to relax and, if he could, to sleep. He had to control everything, to drive the whole ship himself: he had to act on signals, to fix their position, to
5   keep his section of the convoy together, to use his seamanship so as to ease "Compass Rose's" ordeal as much as possible. He was a tower of strength, holding everything together by sheer unrelenting grit. The sight of the tall tough figure hunched in one corner of the bridge now seemed essential to them all: they needed the tremendous assurance of
10 his presence, and so he gave it unstintingly, even though the hours without sleep mounted to a fantastic total.

He was tired—he could not remember ever having been so tired—but he knew that he was not too tired: there were always reserves. . . . It was part of the job of being Captain, the reverse side of the prestige
15 and the respect and the saluting: the tiny ship, the inexperienced officers, the unbelievable weather—he had taken these on as well, and they would not defeat him. So he dealt with everything that came, assuming all cares out of an overflowing strength: he was a professional—the only one among amateurs who might in the future become considerable
20 assets to him but at the moment were not very much help—and the professional job, at sea, was not without its rewarding pride. It had to be done, anyway: he was the man to do it, and there was no choice and no two answers.

They grew, almost, to love him, towards the end of the voyage: he
25 was strong, calm, uncomplaining, and wonderfully dependable. This was the sort of Captain to have: "Compass Rose" could have done with nothing less, and "Compass Rose", butting her patient way homewards under the blows of the cruel sea, was lucky to have him.

No voyage can last for ever, save for ships that are sunk: this voyage
30 ran its course, and presently released them. There came an afternoon— the afternoon of the sixteenth day—when the horizon ahead was not level, but uneven; not the pale grey of the sky, but the darker shadow that was the land. The foothills of Scotland came up suddenly, beckon- ing them onwards: their rolling lessened as they came under the lee of
35 the northern coastline: presently, towards dusk, they were in shelter, and running towards the home port that promised them rest and peace at last.

From *The Cruel Sea*, by Nicholas Monsarrat

1   Briefly explain the following phrases·

> a tower of strength   (6–7)
> sheer unrelenting grit   (7)
> the tremendous assurance of his presence   (9–10)
> considerable assets   (19–20)
> its rewarding pride   (21)

2   Give a word or phrase that could be used here instead of the following:

> ordeal   (6)
> unstintingly   (10)
> reserves   (13)
> dependable   (25)
> butting   (27)

3   Review, in about forty words, the qualities required in a wartime ship's captain, as revealed in this passage.

4   What hints are there in this passage of the lurking dangers that threatened ships at sea during the war?

5   What personal "philosophy" helped the Captain bear all the stresses of his command?

6   What do you think a sailor would enjoy about his life, in peace-time, and what would be the disadvantages?

7   Write a vivid paragraph, describing the sea in its most cruel mood.

20   SCIENTIFIC PROGRESS

It is sometimes said that civilised life has nothing to do with scientific achievements, and that these achievements have in fact made us less civilised than we used to be and ought to be. When you think of the appalling destruction of war, which takes such terrible advantage of
5 science and invention, you may be tempted to agree with this view.

In fact, the reverse is true. War or none, the progress of civilisation depends upon scientific and mechanical advance, which in turn calls for a continual expansion of power. Only by knowledge can life be improved: only by invention can knowledge be enlarged.

10 The fact that man has too often used his power in destructive ways proves only that he is still a very imperfect creature. Ignorance will not remedy his imperfections. In any case, he cannot be denied access to knowledge. Nature has given man an enquiring mind, and nothing will prevent him from using it.

15 It is worth remembering that the greater part of the world's technical development has taken place during the last 200 years. Before that time, there were no steam railways or steamships, no cars, no aeroplanes, no supply of electricity or gas, no big factories, no greater mechanical power at hand than the turning of a water-wheel or windmill, or an
20 atmospheric engine rocking a sleepy beam. Two hundred years is a small fraction of the 5,000 centuries of man's existence in human shape. It is equivalent to a little more than ten seconds in an eight-hour working day. There has not been much time to think.

Looking back over the long story, you can see how development has
25 swung back and forth, leaving one principle for another, only to return again at the next stage to the old principle in a new form.

Man's first power engine was his own body. It was an engine of the reciprocating type, operated by the alternate stretching and contracting of his muscles. Improving on this, he made watermills and windmills, in
30 which reciprocating motion was replaced with direct rotation. The piston steam engine set reciprocation above rotation once again, until the invention of the turbine brought back rotation in a new and powerful form.

The old mill wheels made use of the moving energy of water and
35 wind, but the coming of the steam and internal combustion engines seemed to prove that greater power could be won from heat. Now the development of hydro-electric plant and the prospect of tidal schemes and wind generators threatens to turn the scales once again.

From *Growth of Mechanical Power*, by Miles Tomalin

1 Explain simply and briefly the meaning of each of these phrases:

> a continual expansion of power (8)
> a very imperfect creature (11)
> an atmospheric engine (20)
> internal combustion engines (35)

2 In the last two paragraphs we are told of two types of "engine"—those involving "rotation" and those involving "reciprocating motion". Explain in very simple terms what you think is meant by the principle of reciprocating motion. You may look up the word "reciprocating" in the dictionary, if this will help you.

3 Does this writer think that it is right or wrong for men to go on inventing and experimenting? Explain his point of view simply, in about 25 words of your own.

4 Explain the curious pattern which the writer sees in the story of man's inventions, using your own simple words.

5 What is this writer trying to explain about our modern world when he says (23): "There has not been much time to think"?

6 Summarise this extract, in 140–60 words.

7 Would you have preferred to live 200 years ago or today? Write a paragraph explaining your attitude and considering some of the ideas presented here.

8 Write a fanciful description in one paragraph, entitled: "A quaint old machine".

9 Write a concise statement explaining the principle on which the internal combustion engine works.

21 TRY SAILING?

The best blood-sports are those where the only life in jeopardy is the sportsman's. Rock-climbing is one of these—but perhaps too lethal an example, since real addicts do not commonly live beyond middle-age. Single-handed cruising is another.

5   There is, of course, nothing foolhardy about such sports: that would be uninteresting except to boys. Rather it is a match between measured skill and measured danger. If at times the achievement seems foolhardy, that is because the adept can bank on a skill beyond common understanding and almost beyond belief. For skill of the first order does not
10   come only from practice and study: it is inborn. Physical genius is as wide of average ability as mental genius is; and indeed if the hand on the paint-brush or the piano-keys can be inspired, why not the hand on the tiller?

Slocum was the father of the sport, and it was born in a New England
15   apple-orchard. Slocum was an elderly Yankee sea-captain without a ship when, towards the end of the last century, an acquaintance offered him a new command. The offer was a wry joke; for the little *Spray* was hauled up rotting among the trees, riper than the windfalls around her. But Slocum had accepted the command and refused to see any joke in it
20   —thereby turning it on the joker.

He rebuilt *Spray* from stem to stern with his own hands, launched her, embarked alone, and set her on an easterly course. The Banks fishermen were left behind. Encouraged by a vision (visions are not uncommon among single-handed seamen), he made Gibraltar. There
25   he was warned not to enter the Mediterranean because of Barbary pirates—still active even then, in a diminished way. So Slocum turned about, and sailed for the Straits of Magellan. Here, too, his dangers came in part from Man: the wild Fuegians. But Slocum sprinkled his decks with carpet-tacks, and so slept easy, having made each barefoot
30   savage his own burglar-alarm. After appalling battles with contrary winds he at last burst out into the Pacific, and by way of Australia and Africa arrived home again—the first man in the history of Man to circumnavigate the globe alone.

From *Sailing*, by Richard Hughes

1   What do you normally understand by a "blood-sport"?   (1) Why does this writer regard sailing as a blood-sport?

2   Explain the definition of sailing as ". . . a match between measured skill and measured danger. . . ."   (6–7)

3   Give a word or short phrase to suggest the meaning of each of the following, as used here:

> addicts   (3)
> foolhardy   (7)
> adept   (8)
> circumnavigate   (33)

4   What does the writer mean when he says: "the adept can bank on a skill beyond common understanding and almost beyond belief"?   (8–9)

5   Give a short phrase that could be used here in place of each of the following:

> physical genius   (10)
> skill of the first order   (9)
> in a diminished way   (26)
> with contrary winds   (30-1)

6   What is meant by "Physical genius is as wide of average ability as mental genius is"?   (10–11)

7   Write a summary of this passage, in 120–40 words.

8   Write a vivid pen-portrait of Joshua Slocum, as you imagine he may have looked rebuilding his boat, *Spray*.

9   What was it about Slocum that interested Richard Hughes?

22 SUPERMARKET SHOPPING HABITS

For some years the DuPont company has been surveying the shopping habits of American housewives in the new jungle called the supermarket. The results have been so exciting in the opportunities they suggest to marketers that hundreds of leading food companies and ad agencies
5 have requested copies. Husbands fretting over the high cost of feeding their families would find the results exciting, too, in a dismaying sort of way.

The opening statement of the 1954 report exclaimed enthusiastically in display type: "Today's shopper in the supermarket is more and more
10 guided by the buying philosophy: 'If somehow your product catches my eye—and for some reason it looks especially good—I WANT IT'." That conclusion was based on studying the shopping habits of 5,338 shoppers in 250 supermarkets.

DuPont's investigators have found that the mid century shopper
15 doesn't bother to make a list or at least not a complete list of what she needs to buy. In fact less than one shopper in five has a complete list, but still the wives always manage to fill up their carts, often while exclaiming, according to DuPont: "I certainly never intended to get that much!" Why doesn't the wife need a list? DuPont gives this blunt
20 answer: "Because seven out of ten of today's purchases are decided in the store, where the shoppers buy on impulse."

The proportion of impulse buying of groceries has grown almost every year for nearly two decades, and DuPont notes that this rise in impulse buying has coincided with the growth in self-service shopping.
25 Other studies show that in groceries where there are clerks to wait on customers there is about half as much impulse buying as in self-service stores. If a wife has to face a clerk she thinks out beforehand what she needs. . . .

In this beckoning field of impulse buying psychologists have teamed
30 up with merchandising experts to persuade the wife to buy products she may not particularly need or even want until she happens to see them invitingly presented. . . . On 18 May 1956 the *New York Times* printed a remarkable interview with a young man named Gerald Sahl, executive vice-president of the Package Designers Council. He stated: "Psychia-
35 trists say that people have so much to choose from that they want help —they will like the package that hypnotizes them into picking it." He urged food packers to put more hypnosis into their package designing,

128

so that the housewife will stick out her hand for it rather than one of many rivals.

From *The Hidden Persuaders*, by Vance Packard

1 The phrase "impulse buying" is used several times here. Explain carefully what it means, in about 25 words.

2 Explain why a self-service store is more likely than an ordinary shop to persuade housewives to spend recklessly.

3 Briefly explain the meaning of each of the following phrases:

> display type (9)
> buying philosophy (10)
> this beckoning field of impulse buying (29)
> merchandising experts (30)
> the package that hypnotizes them (36)

4 What is the importance of attractive wrappings in helping to sell goods?

5 Why might husbands be excited, "in a dismaying sort of way", to learn about the DuPont survey of shopping habits? (5–7)

6 Why do you suppose the writer refers to the supermarket as a "jungle"? (2) Give full reasons, in about 30 words.

7 Write a summary of this piece, in 140–60 words.

8 Say what you have noticed yourself about the ways in which manufacturers try to persuade people to buy their products.

9 Do you think that boys and men shop more wisely than girls or women? Give reasons for your opinion.

23 RODEO SCENE

Gay helps as Perce descends and straddles the bull. Mounted, he turns up to Roslyn. "You watch me now, sport!"

A handler yanks the bucking belt up tight. The bull shoots its head up, the gate opens, and Perce goes charging out into the arena.

5 Standing so close to the chute, Roslyn can feel the earth shake as the bull pounds out across the arena, and once having felt the thunder of its weight she nearly goes blind, seeing only tattered impressions that filled her through her fear: the bull's corded neck, its oddly deadened eyes fixed on some motionless vision of vengeance, the pounding on the earth 10 that seems to call up resounding answers from deep below the ground. The beast humps into the air and shifts direction, coming down, and Perce's body twists and doubles over, straightening only to be wracked again, flung and compressed as though he were tied to the end of a whip. A grimace of teeth-clenching anguish spreads over his face, and when he 15 comes down from a leap his head is thrown back against the darkening sky like that of a supplicant. The crowd is roaring, but she does not hear it; customers are fighting the air with their fists and tearing with bared teeth at a hundred imagined demons, dogs are barking, pop bottles smash, strangers are squeezing one another's arms, a portable radio in 20 the stands is loudly advertising an airline's cuisine, and the sun itself is setting behind the blind mountains; she is in a void, a silence of incomprehension, glimpsing only the bull's steady, remorseless stare and Perce's head snapping back like a doll's, the manly determination of his mouth belied by the helpless desolation in his eyes.

25 Guido has stopped cheering. Out of his half-drunken lethargy a new inner attention has straightened him, and he turns to her as though to comfort her, but she runs into the crowd behind her. A coarse call, a roar, an "Ohhh" from the crowd turns her around towards the arena.

Perce is lying in the dirt, his shoulder twisted over half his face. The 30 silence of the mountains spreads over the arena and the stands. The barebacked bull is lunging and blindly kicking near Perce's body, and the outrider is trying to manoeuvre it towards the chute, his expression drained of sport, his body pivoting his horse with every threatened feint of the white bull.

From *The Misfits*, by Arthur Miller

1   Give a word or short phrase to explain the meaning of each of the following words used here:

> straddles   (1)
> corded   (8)
> vengeance   (9)
> supplicant   (16)
> remorseless   (22)

2   Comment in about 25 words on the way in which the bull's massive strength is emphasised in the first half of the third paragraph. (5–13)

3   What are Roslyn's feelings as she watches Perce riding the steer? Quote from the passage to illustrate your answer.

4   Briefly explain the following phrases:

tattered impressions   (7)
a grimace of teeth-clenching anguish   (14)
the manly determination of his mouth belied by the desolation in his eyes   (23–4)
his expression drained of sport   (32–3)

5   What impression do you gather of the writer's attitude to this kind of sport, and to the crowds that enjoy watching it? Give your answer in about 40 words, with ample reference to the passage itself.

6   Explain the description of the onlookers as "tearing with bared teeth at a hundred imagined demons". (17–18)

7   Write a summary of this passage, in plain language, using the past tense and between 120 and 140 words. Compare your final version with the original, to see how much this action description depends on clever writing for its effect.

8   Do you think there is anything significant in the Americans' love of "tough" sports like this? (Compare their favourite sports with our own!)

9   Write a dramatic paragraph describing Perce's feelings and view of the scene around him as he rides on the bull.

24 PERFUME INDUSTRY

Perfume is Very Big Business in France and any man who thinks of it in terms of triviality (no woman would) is sadly underestimating it. The story of perfume is one of the most exciting strands in the whole tapestry of France. Secrets of fragrance, not fully understood even by science,
5 have monopolized the attention of many a chemist for decades past. The manufacture of perfume employs many thousands of workers throughout France, especially in the South and in Paris. Its sale has carried the name and fame of France to every distant corner of the globe.

Great perfumes are as rare as great wines, for most blends lose their
10 potency after a time. Permanence, quite as much as distinction and subtlety, concerns the searcher for new fragrances. . . .

The town of Grasse, near Cannes, is the chief perfume town of France, since something in the soil of the region seems to give, even to common flowers, a peculiar strength of fragrance. The world's best
15 "attars" (that is, "greases" or bases for perfume), not excepting Bulgaria's celebrated attar of roses, are produced at Grasse, and many of the perfumiers maintain factories here. Four thousand tons of roses and orange blossoms, as well as countless other blooms, are crushed into oil in Grasse every year and the whole town fairly reeks with their pungent
20 sweetness. You can smell it miles before you reach the town if you drive in against the breeze. I shall never forget an afternoon once spent at Grasse. It was fascinating to watch petals by the billion being crushed into various attars; to see them stored in thousands of jars; to see powders being mixed according to various formulae; and liquid rouge
25 being poured into moulds.

The perfumes themselves are sometimes boxes of paste, but more often liquid, and one may watch them being poured by hand from large copper pitchers into fancy and fancier bottles, ready for marketing. France does not sell by any means all of this liquid wealth abroad. Ten
30 thousand shops—it seems a very tall story—are said by publicists of the trade to exist in Paris for the sale of perfume *alone*. In many more than ten thousand establishments, especially those of coiffeurs and couturiers, it is sold as a sideline. Perfume, one quickly grants, is a major item of French industry and commerce.

From *All the Best in France*, by Sydney Clark

1 Give a word or short phrase that could be used here in place of the following:

> monopolized (5)
> potency (10)
> pungent (19)
> formulae (24)
> sideline (33)
> major (33)

2 Rewrite the following sentence in your own words, so as to make its meaning quite clear: "Permanence, quite as much as distinction and subtlety, concerns the searcher for new fragrances." (10–11)

3 Briefly describe the method of perfume manufacture, in so far as it is explained here. Restrict your answer to about 40 words.

4 Explain the difference between the terms "industry" and "commerce". (34)

5 Briefly explain the following phrases:

> in terms of triviality (2)
> the whole tapestry of France (3–4)
> liquid wealth (29)
> publicists of the trade (30–1)
> coiffeurs and couturiers (32)

6 Explain in your own words what you understand by the word "attar". (23)

7 Write a summary of this passage, in 140–60 words, remembering the need for indirect speech.

8 Do you think it is right that so much money should be involved in a luxury trade like this one?

9 Write a paragraph vividly describing the scene "at the flower receiving end" in the perfume factory.

25 CRATERS ON THE MOON

The Moon has no detectable atmosphere, and its surface is severely pockmarked, looking as if it had been bombarded by a host of celestial missiles. And this is very likely just what has happened. At one time it was thought that the lunar craters were extinct volcanoes, but for the
5 following reasons this now seems unlikely. Some of the craters are over a hundred miles across and do not show the same uniformity of structure. Besides, it is certain that volcanic activity on the Moon is quite negligible at the present time.

   Perhaps the strongest argument in favour of the bombardment theory
10 is that the amount of material in the walls surrounding a crater can actually be estimated, and it turns out to be just the amount required to fill in the hole in the floor of the crater. But in spite of this patent clue the bombardment theory has not gained general currency because it was thought that a crushing argument could be brought against it. There are
15 large areas of the Moon where no craters can be found. How have all the missiles contrived to miss these areas, whereas in other places the craters are almost overlapping each other? Only the other day the way round this apparent difficulty was pointed out to me by my colleague, Gold. The fierce heating of the lunar surface rocks by day and the
20 cooling by night must lead to an alternate contraction and expansion which causes small bits of rock to flake away from the surface. These particles of dust tend to work their way to the lower parts of the Moon where they have accumulated as gigantic drifts that cover the underlying craters. I think that this brand new idea is almost certainly correct,
25 because it not only overcomes the old objection, but it also explains those cases where the walls, or only a portion of the walls, of a crater stick straight out of an apparently flat plain. These are simply the cases where the drift of dust is not sufficiently deep to cover the craters entirely.

From *The Nature of the Universe*, by Fred Hoyle

1   Give a word or phrase of similar meaning to the following, as used in the passage:

> celestial missiles   (2–3)
> extinct   (4)
> general currency   (13)
> contrived   (16)
> accumulated   (23)

2   What is the bombardment theory referred to in line 9?

3   State in your own words three reasons that make the writer reject the idea that the moon's craters are of volcanic origin.

4   Explain simply why huge quantities of dust have been formed on the moon's surface.

5   What connection is there between this lunar dust and the areas on the moon that show no craters?

6   Briefly explain the meaning of the adjective in each of the following phrases:

> *patent* clue   (12)
> *crushing* argument   (14)
> *alternate* contraction and expansion   (20)

7   Write a summary of this piece, in your own words, covering all the main points and using indirect speech (120–40 words).

8   The writer of this piece is a well-known astronomer. Write down what you know about astronomy.

9   Another (so-called) science which is supposed to be connected with the stars is called "astrology". Say what you think about those who "follow what the stars foretell".

26 THE SPIRIT OF CRICKET

Cricket is, in a sense, warfare in miniature and a cricket match should be fought out by both sides with all the resources of spirit and technique at their command. At the same time it should always be a recreation, a game to be played not only according to written laws but in harmony
5 with an unwritten code of chivalry and good temper.

A cricket team should feel that they are playing with, as well as against, their opponents. The home side should remember that they are hosts, the visitors that they are guests, and both should realize that the true greatness of the game lies in combat and comradeship combined.
10 Pursued in such a spirit, victory, and nothing short of victory, should be the object of both teams from the first over of the match. The bowlers and fielders of the one, the batsmen of the other, should go on to the field determined to attack and to go on attacking until they are really forced to fall back on defence, and even then to resume the offensive
15 directly the balance of the game permits.

It would seem that of recent years this instinct for attack has tended to give place to a premature concern with defence in which the batsman's chief aim is to stay at the wicket rather than to make runs and the bowler's is to keep down the rate of run-getting rather than to get
20 wickets. With the resulting development of defensive technique in batting, bowling, and field-placing the game is in danger of becoming less vital and less enjoyable for players and spectators alike.

The coaches of today can do cricket no greater service than by helping the cricketers of the future to recapture the spirit and the
25 armoury of attack: only so can they win from the game the best that it has to give them.

In no other game perhaps is the individual and his team so closely integrated. One man can virtually win a match, not necessarily by technical skill, but by intelligence, concentration and character; one
30 man can lose it by a failure in those qualities. Conversely, the morale of each member of an eleven can be largely built up and sustained by the atmosphere of the whole.

From *The M.C.C. Cricket Coaching Book*

1   Give a word or short phrase of the same meaning as the following:

> technique   (2)
> combat   (9)
> premature   (17)
> vital   (22)
> integrated   (28)
> virtually   (28)
> morale   (30)

2   The first ten lines of this passage explain that cricket involves a blend of two main attitudes to one's opponents. State in your own words what these two attitudes are.

3   Briefly explain what is meant by each of the following phrases:

> an unwritten code of chivalry   (5)
> defensive technique   (20)
> to recapture the spirit and the armoury of attack   (24–5)

4   What does the writer of this passage consider to be wrong with modern cricket?

5   Explain simply how one member of a cricket team may influence the whole outcome of a match.

6   In what way may cricket be thought of as "warfare in miniature" (1), and in what main sense does it differ from war?

7   Write a summary of this passage, in 120–40 words.

8   Write a paragraph that might continue this extract, offering advice to boys keen on the game as to how they can become worthy of a place in their school first eleven.

9   Do you enjoy cricket or not? Give your reasons.

27 WELSH SEASIDE TOWN

Quite early one morning in the winter in Wales, by the sea that was lying
down still and green as grass after a night of tar-black howling and
rolling, I went out of the house, where I had come for a cold unseasonable holiday, to see if it was raining still, if the outhouse had been blown
5 away, potatoes, shears, rat-killer, shrimp-nets, and tins of rusty nails
aloft on the wind, and if all the cliffs were left. It had been such a fero-
cious night that someone in the smoky shipped-pictured bar had said he
could feel his tombstone shaking even though he was not dead, or at
least was moving; but the morning shone as clear and calm as one
10 always imagines tomorrow will shine.

The sun lit the sea town, not as a whole—from top-most down—
reproving zinc-roofed chapel to empty but for rats and whispers grey
warehouse on the harbour, but in separate bright pieces. There, the quay
shouldering out, nobody on it now but the gulls and the capstans like
15 small men in tubular trousers. Here, the roof of the police-station, black
as a helmet, dry as a summons, sober as Sunday. There, the spla shed
church, with a cloud in the shape of a bell poised above it, ready to drift
and ring. Here the chimneys of the pink-washed pub, the pub that was
waiting for Saturday night as an over-jolly girl waits for sailors.

20 The town was not yet awake. Birds sang in eaves, bushes, trees, on
telegraph wires, rails, fences, spars, and wet masts, not for love or joy,
but to keep other birds away. The landlords in feathers disputed the
right of even the flying light to descend and perch.

The town was not yet awake, and I walked through the streets like a
25 stranger come out of the sea, shrugging off weed and wave and darkness
with each step, or like an inquisitive shadow, determined to miss nothing
—not the preliminary tremor in the throat of the dawn-saying cock or
the first whirring nudge of arranged time in the belly of the alarm clock
on the trinketed chest of drawers under the knitted text and the done-
30 by-hand water-colours of Porthcawl or Trinidad.

From *Quite Early One Morning*, by Dylan Thomas

138

1 Quote two examples from this passage of Dylan Thomas's love of giving long lists of items. Why do you think he should do this?

2 Choose two similes and two metaphors (see p. 210) from this passage that seem to you effective, and briefly comment on the effectiveness of each.

3 Briefly explain the following phrases:

a night of tar-black howling and rolling   (2–3)
the quay shouldering out   (13–14)
the landlords in feathers   (22)
the first whirring nudge of arranged time in the belly of the alarm
    clock   (28)

4 Explain the statement that the sun lit the town "in separate bright pieces" (13)

5 Briefly explain the significance of the adjectives in the following phrases:

unseasonable holiday   (3–4)
shipped-pictured bar   (7)
inquisitive shadow   (26)
preliminary tremor   (27)
trinketed chest of drawers   (29)

6 Continue this extract with another paragraph, in similar style, describing the old retired ship's captain snoring in his bed.

7 What sort of man do you imagine Dylan Thomas to have been? Do you think he must have loved the seaside town he writes about here?

28 TOBY JUGS

Time was when old Toby jugs could easily be procured in antique shops and salerooms, or they might often be found upon cottage shelves from which places their unsuspecting owners would frequently be induced to remove them in exchange for a modest sum. But that day has long since
5 passed. The majority of collectors of old Staffordshire pottery endeavour to acquire at least one good example, and nowadays the bidding at auction for a genuine Toby jug by Ralph Wood or Thomas Whieldon may reach a large figure. These "aristocrats" of the Toby world are not for the average collector of limited income who, while not lacking in
10 enthusiasm, unfortunately cannot afford to pay prodigious prices. Nevertheless, there are still rewards to be found for patient search.

A collection of Toby jugs will be perforce limited in scope and character. Since the appearance of the original eighteenth century Toby jugs made in Staffordshire down to the present day popular mass-
15 produced jugs portraying political or otherwise notable personages, their general design has remained fundamentally unaltered. The Toby jug was at the zenith of its popularity during the period extending approximately from 1775 to 1825. Even so late as the beginning of the Victorian era some quite amusing jugs were produced, but in general they were crudely
20 modelled and excessively decorated and do not receive the attention of the serious collector. The jugs most desired by collectors are those made in the later eighteenth century.

There can hardly be anything else among English antiques more cleverly reproduced or more often crudely imitated by Continental
25 pottery manufacturers. After the fine jugs of the eighteenth century, the nineteenth century opened with brilliantly enamelled but less artistic productions. The quality of English Toby jugs, as with other forms of pottery, rapidly declined with the advance of the new century. In time the Toby jug became outmoded as a drinking vessel and survived solely
30 as an ornament, usually considered more suitable for cottage shelves. Many grotesque forms evolved, the majority of which have vanished.

From *Old English Toby Jugs*, by C. P. Woodhouse

1 Give a word or short phrase that could be used in this passage instead of each of the following:

> induced (3)
> prodigious (10)
> perforce (12)
> fundamentally (16)
> grotesque (31)

2 Give two reasons why it is rather difficult nowadays to obtain one of the best types of Toby jug.

3 What do you understand by the term "aristocrat of the Toby world"?

4 Briefly explain the meaning of the following phrases as used in this passage:

> the zenith of its popularity (17)
> crudely imitated (24)
> less artistic productions (26-7)

5 For what use were Toby jugs first intended? What were they later used for?

6 Why did the quality of the Toby jug decline in the nineteenth century?

7 Write a summary of this passage, in about 120-40 words.

8 What quaint relics of our age do you suppose people will want to collect in, say, two hundred years from now?

9 What do you think are the pleasures of collecting antiques?

29   GHOSTLY VISIONS

Last summer, on a remote island off the north-west coast of Scotland,
I saw a light shine clear from the headland, blinking peacefully in the
clear-etched Hebridean sky. It cut sharp through the darkness of night,
even as it had gleamed in the war years of blackout, because it could not
5 be extinguished. A ghost light it was, which must burn steadily the night
through, for no human hand kindled it and none could put it out.

I saw this light, which shone bravely in the distance, which flickered
and died if approached by man. It shook me a little; but to the islanders,
my hosts, it was as friendly as a sweet burning lamp, as harmless as the
10 sun. This is their attitude to the supernatural, and to those who have
the "sight".

Maybe their isolation has something to do with it, living in a world
where the postman calls only three times a week, where wireless batteries
die and lie useless for months on end. Maybe this indifference to squalid
15 civilization is a reason why the "sight" still lingers in the Hebrides; it is
certainly a very natural phenomenon to the islanders, who regard it with
tolerant good humour, as a southerner might regard a man known to be
colour blind or afflicted with a stammer. A physical characteristic, in no
way alarming or unusual, but an attribute about which one prefers not
20 to talk. It is understood that those who have the "sight" would rather
not be thus set apart, and good manners demand it shall not be discussed
with strangers.

On the other hand, should a stranger display the necessary reserve,
yet contrive to suggest respectful interest, the islanders make no bones
25 about disclosing their knowledge.

. . . The visions take many forms. The shroud features again and
again; seen round a living body, it is a sure sign of death. Phantom
funerals are the commonest manifestation of all. There is ample,
authenticated evidence that people still living in the Highlands today
30 have seen them. The "taibseer" can describe, in minute detail, a spectre
funeral, down to the identity of the mourners and the conversation of
the men who throw earth upon the coffin. . . .

These visions cannot be explained; the elaborate theories of philoso-
phers and scientists are no more than theories, and often of such com-
35 plexity as to be equally incomprehensible. Human knowledge today
cannot explain the "sight", though Dunne and his experiments with
time may go some of the way. That it is a gift of God is an explanation
142

which has satisfied many, but the unbeliever must nail his colours to a
more material mast. In this at least he has the support of the Society for
40 Psychical Research, which recognises second sight as a possession or a
faculty within the category of scientific fact; and there is some evidence
that visions are more than images of the mind.

From *Second Sight*, by Elizabeth Nicholas

1 Explain, in about 25 words, what you understand by the expression
"the sight".

2 What was the writer's first experience of "the sight"? Mention also
what other forms it might take, as described here.

3 What reason is suggested for so many Hebridean islanders having
this strange power?

4 Briefly explain the following phrases;

> the clear-etched Hebridean sky (3)
> indifference to squalid civilisation (14–15)
> display the necessary reserve (23)
> contrive to suggest respectful interest (24)

5 Give a word or phrase of the same meaning as each of the following:

> supernatural (10)
> phenomenon (16)
> attribute (19)
> manifestation (28)
> authenticated (29)

6 Clearly explain the statement ". . . the unbeliever must nail his
colours to a more material mast. . . ." (38–9)

7 Write a summary of this passage in 160–80 words, remembering the
need for indirect speech.

8 What are your views on this piece? Do you think it belongs with the
"fairy-tales" of Ireland or stories of the Loch Ness Monster, or do you
think there may be something in it? Give your reasons for thinking as
you do.

9 Write a short story, in not more than 100 words, using an idea
borrowed from this piece.

143

30 ENERGY FROM ATOMS

The study of the insides of atoms, or of atomic nuclei, is called "nuclear science", or "nucleonics". Men have built amazing instruments in their attempts to learn more about nuclear structure. For nuclear knowledge can be put to work in many ways for the benefit of mankind. Already
5 we have learned to split atoms in such a way as to obtain huge amounts of energy. This atomic energy is already propelling submarines and driving generators in electric power plants. . . .

First let us discuss one type of atom smasher; it is a circular device. Inside there is a hollow ring; a vacuum pump maintains a very high
10 vacuum in the ring. Along the ring are heavy electromagnets. '

Here is how the atom smasher works: protons, or other atomic particles, are shot into the ring. There, alternating magnetic fields from the electromagnets urge the particles on. The particles circle faster and faster, getting an additional magnetic boost with every revolution.
15 Finally, when they are going at the desired speed, which may be well above 100,000 miles a second, they fly from the ring into a target This target is made up of atoms to be smashed.

The atomic particles act differently on different kinds of atoms, depending upon the type of particles, their speeds, and the type of atoms
20 they hit. In some cases, the target atoms are actually smashed, or broken into smaller atoms. In other cases, atomic particles may combine with target atoms to make larger, and more complex, atoms.

When atoms split, the process is called "fission". When atomic particles enter atoms to make new, more complex atoms, the process is
25 called "fusion". With either process energy is released—energy in huge amounts. This release of energy is the basis of atomic power and atomic bombs.

In 1905 Albert Einstein, the famous German-Swiss scientist, formulated a theory about the amount of energy that can result from fission
30 or fusion. This is the theory of the equivalence of mass and energy. In simple language, it means that any material substance can be converted into energy, and, conversely, that energy can be changed into material substances. According to Einstein's formula, when a substance is converted into energy, the atoms vanish. They become changed into light,
35 heat, and other electromagnetic waves, all of which are forms of energy.

Einstein's simple formula states that the energy to be obtained equals the mass (or weight) of the substance being converted, times the velocity of light, times the velocity of light. Or, in the form of an equation:

$$e = mc^2$$

o where *e* is the energy, *m* the mass, and *c* the velocity of light. This formula means that one pound mass of any substance, if completely converted into energy, would produce the same amount of heat as would be produced by the burning of 2,800,000,000 pounds of coal!

From *Understanding Science*, by William H. Crouse

1   What do you think is the enormous advantage of producing energy from an atomic-power station, rather than by any other means?

2   This extract contains a hint that perhaps "atom smasher" may not be an entirely suitable phrase for the device described. Explain simply why another term might be more appropriate. Can you invent your own name for the device?

3   Explain simply what you understand by the following scientific terms:

nucleus, *pl.* nuclei   (1)
vacuum pump   (9)
electromagnets   (10)
revolution   (14)
target atoms   (22)

4   Explain simply the difference between "material substances" (31) and "energy" (32). What is the connection between them?

5   Do you think it is right for mankind to experiment with atoms in this way? Review the possible dangers and benefits.

6   Do you think there could be any connection between Einstein's theory as outlined here and the existence of planets in the universe? Explain your point of view.

7   Write an imaginative paragraph, describing an "atom smasher" at work.

8   Explain in your own simple terms what you understand by Einstein's equation: $e = mc^2$.

9   Summarise this piece, in 180–200 words.

31 VOLCANIC LANDSCAPE—MOUNT ETNA

The mountain does not stand alone, as so many extinct volcanoes do—mere monuments posing to be admired—but hunts with a whole pack of lesser monsters, their jaws foaming. The whole volcanic mass is in fact a great military fortress, connected by underground tunnels. Mt. Etna
5 is the highest tower, guarded by a network of subsidiary forts, some dangerous, others ruined. The perimeter of the whole military system measures some hundred and fifty miles, and the slope is correspondingly gentle. The ascent is unsensational, considering the mountain's great height: orange groves give way reluctantly to cherry and apple trees, and
10 these in turn to oaks and beeches, which once entirely covered the middle reaches of the mountain but are now sparsely sprinkled. Higher still lies the desert, lava too overwhelming for anyone to clear and pile into neat walls, lava in boulders, fragments, slabs, waves; brute matter, prime substance devoid of all shape and even of all colour, for this dark grey
15 does not merit such a name. It might seem to be a petrified sea of lava, yet a sea has form, while this nameless stuff has refused all shape. Here it rises in the shape of a crater, there it falls in a valley, like grey, useless slag; solidified in monstrous chunks, and broken into particles. This, then, is the beginning of everything: this is the world still in creation,
20 this is the underlying enduring substance—cold grey lumps of molten rock, formless as ghosts, crushing as millstones, and all the rest, brown earth, green grass, even the rugged mountains which at one time seemed so forbidding and shapeless but which now appear almost graceful, are mere superficial ornaments which conceal the essential horror. For this
25 scene is horrible—brute, devoid of vegetation or flower, of any animal or human trace whatever—it might be a meteor, it might be a moon. Such a grey wilderness was not designed for men, or is it true that the whole world was once like this before mankind softened and humanised it, giving it a tolerable, inhabitable form. Were the poets of nature, the
30 singers of flower and tree and the beauties of Mother Earth, to look beneath the surface, at the lava of Etna, at the basis of living things, they would be shocked.

From *The Golden Honeycomb*, by Vincent Cronin

1 How does the writer suggest from the very start of his description that he regards this landscape as fearsome and horrible?

2 Comment, in about 30 words, on the way in which he emphasises this impression between lines 11 and 26.

3 Briefly explain the following phrases:

orange groves give way reluctantly to cherry and apple trees (9)
a petrified sea of lava (15)
the underlying enduring substance (20)
mere superficial ornaments (24)
a tolerable, inhabitable form (29)

4 Why do you think the writer describes the volcanic mass which towers above the slope as "a great military fortress"? (4)

5 Give a word or short phrase that might replace the following in this passage:

subsidiary (5)
perimeter (6)
sparsely (11)
devoid (14)
humanised (28)

6 Write down a list of 10 words or short phrases from this passage which serve to emphasise the great weight and repulsive strength of the volcanic rocks.

7 Write a summary of this passage, in 120–40 words, condensing all this elaborate description into a plainer statement of the main features.

8 Write a paragraph describing the feelings of horror aroused in you as you walked at night amidst this volcanic landscape.

9 What signs are there in the passage that the writer probably loves and believes in his fellow men?

32 THE SENSE OF MYSTERY

It was not, I think, until my eighth year that I began to be distinctly conscious of something more than this mere childish delight in nature. It may have been there all the time from infancy—I don't know; but when I began to know it consciously it was as if some hand had surrep-
5 titiously dropped something into the honeyed cup which gave it at certain times a new flavour. It gave me little thrills, often purely pleasurable, at other times startling, and there were occasions when it became so poignant as to frighten me. The sight of a magnificent sunset was sometimes almost more than I could endure and made me wish to
10 hide myself away. But when the feeling was roused by the sight of a small and beautiful or singular object, such as a flower, its sole effect was to intensify the object's loveliness. . . .

The feeling, however, was evoked more powerfully by trees than by even the most supernatural of my flowers; it varied in power according
15 to time and place and the appearance of the tree or trees, and always affected me most on moonlight nights. Frequently, after I had first begun to experience it consciously, I would go out of my way to meet it, and I used to steal out of the house alone when the moon was at its full to stand, silent and motionless, near the group of large trees, gazing at
20 the dusky green foliage silvered by the beams; and at such times the sense of mystery would grow until a sensation of delight would change to fear, and the fear increase until it was no longer to be borne, and I would hastily escape to recover the sense of reality and safety indoors, where there was light and company.

From *Far Away and Long Ago*, by W. H. Hudson

1 Give a word or short phrase that means the same as each of the following:

> consciously (4)
> surreptitiously (4–5)
> poignant (8)
> singular (11)
> evoked (13)

2 Briefly explain the following phrases:

> distinctly conscious of (1–2)
> to intensify the object's loveliness (12)
> dusky green foliage silvered by the beams (20)
> to recover the sense of reality and safety (23)

3 What was the most powerful emotion aroused in the writer by nature, and what aspect of nature was most effective in arousing it?

4 Why do you think this extract has been called "The Sense of Mystery"?

5 Explain the idea of "a honeyed cup" into which was dropped something which gave it at times a new flavour. (5–6)

6 What qualities did the writer probably possess as a child?

7 Write a summary of this passage, in about 120–40 words, using indirect speech.

33 INTO A WORLD OF BEAUTY AND DELIGHT

Ballet is not a realistic art. It is further removed from everyday life than
any other branch of the theatre, save only opera. Its business is with
illusion. That is its strength, and one of the reasons for its great popularity. People are tired of queues and crises, they ask nothing better than
to be transported into a new world where beautiful people seem to defy
the laws of gravity, where enchanted princesses and not our drab selves
are the chosen inhabitants. Some people despise this flight from reality
and use the word "escapism" to express their contempt. I have never
exactly understood what escapism is, and why it should be such a bad
thing to refresh one's spirit from time to time. Always to live in a fantasy
world may be escapism and, if that is carried to its logical conclusion,
the dreamer ends up in an asylum. But to visit a picture gallery, listen to
a symphony orchestra, or spend a couple of hours at the ballet is a
positive good, since it enables one to face the real problems of the day
in better heart. We must in any case differentiate between true escapism,
such as using the cinema as a kind of dope or reading bad fiction, and
what the Greeks called Re-creation, that is, the gaining of strength
through contact with a work of art.

The "anti-escapists" wish to use art to enlighten us on present-day
life. "Why enchanted princesses?" they say. "What about housing, war,
famine, and pestilence? These are the things to show in the theatre
today." They want to use the arts for propaganda. But art cannot be
made use of in this way. Even in Soviet Russia, which has attempted the
crime against freedom of harnessing the arts to a political ideal, the
enchanted princess still dances almost nightly to enthusiastic audiences,
while the other arts have suffered serious damage through being harnessed to politics.

From *Going to the Ballet*, by Arnold Haskell

1 Explain simply, in about 25 words, why the writer believes it is a good idea to look at paintings, or hear good music, or visit the ballet.

2 Why is ballet looked upon by some with disapproval, as an "escapist" art?

3 Give a word or phrase which means the same as each of the following:

> realistic (1)
> crises (4)
> drab (6)
> differentiate (15)
> propaganda (22)

4 Explain briefly in your own words what use the writer believes has been made of the arts in Soviet Russia.

5 Explain briefly the meaning of each of the following phrases used here:

> flight from reality (7)
> fantasy world (10–11)
> harnessed to politics (26–7)

6 Explain why the writer disapproves of art that concerns itself with the realistic problems of our lives today.

7 Write a summary of this passage, in 120–40 words.

8 What is your personal view of this branch of the arts? (Boys, before condemning out of hand, should know that ballet dancers are probably tougher and fitter than they will ever be themselves!)

9 Do you think any of the serious arts are really needed—ballet, music, opera, painting, sculpture, drama, etc.? Give reasons for your point of view.

34 KNOTS

Before commencing to tie these knots memorise the following: **The part of a rope which is attached to something is called the standing part. The end of a rope beyond a knot is called the fall. A loop formed in a rope is known as a bight.**

5   *Now to tie the first knot:* Hold the rope in your two hands, an end in either hand. Pass the end in your right hand over the end in your left hand. Then pass the end in your left hand over the end in your right hand:

"First right over left, then left over right."

10   This knot can be depended on only when two ends of the same rope or ropes of the same size are tied together. It is not safe to tie a large rope to a small one by means of this knot.

The second knot: Take a post; the leg of an upturned chair will do. Secure one end of the rope. Imagine that this end is now attached to

15   your boat and you are about to secure her to a bollard on the quay-side by means of this knot. The end secured is the standing part and the opposite or loose end is the fall. Take the rope and pass it round the post, keeping the fall underneath the standing part. Then take hold of the fall and pass another loop over the post, keeping the fall underneath

20   as before. Pull taut. You must remember that it is the strain on the standing part that keeps the knot tight. If there is no strain on the standing part, the knot will not be safe and will slip.

The third knot: Take your rope and make one end fast to something. That is the standing part. Now holding the fall in your right hand place

25   it above the standing part which you hold in your left. Then, without letting go the part held in your left hand, move the left hand higher up on the standing part and form a loop. Notice at this stage, that you have the loop in your left hand and the fall in your right hand and that the fall goes up through the loop. The standing part is underneath the loop.

30   Finally, pass the fall under and around the standing part and **down** through the loop and pull tight.

From Sailing, by Peter Heaton

For this comprehension exercise you need no pen and paper: a couple of yards of clothesline are needed instead, for these are exercises in tying certain knots used in sailing:

1 Try to tie each knot in turn, following the instructions carefully. When you have tried, your teacher (or a convenient Boy Scout) will demonstrate slowly, as each stage is read out aloud. You will see that the instructions given here really can be followed.

2 The names of these knots are: bowline, reef knot, and clove hitch— but not in that order. Find out which is which, and what each one is used for.

3 Write in not more than 120 words simple instructions for tying a shoelace into a bow.

35 KNOW YOUR BUOYS WHEN SAILING

These notes are based on the system of buoys placed round our coasts to direct ships along a safe course—water traffic signals if you like. Study the facts, and then answer the questions below. Be sure not to wreck your ship!

5   *The basic rule:* A port hand buoy is left to port and a starboard hand buoy to starboard when you are moving with the main flood stream. (Port hand is *left* hand; starboard is *right*.)

    Starboard hand buoys: Conical in shape, painted in black, or black and white checks. They may have a black cone pointing upwards on top, 10 and at night a white light, flashing regularly in groups of 1, 3, or 5 flashes.

    Port hand buoys: Can-shaped, painted in red, or red and white checks. They may have a small red can on top, and at night a red light flashing in groups of 1, 2, 3, or 4 flashes, or a white light flashing in groups of 2, 4, or 6 flashes.

15   *Middle ground buoys:* Spherical in shape, painted in two ways:

(*a*) red and white horizontal bands where the main channel is to starboard when moving with the main flood stream, or where the channels on either side are of equal importance.

(*b*) black and white horizontal bands, where the main channel is to port 20 when moving with the main flood stream.

    If the main channel is to starboard, the seaward middle ground buoy may have a red can on top; the landward buoy a red T-shape. If the channels to either side are of equal importance, the seaward may have a red sphere on top and the landward buoy a red St. George's Cross. If 25 the main channel is to port, the seaward buoy may have a black cone on top, and the landward buoy a black diamond. Lights, if carried, may be white or red.

    Wreck buoys: Any of above three shapes, painted green, possibly with green flashing light.

1 What do you think is the purpose of middle ground buoys, and why are there "seaward" and "landward" ones?

2 Should you always leave a port hand buoy to port and a starboard hand buoy to starboard? If not, why not?

3 How would you distinguish between port and starboard hand buoys at night? Would the flashing lights not confuse you?

4 What is a green buoy used for? How would you pass: (a) a conical buoy, (b) a spherical buoy, and (c) a can-shaped green buoy?

5 What would you do when moving with the tide if you saw a spherical buoy ahead, painted in red and white horizontal bands and carrying a red can on top?

6 You are moving against the tide at night, and see ahead a red light flashing singly at intervals. What would you do?

7 You are moving with the tide and are about to pass a black conical buoy, leaving it to port. Is this correct?

Most of your work in comprehension will be concerned with prose. The next few pieces are poems, however, to offer a change and to help you with your appreciation of poetry.

36 THE ZEBRAS

From the dark woods that breathe of fallen showers,
Harnessed with level rays in golden reins,
The zebras draw the dawn across the plains
Wading knee-deep among the scarlet flowers.
The sunlight, zithering their flanks with fire,
Flashes between the shadows as they pass
Barred with electric tremors through the grass
Like wind along the gold strings of a lyre.

Into the flushed air snorting rosy plumes
That smoulder round their feet in drifting fumes,
With dove-like voices call the distant fillies,
While round the herds the stallion wheels his flight,
Engine of beauty volted with delight,
To roll his mare among the trampled lilies.

Roy Campbell

1 What idea does the poet convey by using the word "breathe" to describe the woods?

2 Explain, in about 25 words, *either*:

   (a) how rapid, sudden movements are contrasted with slower, more deliberate movements in this poem, *or*

   (b) what you think about the suggestions of colour-effects in the poem.

3 Explain the phrase ". . . zithering their flanks with fire. . . ." (A zither is a multi-stringed musical instrument, not unlike a small harp, but held horizontally and having a wooden sounding-box underneath.)

4 In what ways does the poet suggest the strength and power of the zebras?

5 Describe, in about 25 words, the scene we are meant to imagine in the first three lines of this poem.

6 Write down and name two different figures of speech (see pp. 209–12) that seem to you effective in the poem.

37 THE KINGFISHER

It was the Rainbow gave thee birth,
And left thee all her lovely hues;
And, as her mother's name was Tears,
So runs it in thy blood to choose
For haunts the lonely pools, and keep
In company with trees that weep.

Go you and, with such glorious hues,
Live with proud peacocks in green parks;
On lawns as smooth as shining glass,
Let every feather show its marks;
Get thee on boughs and clap thy wings
Before the windows of proud kings.

Nay, lovely Bird, thou art not vain;
Thou hast no proud, ambitious mind;
I also love a quiet place
That's green, away from all mankind;
A lonely pool, and let a tree
Sigh with her bosom over me.

W. H. Davies

1 Give a concise account, in about 40 words, of what this poem is about.

2 Why does the poet think of the kingfisher in connection with the rainbow? (There are two reasons.)

3 What do we learn about the poet's own temperament from this poem?

4 Why does the poet say, of the rainbow, that "... her mother's name was Tears ..."?

5 Why does the poet urge the kingfisher to live with peacocks and perch outside the windows of proud kings?

6 Give some examples of the poet's use of long, slow vowel-sounds, and say why you think he uses so many in this poem.

38 WORLDS

Through the pale green forest of tall bracken-stalks,
Whose interwoven fronds, a jade-green sky,
Above me glimmer, infinitely high,
Towards my giant hand a beetle walks
In glistening emerald mail; and as I lie
Watching his progress through huge grassy blades
And over pebble boulders, my own world fades
And shrinks to the vision of a beetle's eye.

Within that forest world of twilight green
Ambushed with unknown perils, one endless day
I travel down the beetle-trail between
Huge glossy boles through green infinity . . .
Till flashes a glimpse of blue sky through the bracken asway,
And my world is again a tumult of windy sea.

W. W. Gibson

1 Briefly explain the meaning of the following phrases:

interwoven fronds; glossy boles; green infinity

2 With what words does the poet suggest that he begins to see his surroundings from the beetle's point of view?

3 What words and phrases in lines 1–8 suggest great size? Say briefly why the poet wishes to stress this idea of size.

4 Why is this poem called "Worlds"?

5 Explain the meaning of the phrase "Ambushed with unknown perils".

6 What is the poet probably looking at when, at the end of his poem, he describes his surroundings as "a tumult of windy sea"?

39 THE SHINING STREETS OF LONDON

Now, in the twilight, after rain,
The wet black street shines out again;
And, softening through the coloured gloom,
The lamps like burning tulips bloom.

Now, lighted shops, down aisles of mist,
Smoulder in gold and amethyst;
And paved with fragments of the skies
Our sooty town like Venice lies.

For, streaked with tints of cloud and moon,
The tides of a bewitched lagoon
Into the solid streets we know
And round the shadowy minster flow;

Till even that emperor of the street,
The bluff policeman on his beat,
Reflected there with portly pride
From boots to helmet, floats enskied.

Now every woman's face is fair,
And Cockney lovers walk on air,
And every road, in broken gleams,
Mirrors a travelling throng of dreams.

Like radiant galleons, lifting high
Their scutcheoned prows against the sky,
With lamps that near you, blazing white,
Or dwine in crimson through the night,

Buses (with coloured panes that spill
A splash of cherry or daffodil)
And lighted faces, row on row,
From darkness into darkness go.

O Love, what need have you or I
Of vine and palm and azure sky?
And who would sail for Greece or Rome
When such a highway leads him home?

Alfred Noyes

159

1   Why does the poet describe his town as being "paved with fragments of the skies"?

2   A similar idea occurs in several places later in the poem. Quote *one* of these places, and explain the effect achieved.

3   Briefly explain the following phrases:

portly pride; walk on air; mirrors; a travelling throng of dreams

4   To what does the poet compare the passing buses? Do you think this comparison is effective or not? Give reasons.

5   What idea does the poet express in the last stanza?

6   Name the figures of speech used in lines 4, 5–6, and 9–12, and briefly comment on their effectiveness.

7   Comment, in about 40 words, on the poet's use of *either* colour, or light-effects in his poem.

40 THE BARN

Half-hidden by trees, the sheer roof of the barn
Is warped to a river of tiles
By currents of the sky's weather
Through long damp years.

Under the leaves, a great butterfly's wing
Seems its brilliant red, streaked with dark lines
Of lichen and rust, an underwing
Of winter leaves.

A sapling, with a jet of flaming
Foliage, cancels with its branches
The guttered lower base of the roof, reflecting
The tiles in a cup of green.

Under the crashing vault of sky,
At the side of the road flashing past
With a rumour of smoke and steel,
Hushed by whispers of leaves, and bird song,
The barn from its dark throat
Gurgitates with a gentle booming murmur.

This ghost of a noise suggests a gust
Caught in its rafters aloft long ago,
The turn of a winch, the wood of a wheel.

Tangled in the sound, as in a girl's hair
Is the enthusiastic scent
Of vivid yellow straw, lit by a sun-beam
Laden with motes, on the boards of a floor.

Stephen Spenaer

1   Why do you think the old roof of the barn reminds the poet of a
butterfly's wing?

2   Give a word or phrase similar in meaning to each of the following,
as they are used in this poem:

cancels, vault, rumour, gurgitates

3   What is the poet thinking of when he uses the following descriptive
words?

a cup of green
the *crashing* vault of sky
the *enthusiastic* scent of vivid yellow straw

4   Name the following figures of speech, and explain them:

a river of tiles
an underwing of winter leaves
tangled in the sound, as in a girl's hair, is the enthusiastic scent of
vivid yellow straw

5   Use some of the poet's ideas, with some of your own, to write a prose
description of the old barn, in about 100 words.

41   THE LITTLE DANCERS

Lonely, save for a few faint stars, the sky
Dreams; and lonely, below, the little street
Into its gloom retires, secluded and shy.
Scarcely the dumb roar enters this soft retreat;
And all is dark, save where come flooding rays
From a tavern-window; there, to the brisk measure

Of an organ that down in an alley merrily plays,
Two children, all alone and no-one by,
Holding their tattered frocks, thro' an airy maze
Of motion lightly threaded with nimble feet
Dance sedately; face to face they gaze,
Their eyes shining, grave with a perfect pleasure.

Laurence Binyon

1 Briefly explain the following words, as used in this poem:

secluded, measure, nimble, sedately, grave

2 Name the figure of speech used twice in the first three lines. How do these lines help to prepare for the description of the dancing?

3 What is the "dumb roar" mentioned in line 4?

4 What effect of light does the poet use to "set the stage" for the young dancers?

5 What words and phrases does the poet use to suggest the delicate character of the children's dancing?

42 THE BLACKBIRD

He comes on chosen evenings,
My blackbird bountiful, and sings
Over the gardens of the town
Just at the hour the sun goes down.
His flight across the chimneys thick,
By some divine arithmetic,
Comes to his customary stack,
And couches there his plumage black,
And there he lifts his yellow bill,
Kindled against the sunset, till
These suburbs are like Dymock woods
Where music has her solitudes,
And while he mocks the winter's wrong
Rapt·on his pinnacle of song,
Figured above our garden plots
Those are celestial chimney-pots.

John Drinkwater

1   Give a word or phrase of similar meaning to each of the following, as used in this poem:

   bountiful, customary, couches, kindled, celestial

2   What does the poet mean when he thinks of the bird's visit as being governed "by some divine arithmetic"?

3   Why is the poet reminded of "Dymock woods"?

4   What is meant by "while he mocks the winter's wrong"?

5   Explain the phrase "Rapt on his pinnacle of song".

43   from STREET SCENE

Between March and April when barrows of daffodils butter the pave-
      ment,
The colossus of London stretches his gaunt legs, jerking
The smoke of his hair back from his eyes and puffing
Smoke-rings of heavenward pigeons over Saint Paul's,
While in each little city of each individual person
The black tree yearns for green confetti and the black kerb for yellow
      stalls.
Ave Maria! A sluice is suddenly opened
Making Orchard Street a conduit for a fantastic voice;
The Canadian sergeant turns to stone in his swagger,
The painted girls, the lost demobbed, the pinstriped accountant listen
As the swan-legged cripple straddled on flightless wings of crutches
Hitting her top note holds our own lame hours in equipoise,

Then waddles a yard and switches *Cruising down the river*
Webbed feet hidden, the current smooth *On a Sunday afternoon*
Sunshine fortissimo; some young man from the desert
Fumbles, new from battle-dress, for his pocket,
Drops a coin in that cap she holds like a handbag,
Then slowly walks out of range of *A sentimental tune.*

                                                       Louis Macneice

1   Write a descriptive prose paragraph of about 40 words, outlining the scene described in this piece of poetry.

2   Why are the barrows of daffodils said to "butter" the pavement?

3 Explain the ideas suggested by the following:

> Smoke-rings of heavenward pigeons
> The black tree yearns for green confetti
> *Ave Maria!* A sluice is suddenly opened
> The Canadian sergeant turns to stone

4 To what is the crippled street-singer compared? Quote the words and phrases which make this comparison and say how the singer's crutches help to make this comparison effective.

5 What is meant by "each little city of each individual person"?

6 Who were "the lost demobbed", and why are they described as "lost"?

44 NOW THE FULL-THROATED DAFFODILS

> Now the full-throated daffodils,
> Our trumpeters in gold,
> Call resurrection from the ground
> And bid the year be told.
>
> Today the almond-tree turns pink,
> The first flush of the spring;
> Winds loll and gossip through the town
> Her secret whispering.
>
> Now too the bird must try his voice
> Upon the morning air;
> Down drowsy avenues he cries
> A novel great affair.
>
> He tells of royalty to be;
> How with her train of rose
> Summer to coronation comes
> Through waving wild hedgerows.

Cecil Day Lewis

1 Express simply, in about 25 words, the contents of this poem.

2 Why are the daffodils described as "full-throated"?

164

3   Briefly state the two ideas expressed in lines 3 and 4.

4   In stanza 3 of this poem, the poet makes the bird seem a little amusing. How does he suggest this?

5   What is meant by "royalty to be"?

6   What impression is conveyed by the words "loll and gossip" in describing the winds?

45   from WHITEHAVEN

In this town the dawn is late.
For suburbs like a waking beast
Hoist their backbones to the east,
And pitheads at the seaward gate
Build barricades against the light.
Deep as trenches streets are dug
Beneath entanglement of fog
And dull and stupid the tide lies
Within the harbour's lobster claws.
Curlews wheel on the north wind,
Their bills still moist with Solway sand,
And waves slide up from the wide bays
With rumours of the Hebrides.
But anchored to the jetty stones
Bladderwrack gnaws at the town's bones;
Barnacle, cockle, crab and mussel
Suck at the pier's decaying gristle;
And limpet keeps its tongue and dream
Riveted to an inch of home.
At the Atlantic's dying edge
The harbour now prepares for siege.
The mole intimidates the sea,
The bastions of the colliery
Are battlemented like a fort—
This is the last invasion port.

                              Norman Nicholson

1   Quote four phrases or words which give the impression of this port being defended or fortified against invasion. What is the enemy referred to in the first part, and what enemy does the poet have in mind later on?

2 Explain fully why the poet thinks of the suburbs as "like a waking beast".

3 What is meant by the following phrases?

> Within the harbour's lobster claws
> With rumours of the Hebrides
> the pier's decaying gristle
> The mole intimidates the sea

4 Quote phrases which suggest the slowly approaching death of this town.

5 What effect is suggested by the description of the streets in line 6?

OTHER KINDS OF COMPREHENSION

Interpreting information

This is a rather specialised form of comprehension, and it consists of gleaning information from a set of tabulated figures, called "statistics" or "statistical information". Facts and figures are often conveniently presented in this way, and it is useful to be able to "interpret" them.

The best way to learn simple "statistical analysis" is by working through examples with your teacher's help. It is not easy to give clear-cut advice, as statistical tables vary so much in form, but here are some general hints:

1 Look first at the column headings of the figures: it is the *interrelation* of these that will suggest your talking-points. In Question 1, for instance, below, you will compare the sums taken by the various fête attractions; in Question 5, the profits of each branch of the firm will be compared, in relation to various seasons and perhaps also to one another.

2 You will find your talking-points, therefore, by studying the inter-relation of column-headings. Be selective, though: choose the most significant relationships. In Question 2, for example, do not waste time on a close study of, say, Miss Z's personal voting, but look for more startling facts: the apparent dislike by all of our hotels and food; the popularity of our "pubs" amongst the men visitors, etc.

3 Practise writing in each case about 200–250 words of concise interpretation of the figures, stressing the most important facts or trends which they reveal. Sometimes you have to choose your own talking points, but sometimes specific questions are asked.

166

Exercises

1 The details below relate to a youth club's annual Garden Fête.

(*a*) Write an account for the local paper in about 150 words, summarising the fête's chief attractions and the most interesting facts about the receipts.

(*b*) Consider how the fête would have been affected by heavy rain all afternoon, and write a report of the event under these circumstances. Attendance and some items would be affected, of course, but most stalls could continue under cover.

Fête Proceeds	£	*Less Expenses*	£	*Profit*
Entrance programmes (629 at 10p)	62·90	Printing and advertising	13·80	
Snack bar	80·30			
Set teas (150 at 20p)	30·00	Catering	44·90	
Pony rides	6·40			
Swing boats	14·45	Transport	4·20	
Racing cars	18·90	Petrol	2·25	
24 stalls and sideshows	326·85	Prizes etc.	65·00	
2 raffles	108·35	Prizes, tickets	42·50	
		Insurance	3·00	
		Hire, hall, field	21·00	
	£648·15		£196·65	£451·50

2 Six young foreign visitors to England were asked to give their views on various aspects of English life, giving a score out of *five* for each item, or leaving a blank where a particular item did not interest them. The results are below, and you should analyse them concisely, considering the most popular and least popular features, major differences in voting between the men and women, etc.:

	Mr. A	*Mr. B*	*Mr. C*	*Miss X*	*Miss Y*	*Miss Z*
English people	3	4	5	4	3	5
Countryside	4	4	5	4	4	5
Old buildings		2	3	5	4	5
Pubs	4	5	3		1	
Hotels	1	1	2	1	0	1
Shops		2	2	4	4	5
Seaside resorts	2	1	3	2	2	1

167

	Mr. A	Mr. B	Mr. C	Miss X	Miss Y	Miss Z
Food	0	0	1	0	1	1
Travel facilities	2	2	3	2	2	2
Cleanliness	3	3	3	2	3	4
Gardens		4	5	4	4	5
English currency	1	2	1	0	1	2

3 These figures are the results of an investigation into the reading habits of pupils in a secondary modern school. Analyse them concisely, considering:

(a) significant changes in reading habits as age increases.

(b) comparison of the use made of school library and public library.

(c) relative popularity of fiction and non-fiction.

In each case, suggest possible reasons for the trends noted.

Age	Regular Borrowers	Occasional Borrowers	Never Borrow	Use Public Libraries	Prefer Fiction	Prefer Non-Fiction
12–13	50%	30%	20%	40%	70%	20%
14–15	30%	25%	45%	20%	60%	20%
16+	15%	20%	65%	45%	50%	30%

(School Library) (Regular borrowers, School and Public Libraries)

4 Consider these figures, which summarise the enrolment of students at an Evening Institute, and write about 200 words, explaining concisely the significant features which the figures convey:

Classes	Men				Women				Totals
	aged 15–18	aged 18–21	aged 21+	total	aged 15–18	aged 18–21	aged 21+	total	
36 weeks									
Woodcraft	6	3	8	17			2	2	19
Metalcraft	4	6	8	18		1		1	19
Dressmaking					5	6	6	17	17
Typing	2	2		4	8	7		15	19
Shorthand	2	2		4	6	5	3	14	18
English	1	1	1	3	6	4	1	11	14
6 or 12 weeks									
French	1		3	4	4	8	4	16	20
German			1	1	1	5	2	8	9
Art		3	4	7	3	5	6	14	21
Photography	5	5	5	15			3	3	18
Cookery			2	2	1	4	12	17	19
Totals	21	22	32	75	34	44	40	118	193

5 These figures show the profits of a catering firm with many branches in several popular sea-coast resorts. What comments can you make about-them? The figures represent £1,000's.

Season	Ices	Sweets/ Chocs	Teashops/ Snacks	Restaurants	Special Catering	Totals
Jan./March	·3	·8	1·7	3·5	2·3	8·6
April/June	·9	1·5	2·2	4·7	2·7	12·0
July/Sept.	1·8,	2·3	3·5	5·8	2·8	16·2
Oct./Dec.	·6	1·2	2·1	3·9	2·8	10·6
						47·4

6 Say what ideas you form from these figures about newspaper-reading habits in Britain:

Year	Copies sold (in millions)		No. of papers published National		Local
	Dailies	Sundays	Dailies	Sundays	
1920	5½	13	12	21	42
1930	8½	14½	(Figures not available)		
1937	10	15½	9	17	28
1947	15	29	9	16	25
1957	17	27	9	15	23

Spotting the artful persuaders

Yet another special kind of comprehension involves examining a piece of writing for signs of any attempt to deceive or influence the reader unfairly. Ours is an age of propaganda, with politicians, advertisers, and journalists all skilled in the art of persuading people to accept their points of view. It is very important to distinguish between honest argument and attempts to deceive.

Unfortunately, the "persuaders" are very skilful, and their use of language plays in so many cunning ways on our emotions. In politics particularly, one needs considerable knowledge and experience to decide what is the truth. You have to make a start somewhere, however, and the notes that follow should enable you to spot some of the tricks.

The artful persuader relies on a series of gentle suggestions, subtle hints, words that arouse a desired response in the reader, to achieve his aim. Nothing may be bluntly stated; on the surface, his writing must seem quite ordinary, but here and there will be the skilful touches, persuading, influencing the reader to adopt a certain point of view. Consider this short extract: a gallant piece of sporting prose!

169

Yes, Ivan Ivanovitch and his sturdy fellows have done very nicely, thank you, in the current Olympics—may they enjoy all the credit due to them. They came—to fight and win—or else! And they have bravely fought, and won. So now they return, closely shepherded by their managers, trainers and other supervisors, home to their posy-throwing welcoming committees of blonde, broad-featured Russian beauties.

And souvenirs they will take home in plenty from Rome. "Mamma mia!" said one bewildered, overjoyed shopkeeper to me. "They buy everything! The size, the colour—no matter; only the price they haggle over." So it may have been glass I heard chinking against the three gold medals in Ivan's suitcase this morning. Perfume, perhaps? Or a bottle of something else? Ivan was giving nothing away—not even a smile. His broad, flat, sallow features seemed filled only with a yearning to leave this sun-drenched land of happy people, to return to some cold, remote township that he calls home.

Here now is a list of the tricks to look out for in biased writing:

(*a*) Beware the writer who flatters your intelligence and ability: "All thinking people will agree that . . .", "We need hardly tell you . . ."

(*b*) Watch out for the clever hinting conveyed by words carefully chosen to influence your attitude. The piece above has plenty of these touches, as has Question 7 below, passage (*a*). "bulbous", "shambled", "pudgy"— there is a wealth of difference between these and "stout", "walked", "plump". Evil, stupidity, disgusting habits—all can be hinted at.

(*c*) Compare different accounts of the same news item, to see how slight twisting of the facts, or even suppression of some, can help the writer to mislead his readers. This is a common practice, unfortunately; compare your newspapers to find out!

(*d*) See how often the clever "half-truth" or vague generalisation is used to influence the reader's viewpoint: often a statement just will not stand up to close examination, but it is used to hint, nevertheless: are all Russian girls blonde and broad-featured (and therefore *not* beautiful)? Do all the Russians really buy "everything"?—without taste or good sense?

Your best approach is to judge all ideas on their merits, trying to rid your mind of all personal bias and prejudice. This is the whole art of straight thinking—to cut through mistaken viewpoints and confused or misleading argument, and arrive at the real truth of a matter.

Judging advertisements

(a) View with suspicion the advertisement that screams at you with a wealth of words like "Super!", "Miracle!", "Fabulous!".

(b) Similarly, beware the "caressing" type of advertisement, promising you quiet joy and comfort: "Give yourself the serene joy of a bath in— SPLURGE!"

(c) Vague recommendations such as "All busy housewives welcome X", or "Tested and passed by scientists" do not necessarily mean anything.

(d) Flattering the reader is another approach: "The peppermint for people of taste", or "The soap for delicate skin—like yours".

(e) Some advertisements seem to offer something for nothing—rarely a genuine offer, it is usually a dodge to persuade you either to buy goods that are not selling well, or to buy more than you otherwise would: "3p off!", "2 for the price of 1!", or "This lovely bowl at half price, with three packet tops!" are all variations.

(f) Attention is often drawn to the package: "In the new, bigger packet!" does not always mean that you get more.

(g) Often claims are made which, on close study, seem incredible: How *can* whites go on growing whiter—and whiter—and whiter—and whiter?

Exercises

7 Study these two accounts of a meeting with the Minister for State Security of a foreign power, and comment in some detail on the impressions you gain from the first account, in contrast to the second:

(a) As I entered the dingy office, in which a watery ray of sunlight was fighting a losing battle with the lingering shadows, the Minister did not at first look at me. A squat, bulbous figure, crouched behind an enormous desk littered with papers, he sat gazing through slitty spectacle-windows, brooding on some awkward problem of state security.

At length, becoming aware of my unwelcome presence, he rose, drawing himself to his full five feet, or less, shambled round the desk—it took an age —and held out a moist, pudgy hand. We shook hands loosely, reluctantly, and I noticed a dark stain on his waistcoat: egg or wine, it was hard to say.

Once he had devoured me with a searching stare, he placed one fat finger in a whiskery ear, scratched, examined and wiped the finger on his waistcoat, and motioned me sharply to sit down.

(b) I was shown into the Minister's rather gloomy office, to find him working hard at his papers, obviously immersed in important affairs. He rose to greet me—a short, rather stout figure, his clothes creased from long sitting.

Nothing was said at first; we eyed one another, as people do at first meeting. I formed the impression of an astute, but tired man, drawing heavily on reserves of will-power and energy. His gaze was frank and direct, almost challenging.

At length, however, he scratched one ear, like an amiable St. Bernard, and with a brief gesture invited me to sit.

8 Here are the points of view of three members of a discussion group, briefly summarised. Study them, and then write about 150 words, summing up the most sensible of the views expressed, and criticising the most stupid:

Subject: Should young people bother to read newspapers?

Speaker 1

1 A waste of time; news on T.V.

2 So gloomy—full of accidents and crises.

3 Politics boring, and hard to understand.

4 Advertisements enjoyable though.

Speaker 2

1 Something to read; don't take so long as books.

2 Some papers "stuffy" though: too sober and difficult.

3 Some entertaining: good articles on various interests.

4 Latest "scandal" and crime reports—juicy.

Speaker 3

1 Politics affect all; our duty to keep informed.

2 Sensational stuff should all be banned.

3 We should take serious papers only, to raise our level of understanding.

4 Too many pictures in most.

You may include a few of your own points of view.

9 Consider these four comments about television and comment critically on each:

A dress-shop manageress, aged 45: "I love television, but carefully select my programmes, allowing myself only the best: plays, musical concerts, ballet, travel programmes, and current affairs. Apart from these, and programmes appealing specially to women, the rest is sheer rubbish."

A coal-merchant, aged 35: "I like my telly, after a day's hard work. I watch everything, but variety, thrillers, and westerns are best. It's a lovely relaxation; sometimes I go to sleep, if the programmes get dull—those brainy folks arguing, for instance, but we keep it on non-stop. I like the sport too."

A lecturer, aged 28: "When you consider the time people waste watching poor stuff on television, it seems appalling. Here is a splendid chance to educate the masses, squandered with endless hours of rubbishy adventures, piffling parlour games and ancient films, acres of sport, and only one or two worthwhile cultural items. I haven't a set—wouldn't give it houseroom."

A typist, aged 18: "Yes, it's very nice, especially if you're interested in people's personalities. I don't watch much, though, as I'm too busy in the evenings, going out with my friends. It's good for older people, who like to sit and be entertained. Those programmes that make you think are good; I'm sorry I miss so many of them."

10 Study the various statements made in this advertisement, and comment critically on them:

Scientists Recommend

F U Z Z

The New, Super Soap-Powder in the
Bigger, Brighter Box

It costs no more, for you use less

Watch your whites grow more white
and dazzling with each and every
wash—your coloureds brighter too

3p OFF, BARGAIN OFFER
for a short time only. Present the
coupon to your retailer NOW, to get
two 10p packets for ONLY 17p!!!

---

11 Comment critically on each of these two advertisements:

Soothe away the cares of
each demanding day with
a ZIZ easy chair

NEVER have you known
SUCH COMFORT!

NEVER will you find
MORE EASE!

YOU OWE IT TO YOURSELF!

Relax and dream by the
firelight's gleam

THERE'S ONE WAITING
FOR YOU!!!

TEEN-TIMERS
GET WITH IT!

Every modern teenager needs one
—for parties, picnics, swinging,
twisting—get groovy, man!

WHAT IS IT?

It's the newest, the latest,
sensational

GROOVYGRAM

portable record-player Mk. 6

Miracle tone, Continental
styling, Fully transistorised

SO CHEAP (£24·75)

(EASY, EASY TERMS!!!)

12 Write brief critical comments on each of the following statements:

"Oh, look! Another red hat! Everybody's wearing them now!"

"I shall vote for Mr. Smith. I feel I can trust him; everything about his appearance and manner seems to inspire confidence."

"What was good enough for your father is good enough for you."

"I don't claim to know anything about art, but I know what I like."

"Why don't you go out with Peter Smythe? He must be nice; his father's a bank manager and his mother is the President of our Women's Institute."

"I don't trust him somehow. He never looks you straight in the eye."

"This product is guaranteed for twelve months after purchase against all faults of workmanship and materials used."

"They say, you know, that people with red hair have fiery tempers."

"Once a crook, always a crook."

"Of course we can afford it. It's only £10 deposit and then you have three years to pay the rest."

6 Vocabulary

In this section you will find advice and exercises to help you master words. It is a great pity that this aspect of English is often dealt with unmethodically. Many students remain poor at spelling, they confuse word-meanings, and have only a pitifully small range of words with which to express themselves.

To master words, you have to *notice* them; some system must be used which will bring you face to face with all the problems concerning spelling and word-usage, and give you plenty of practice over a long period of time. This section covers the main problems systematically, and the material can be used to devise weekly "Twenty Questions" tests, to measure progress.

In addition to these exercises and the weekly tests, there is much you can do for yourself. Keep a special notebook for vocabulary. One end should be for the exercises and tests while the rest should be divided into sections in which you collect words new to you. Details of how to organise this are in the first chapter of this book.

Remember that the real cause of poor spelling and poor vocabulary knowledge is neglect. If you really *notice* words your "word-power" will soon improve. But the effort must come from you.

SPELLING

There are rules about English spelling, but also many exceptions to the rules. You will just have to learn to spell the words as they are. The real secret is to look at words carefully, spot the possible danger-points for spelling, and memorise the right way. When in doubt consult your dictionary, which should always be kept handy. If you can think of any little aid to memory, so much the better. It is not so hard:

disa*pp*oint	one *s* and two *p*'s
sep*arat*e	"a rat" in it
ne*c*e*ss*ary	one *c* and two *s*'s
defin*ite*	"ite", not "ate"

It may help you to know the English words that most people find difficult to spell. If you work hard at the lists that follow and master every word, you will already have made a sizeable step towards good spelling.

English words most commonly misspelt
(Heavy type shows the danger points.)

up 1 (*most frequently used*)

A

absence	accommodation	achieve achievement	across
address	advantageous	aerial	agreeable
amount	anxious	appoint	arctic
argue arguing argument	assistant	association	athlete athletics
author Arthur	autumn·	awkward	

B

beautiful	begin beginning	belief believe	benefit benefited
biscuit business	Britain	build	buoy

C

ceiling	chimney chimneys	changeable	commit committee committing committed
conceit	condemn	conscience conscientious	conscious
cool coolly (wool woolly woollen)	courageous		

D

deceive deceit deceptive	definitely	disappear	disappoint
describe description	desire desirable	despair	develop development
dissatisfied dissatisfying	drunkenness (suddenness keenness)		

E

Edinburgh	eerie	exceed excessive	except
existence existent			

176

F
February   forty
            four

G
gauge   grammar   gramophone   grief
       grammatical   grievous

guard

H
handkerchief   heifer   height   holiday
   handkerchiefs

humour
   humorous

I
immediate   incidentally   independent   insistent
   immediately   dependent
                           dependant

install   irritable
   installed
   instalment

J
judge
   judgment (judgement also acceptable)

K
knowledge
   knowledgeable

L
leisure   library   likeable   lovable

M
maintain   managerial   marriage   Mediterranean
   maintenance   manageable   marriageable

Middlesbrough   mischief   mistake   murmur
               mischievous   murmuring

N
necessary   neighbour   niece   ninety
   necessarily

noticeable

O
occur   organiser
   occurring
   occurred
   occurrence

Vocabulary

P

panic
  panicked
	parallel
	  paralleled
		pastime	picnic
			  picnicking
			  picnicked

poem
  poetry
	possess
	  possession
	  possessive
		preliminary	prescribe
			  prescription

privilege	proceed
	  procedure
	  proceeding
	  (precede
	  preceding
	  recede
	  receding)
		professor
		  profession
			pursue
			  pursuer

Q

queue
  queueing

R

receive
  receipt
	recommend	repetition
		  repeat
			restaurant

rhyme rhythm	ridiculous		

S

secretary secretarial	seize	separate	similar

sincere
  sincerely
	solemn	succeed
		  success
			surprise

T

theatre
  theatrical
	thorough	till
		  until
			transfer
			  transference
			  transferred
			  transferring

true truly			

U

umbrella

V

vegetable	vicious	view

W

Wednesday	weird	whole
		  wholly
			wilful
			  wilfully

Y

yacht   yield

178

Group 2 (rather less common)

A

access	analyse	auxiliary
accessible	paralyse	
	(others -ise)	

C

| category | comparative | corroborate |
| | comparison | |

D

discriminate

E

eligible	embarrass	encyclopaedia	exaggerate
eligibility	embarrassment		
	embarrassed		

exhilaration

I

| indispensable | irrelevant | irresistible |

M

| miscellaneous | misspelling |
| | misspelt |

N

newsstand

P

| perseverance | persistent | predecessor | predictable |

| pronounce | | | |
| pronunciation | | | |

S

| sergeant | siege | sheriff |

T

| tranquil | tyranny |
| tranquillity | tyrant |

Words commonly confused

Another kind of "spelling error" is not really a spelling error at all but a confusing of words that have a similar sound but different meanings. We have so many of these that confusion is hardly surprising. Here is a list of all the most common ones. Work through them with your teacher, who will explain the differences. Make notes on all that cause you most trouble. You should do some on your own, with a dictionary. (If they are to be done as formal written exercises, see the note at the end of the list.)

A

accede	accent	accept	access
exceed	assent	except	excess
	ascent		

adapt	addition	advice	affect
adept	edition	advise	effect
adopt			

all	alley	all ready	all right
awl	ally	already	(alright does
			not exist!)

all together	allusion	aloud	altar
altogether	delusion	allowed	alter
	illusion		

angel	anyone	assistance
angle	any one	assistants

B

bale	base	bare	boarder	borough
bail	bass	bear	border	burrow

boy	brake	bread	breath	buy
buoy	break	bred	breathe	by

C

canvas	capital	carrot	cast
canvass	Capitol	carat	caste

cease	cemetery	cereal	choir
seize	symmetry	serial	quire

cite	clothes	coarse	collar
sight	cloths	course	colour
site			

command	complement	confidant	core
commend	compliment	confident	corps
			corpse

correspondence	council(-lor)	cue	currant
correspondents	counsel(-lor)	queue	current
	consul		

cymbal
symbol

D

deceased	decent	decree	defer
diseased	descent	degree	differ
	dissent		

180

deference	defy	depose	depraved
difference	deify	dispose	deprived
deprecate	descendant	dependant	desert
depreciate	descendent	dependent	dessert
device	diagram	die, dying, died	disapprove
devise	diaphragm	dye, dyeing, dyed	disprove
disburse	disinterested	disorganised	divers
disperse	uninterested	unorganised	diverse
draft	dual		
draught	duel		

E

earnest	eclipse	eldest	elicit
Ernest	ellipse	oldest	illicit
eligible	elusive	emigrant	emigrate
illegible	illusive	immigrant	immigrate
ensure	envelop	era	everyone
insure	envelope	error	every one

F

facial	faint	fair	farther
facile	feint	fare	father
fate	fiancé	final	fineness
fête	fiancée	finale	finesse
flair	for	forbear	formally
flare	fore	forebear	formerly
	four		
forth	freeze	funeral	
fourth	frieze	funereal	

G

gamble	gilt	gorilla	grisly
gambol	guilt	guerrilla	grizzly

H

hair	hear	hence	henceforth
hare	her	thence	hereafter
(air)	here		
him	hoard	hole	holey
hymn	horde	whole	holy
			wholly
human	hypercritical		
humane	hypocritical		

I

idle	illimitable	immanent	immoral
idol	inimitable	imminent	unmoral
idyll		eminent	
immunity	impassable	implicate	impotent
impunity	impossible	implicit	impudent
		explicit	

inane	incidence	incinerate	incite
insane	incidents	insinuate	insight
indicate	ineligible	ingenious	instance
indict	intelligible	ingenuous	instants
intense	intimation	intrude	its
intents	intimidation	obtrude	it's

L

later	licence	lightening	load
latter	license	lightning	lode
loan	loath	loose	loss
lone	loathe	lose	lost
luxuriant	luxuriance		
luxurious	luxury		

M

magnate	marital	marten	maybe
magnet	marshal	martin	may be
	martial		
mean	meat	medal	mews
mien	meet	meddle	muse
miner	moral		
minor	morale		

N

new	no	noes	no-one
knew	know	nose	none
	now	knows	known
notable			
notorious			

O

once
one's
ones

P

packed	pair	passed	peace
pact	pear	past	piece
	pare		
peak	peal	pedal	pedaller
pique	peel	peddle	pedlar
persecute	personal	populace	practicable
prosecute	personnel	populous	practical
			impracticable
			unpractical
practice	precede	precious	prescribe
practise	proceed	precocious	proscribe

presence	principal	profit	prophecy
presents	principle	prophet	prophesy

Q

quay	quiet
key	quite

R

rain	recent	residence	respectfully
reign	resent	residents	respectively
rein			
right	role		
rite	roll		
wright			
write			

S

salvage	sew	someone	sometime
selvage	sow	some one	some time
			sometimes
stationary	statue	steal	sterling
stationery	stature	steel	Stirling
stile	straight	suit	
style	strait	suite	

T

taught	tear	their	to
taut	tier	there	too
		they're	two
		(th*ier* does not	
		exist!)	
treaties	troop		
treatise	troupe		

V

veracity	veracious
voracity	voracious

W

waist	wait	ware	weather
waste	weight	wear	whether
		were	
		where	
witch	who's	woman	
which	whose	women	
(sand*wich*)			

Y

your
you're

Note

There are two main ways in which you might be asked to show that you know the difference between groups of similar words, e.g.:

1 Explain briefly the difference between:

affect	principal	site
effect	principle	sight

Your answer to this question should be given in clear statements, for example:

"affect" is a verb, meaning "to have an influence on".
"effect" is a a noun, meaning "the result".
"effect" can also be a verb, meaning "to carry out, achieve"

2 Use the following words, each in a separate sentence, to show that you clearly understand the difference:

affect	principal	site
effect	principle	sight

Form your sentences with care, to ensure that they really *do* show the difference, e.g.:

I hope the rain will not *affect* this wet paint. (V)
The *effect* of the rain was to spoil the wet paint. (N)
He hopes to *effect* the repairs as soon as possible. (V)

Other spelling errors

Here are some real blunders, made by people who try to spell as they hear the words pronounced. It is unwise to do this in English; the result might be as follows:

the safternoon (this afternoon)
the smorning (this morning)
I sore it (I saw it)
yestaday (yesterday)
We arnt going (We aren't going)
I havnt one (I haven't one)
A cuppa tea (a cup of tea)
She dint see me (She didn't see me)

Obviously this kind of error is very bad; it shows that the writer never really looks at words at all.

Some other bad slips, all too common, are listed below:

brocken (broken)	siting (sitting)
bitting (biting)	equiped (equipped)
writting (writing)	runing (running)

Some simple spelling rules

As was stated earlier, the rules of English spelling are not as helpful as they might be, because of the many exceptions. It may be of some help, however, if you remember these simplified rules:

1 Write *i* before *e* except after *c*, when the sound is "ee", e.g.:

believe	thief	chief	grief
ceiling	perceive	receive	receipt

Exceptions: seize   weird   weir   sheik

The following words are spelt with *ei* but do not disprove the rule, as their sound is not "ee":

rein	skein	heinous
neighbour	height	weight
heir	reign	eight
their	feign	eighty
sovereign	foreign	neigh
feint	heifer	vein
freight	veil	counterfeit

2 Words ending in *l* and adding *-ly*, then have *-lly*, e.g.:

faithful, faithfully
beautiful, beautifully
incidental, incidentally

3 Words ending in *y* change it to *i* when -*ly* is added, e.g.:

> merry, merrily
> gay, gaily
> pretty, prettily

Exceptions: shyly, slyly

4 Nouns ending in *y* (sounded "i" as in "pit") have plural ending -*ies*, e.g.:

> jetty, jetties
> forty, forties
> laboratory, laboratories

5 Endings are -*ise* for verbs, -*ice* for nouns, e.g.:

	verbs	*nouns*
	practise	practice
	advise	advice
	devise	device
also	license	licence
	prophesy	prophecy

6 Words ending in a silent *e* lose this *e* when an ending that starts with a vowel follows, e.g.:

> love, loving, lovable

If the ending added starts with a consonant, they do not drop the *e*, e.g.:

> like, likely   hate, hateful

Exceptions: some short words, such as truly, duly.

Words ending in -*ge* and -*ce* also keep the *e* when an ending is added; this is to keep the *g* or *c* sound soft, e.g.:

> changeable   noticeable
> courageous   marriageable
> advantageous   manageable
> knowledgeable

Note, also, dyeing, singeing, to distinguish from dying, singing.

7   Words that double their final consonant before an ending is added:

(a) All words of one syllable ending in a single consonant, e.g.:

> sit, sitting
> knit, knitting
> rob, robbing

(b) Longer words with the stress on the last syllable and ending in a single consonant, e.g.:

> occúr, occurring
> prefér, preferring

It is *not* done, however, if the stress is not on the last syllable, or if the vowel is not single, e.g.:

> differ, differing
> wheel, wheeling
> fócused, bíased, préferable

There are many other "rules", but these are the most useful. The most important task is to look closely at individual words and memorise their individual spelling.

A final hint to help your spelling

A common source of spelling error is the confusing of word-endings such as *-ant* and *-ent*, *-ance* and *-ence*, *-er* and *-or*. Here is a list of all such danger-points, and some exercises to test your skill. Be sure to underline these awkward endings whenever you note down words containing them, e.g. assist*ant*, correspónd*ence*, leg*ible*.

Endings often confused

-able	-an	-ain	-ance	-ant
-ible	-en	-ian	-ence	-ent
-ary	-ate	-ace	-ice	-pal
-ery	-ite	-ice	-ise	-ple
-er	-or	-er	-al	
-eer	-our	-or	-el	
-ier	-ur	-ar	-le	
-ere	-ure			

187

Exercises

Add the necessary endings (dots denote missing letters):

1	2	3
eat	Brit ...	illeg ....
ed	popul ...	legitim ...
second ...	avar ...	endeav ...
separ ...	centr ...	necess ...
harb ...	pract ... (*verb*)	hum ...
carr ...	restaur ...	station ... (*noun*)
car ...	immin ...	princi ... (*adj.*)
rapt ...	natur ..	parliament ...
calend ..	fin ...	propell ..
artic ..	brigad ...	agricultur ..
univers ..	invis	overs ...
coward ...	dev ... (*noun*)	librar ...
promin ...	orat ..	dictat ..
dorm ...	command ...	depend ... (*noun*)
engin ...	manag ..	savi ...
survey ..	debt ..	histor ...
superintend ...	demonstrat ..	independ ...
machin ...	terr ..	inspect ..
bandol ...	theat ..	toler ....
vit ..	cent ..	viol ....
gramm ..	accumulat ..	wom .. (*plural*)
arm ...	abund	interf ...
cult ...	corrupt	intellig ...
vend ..	develop ..	horizont ..
organis ..	coug ..	perpendicul ..

PREFIXES

English has been greatly enriched in words by the use of "prefixes"—small particles added to the front of words in order to give them different meanings, e.g.:

> form: *per*form, *de*form, *re*form, *trans*form, *con*form, *in*form
> take: *mis*take, *in*take, *under*take, *par*take, *re*take
> plane: *mono*plane, *bi*plane, *aero*plane

All these particles or prefixes have a certain meaning, and it will help you in your study of word-meanings to know the most common ones. Here is a list:

in-		hypo-	*under*
im-		in-	*into (also* il-, im-, ir-,
il-	*all these give words an*		em-, en-). *See also* in-
ir-	*opposite meaning*		*as negative meaning*
un-		inter-	*between*
dis-		intro-	*within*
ab-	*away from*	mal-	*bad*
ad-	*to (*a-, ac-, af-, ag-, al-,	meta-	*change*
	an-, ap-, ar-, as-, at-, *all*	mis-	*wrong*
	mean the same)	mono-	*single*
ambi-	*both*	ne-	*not*
amphi-		non-	
ante-	*before*	nona-	*nine*
anti-	*against*	ob-	*against, in the way of*
arch-	*chief*		(*also* o-, oc-, of-, op-)
archae-	*ancient*	octo-	*eight*
auto-	*self*	omni-	*all*
bene-	*well, good*	para-	*beside*
bi-	*two*	penta-	*five*
circum-	*around*	quin(qua)-	
con-	*with, together (also* co-,	per-	*through*
	col-, com-, cor-)	peri-	*round*
contra-	*against*	poly-	*many*
de-	*down, away from*	post-	*after*
demi-	*half (also* semi-, hemi-)	pre-	*before*
dia-	*through*	pro-	*for, before*
dis-	*apart, asunder*	pseudo-	*sham*
equi-	*equal*	quadru-	*four*
ex-	*out of, from* (if hyphen-	re-	*back again*
	ated it means *former*)	retro-	*backwards*
extra-	*beyond, special*	se-	*aside, apart from*
fore-	*before*	sub-	*under*
for-	*without*	super-	*above*
hexa-	*six*	sur-	
hepta-	*seven*	trans-	*across*
septa-		tri-	*three*
hetero-	*different*	ultra-	*beyond*
homo-	*the same*	vice-	*in place of*
hyper-	*beyond, above*		

It is not suggested that you learn all these; the list may be useful for reference and you should learn the most common. Some you will rarely encounter. A worthwhile exercise is to choose certain prefixes and find as many words as you can which contain them. A study of the word-meanings will show you why the prefix in question was used.

Example: quadruped, quadrilateral, quadrangle

WORDS WITH DIFFERENT MEANINGS

Some English words have more than one meaning; a short browse through the dictionary will prove this to you:

Liver: 1 Organ purifying the blood.
       2 One who lives.

(Somebody made a joke out of this: Life can be a joyful experience; it depends on the liver.)

In some cases the word is spoken in the same way, whatever its meaning; in other cases stress is put on one part or another part, according to the meaning intended:

désert (a barren place)   desért (to abandon)
cóntract (an agreement)   contráct (to make smaller)

Words of this kind are nouns if the stress is on the first part and verbs if it is on the second part.

Exercises

Use each of these words in two different sentences, showing that each word has two different meanings:

4	date	last	object	row	spring
	roll	frequent	desert	private	absent
5	consort	pad	gore	conduct	stick
	park	tip	society	switch	swallow
6	accent	transfer	contrast	sink	tap
	present	convict	plane	bridle	match
7	progress	conduct	block	smart	cow
	minute	rebel	duck	mark	change
8	invalid	exploit	increase	chip	stamp
	sow	lie	barrow	bow	care
9	project	incense	plain	bore	drive
	saw	attribute	rest	rent	leaf

190

SYNONYMS AND ANTONYMS

A **synonym** is a word that has the same meaning as, or a similar meaning to, another word, e.g.:

> cheerful, happy, merry, gay, jolly, blithe.
> lazy, indolent, inactive, slothful, sluggish, inert.
> fearful, timid, cowardly, frightened, faint-hearted, nervous.

Our language is rich in synonyms and sometimes you can take your pick of six or seven words, any one of which might do for your purpose. Not all synonyms, however, have *exactly* the same meaning as one another, and sometimes you must be careful to choose exactly the right word. The words in the following list all mean "a person who works with another", but their exact meanings vary:

> | | |
> |---|---|
> | colleague | conspirator |
> | workmate | accomplice |
> | collaborator | ally |
> | helper | assistant |

Similarly, we have many words which are synonyms for "robber", but all vary slightly in meaning:

> | | |
> |---|---|
> | bandit | brigand |
> | burglar | pirate |
> | pickpocket | thief |
> | outlaw | highwayman |

Study these "shades of meaning" in synonyms, and always try to choose the word with the exact meaning you need. If you are asked in an examination question to supply a synonym, then choose one which has as near a meaning as possible to the word given.

An **antonym** is a word with a meaning exactly opposite to another word, e.g.:

> | | |
> |---|---|
> | dead | alive |
> | clean | dirty |
> | cheap | expensive |
> | lead | follow |

If the word you choose is not of exactly the opposite meaning, then it is not a true antonym The antonym of "gigantic" (very large) is "minute" (very small). "Small" or "little" would not do.

Another important point to note when working on synonyms and antonyms is that *the word you supply must be the same part of speech as the original word*. If the original word is a noun, your synonym or antonym must also be a noun; if the original word is a verb, then you must supply a verb, e.g.:

> The antonym of "noise" is "silence" (not "to be quiet")
> A synonym of "power" is "strength" (not "strong")

Exercises

10 Give as many synonyms as you can for each of the following words:

(a) abandon	(b) gain	(c) souvenir
behaviour	dishonest	sly
anxiety	enemy	ugly
big	enlarge	surrender
brave	game	suitable
busy	fruitful	quiet
sincere	hinder	unpleasant
danger	injury	tell
catch	necessary	pity
difficult	politeness	education

11 Give an antonym for each of the following words:

(a) fresh	(b) ancestor	(c) abundance
straight	victor	stationary
puny	compulsory	successor
morning	emigrate	assent
praise	sophisticated	ascent
profit	natural	unique
generosity	ignorance	genuine
rejoice	amateur	prologue
proud	confusion	latitude
disperse	antidote	premature

12 Write an antonym and an exact synonym for each of the following words, arranging your answer in three labelled columns:

(a) elevate	(b) unity	(c) celestial
monotony	meritorious	condemn
submissive	disaster	convex

192

(a) obedience	(b) imaginary	(c) intricate
surfeit	optional	pedestrian
passivity	oriental	apex
frequently	remembrance	wavering
harmony	extravagant	novice
engage	opaque	miserly
permanent	bashful	pugnacious

13 Explain the difference in meaning between the words of the following pairs:

(a) luxurious	arrogance	education	wisdom
luxuriant	boldness	instruction	knowledge
(b) official	conspirator	employer	obsolete
officious	accomplice	superior	obsolescent
(c) unique	new	uninterested	unorganised
rare	novel	disinterested	disorganised
(d) sensible	imaginary	counsellor	momentary
sensitive	imaginative	councillor	momentous
(e) ingenious	fatigued	messenger	insolent
ingenuous	exhausted	ambassador	disdainful
(f) enthusiast	fictional	silhouette	biennial
fanatic	fictitious	shadow	perennial
(g) imperial	repellent	loquacious	veracious
imperious	repulsive	eloquent	voracious
(h) discussion	dialogue	talk	annoy
argument	monologue	debate	aggravate

14 Use each of the words of Question 13 in a separate sentence, to show quite clearly that you understand their meaning and use.

Note

It is not enough just to use the word in a simple sentence; your sentence should be carefully worded to show clearly that you fully understand the word's meaning, e.g.:

Meaning not fully clear	*Clearly showing meaning*
This vase is *unique*.	Experts regard this vase as *unique*, for no-one has ever found another one quite like it.

193

Vocabulary

Meaning not fully clear	*Clearly showing meaning*
Some wild animals are *rare*.	So many wild animals have been destroyed by hunters, that some species are now becoming extremely *rare*.

Test your word-power

The next questions ask you to show that you understand the meanings of various long words, either by using them in sentences that clearly show their meaning, or by writing a brief statement of their meaning, suitable for a dictionary. If you are using them in sentences, the sentences must clearly show the meaning. Form your sentences carefully!

Exercises

15 Use each of these words in a sentence that clearly shows its meaning:

precocious	quarantine	stereotyped	anecdote
chronometer	incensed	therapy	antiseptic
surcharge	impetuous	bequest	patron
rigorous	ecclesiastical	monetary	malevolent
pert	whim	wane	envoy

16 Give brief definitions, suitable for a dictionary, of the following words:

somnambulist	impregnable	expeditious	anthropology
ubiquitous	indelible	patriotism	taxidermy
translucent	vertebrate	illiterate	psychology
derivative	incorrigible	amphibian	heresy
glossary	consignment	resurrection	atheist
census	bigoted	mimic	obscure

17 Use each of these words in a sentence that clearly shows its meaning:

vegetarian	ventriloquist	invigilator	analysis
emissary	agnostic	dispensary	pessimist
misogynist	centenarian	anthology	respective
adjudicator	centurion	constellation	obtuse
static	prolific	arid	concave

194

18 Write a short sentence *explaining* the meaning of each of the following words:

transgressor	reticence	continual	insolvent
impetuous	amateur	retrospective	insoluble
taciturn	fraud	discriminating	bankrupt
psychiatrist	versatility	deception	estimate
indiscreet	continuous	contention	predict
peer	revoke	squalid	carrion

19 Write brief notes explaining the meanings of the following words:

antidote	tyranny	stimulant	provoke
astronomer	hereditary	ethereal	blatant
gullible	perceptive	sagacious	inert
synchronise	austerity	culpable	tuition
judicial	stimulus	precedence	porous
justice	omen	raucous	tragic

ONE WORD FOR SEVERAL

You can often economise on words. These exercises ask you to supply single words for the phrases given. Be careful to supply the right part of speech, e.g.:

"a custom long established" calls for a *noun.*
"to wet something completely" calls for a *verb.*
"having a bad reputation" calls for an *adjective.*

Exercises

20 Supply one word for each of the following phrases:

(a) never known to fail
existing underground
meriting rebuke
able to move on land or water
not given to needless speech
of pleasant, friendly personality
careful not to disclose private matters
having plenty of room
the practice of spying
to express the main ideas in concise form

(b) willing to work hard
existing only in the mind
having a vivid imagination
that which deceives the eye
without system or method
having a high opinion of one's abilities
to regard with extreme contempt
to desire that which belongs to another
a book about a person's life
a state of perfect balance

21 Supply one word for each of the following phrases:

(a) to support another's statement
a five-sided figure
denied moisture
one who studies birds
one who digs for ancient relics
to look forward to
one recovering from an illness
a sudden disaster
not permitted by law
cultivation of the soil for food

(b) having a bad reputation
projecting lower edges of a roof
a person who gives much money to charities
the study of the human mind and behaviour
to wet something completely
not given to needless spending
having a circular base, sloping sides, and a pointed top
a circle with radius approaching zero
a school or class for very small children
a period of ten years

22 Supply one word for each of the following phrases:

(a) legal registration of a new invention
a feeling of admiration for another's good fortune
an Eskimo dwelling
a custom long established
a false name used by a writer

all-powerful
all-knowing
a narrow, projecting spit of land
a three-legged support
concerning the ghostly

(b) lying far-distant
able to speak many languages
to think deeply about some matter
abandoned and falling into ruin
the result of some action
one who lives withdrawn from the company of others
given freely and without charge
to destroy by burning
situated close at hand
to restore as new

23 Supply one word for each of the following phrases:

(a) one who receives
a maze of passages
concerned only with surface matters
to seek the support of others, especially in politics
one who collects stamps
the science of numbers
the study of plants
a four-footed animal
a man whose wife is dead
government of the people, by the people, and for the people

(b) one with skilled judgment in artistic matters
one who eats no animal flesh
one who pretends to be what he is not
one who takes over after another in office or employment
one who is in charge of a museum or art gallery
the study of family descent
a disease attacking many people at the same time
cannot be repaired or remedied
incapable of being destroyed
cannot be wounded or injured

MALAPROPISMS

Mrs. Malaprop was a character in a play by Richard Brinsley Sheridan, called *The Rivals*. She was always trying to make an impression by using long words, but unfortunately she was not sure of the right ones:

> I would by no means wish a daughter of mine to be a *progeny* of learning; she should have a *supercilious* knowledge in accounts:—and as she grew up, I would have her instructed in *geometry*, that she might know something of the *contagious* countries; but above all, Sir Anthony, she should be mistress of *orthodoxy*, that she might not misspell, and mispronounce words so shamefully as girls usually do, and likewise that she might *reprehend* the true meaning of what she is saying. This, Sir Anthony, is what I would have a woman know; and I don't think there is a *superstitious* article in it.

There is a lesson for you here. The sentences below came from pupils' exercise-books. Try to correct them, and try to find similar howlers:

Exercise

24 The English were an easy mark for the French archers, as they staggered uphill heavy with amour.

A triangle with equal sides is called equatorial.

We are masters of steam and eccentricity.

Geometry teaches us to bisect angels.

The practice of having only one wife is called monotony.

A mosquito is the child of black and white parents.

A polygon is a man with several wives.

The heart is a comical bag divided by a fleshy petition.

After the politician had been knocked down, he was found to be suffering from discussion.

Heat is transmitted by conviction.

His toothache simply drove him to extraction.

The professor is a real guinness.

I wish he would not make such incinerating remarks.

If you want to run fast you need a powerful physic.

She sat in the field plucking dandy lions.

If you take poison the doctor must give you an antidope.

Two posteriors rode on the back of the coach.

He was delighted to become a centurion on his hundredth birthday.

My uncle keeps a large diary which supplies milk to half the neighbourhood.

The volcano was erupting malt and rock.

I would rather work out of doors than have a sedimentary occupation.

Her afternoon was really a bomb in a bull.

There are two scales of temperature: furry night and centipede.

PARTS OF SPEECH

You can learn to use your language by studying it "in action" rather than by tearing it apart and trying to push the pieces into grammatical pigeon-holes. At the same time, it is very useful to be able to recognise words according to their *types*; we call these types **parts of speech** and there are eight of them.

The first four (you *must* be able to recognise these!)

1 NOUN: another word for the *name* of something. There are four kinds:

(a) *Common nouns:* names of articles and creatures

(b) *Proper nouns:* names of people, places, ships, and all institutions meriting a capital letter

(c) *Abstract nouns:* names of qualities (cannot be touched!)

(d) *Collective nouns:* names given to groups of things

Examples

Common	Proper	Abstract	Collective
plant	Mabel	jealousy	herd
shoe	Globe Theatre	love	committee
box	Birmingham	speed	suite
umbrella	India	weight	company
cow	Hyde Park	fear	squadron
friend	H.M.S. Defiant	newness	set

2 VERB: a "doing word". It says what a person or thing does; *to be, to have* are also verbs. Verbs may be used singly or in groups of "parts".

199

Examples

Single verb in action	Groups of verb parts in action
He *broke* a cup.	We *should have seen* him.
I *visit* him often.	They *will be going* out.
Iris *has* a new coat.	She *is hoping to get* a seat.

3 ADJECTIVE: This tells us something about a noun:

Examples

In front of noun	After noun	These are adjectives also
a *big* mistake	This room is *large*.	Numbers: *three, fourth*, etc.
a *broken* cup	His nose is *red*.	
this *clever* boy	The hat is *new*	*My, your, his, her, its, our, their*
these *red* roses	A needle is *sharp*	
three books		*Much, many, little, few, every, each, either, none*
which pen?		
either hand		
little money		*Which?, What?*
each person		

4 ADVERB: gives more information about a verb, or sometimes about an adjective or another adverb. There are four kinds:

(a) *Adverbs of time:* answer the question *When?*

> He came *early*.
> She read *first*.
> We saw him *once*.

(b) *Adverbs of manner:* answer the question *How?*

> She ran *fast*.
> They sang *badly*.
> He paints *well*.

(c) *Adverbs of place:* answer the question *Where?*

> He sat *down*.
> I ate *there*.
> She went *out*.

(d) *Adverbs of degree:* these tell us more about the adjective or adverb and answer the question *To what extent?*

> an *extremely* large house
> a *very* old house
> he ran *rather* slowly

The second four (it is helpful but not essential to be able to recognise these!)

5 PRONOUN: a word that can stand in place of a noun, to avoid repeating the noun constantly. Instead of writing "the *man* is old and the *man* lives next door. The *man* has a dog . . .", we can make use of the pronoun *he*: "The man is old and he lives next door. He has a dog. . . ." Pronouns commonly used in place of nouns are:

(a) I, you, he, she, it, we, they

(b) me, him, her, us, them

(c) mine, yours, his, hers, its, ours, theirs

(d) this, that, these, those, who, whom, which, that, what, myself, yourself, himself, herself, itself, ourselves, themselves

6 CONJUNCTION: "joining words". These join parts of sentences, which sometimes, but not always, contain their own verbs. Conjunctions in common use are:

and	although	that	and so
but	because	so that	and then
when	since	though	whither
as	where	than	whence
yet	lest	while	in order that
or	unless	before	until
for	provided	after	

Examples

> He found it difficult *but* I helped him.
> They made it for Alice *and* Jane.
> I waited there alone *until* you came.

7 PREPOSITION: these words are positioned just in front of a noun or pronoun, to form a phrase. Prepositions in common use are:

against	along	in, into
around	on, on to, upon	during
for	behind	off
through	before (in front of)	towards
with	below, under	after
without	above, over	since
between	near, beside, at	from
to		

Examples

under the chair   *with* my books
through the door   *into* his garden
for me   *off* it

8 INTERJECTION: another word for an exclamation, e.g.:

Oh!   My goodness!   Dear me!

Exercises

25 Identify the following words as one of the following parts of speech:

N (noun), V (verb), ADJ (adjective), ADV (adverb).

hurricane	fiery	liability
longitudinal	spontaneous	guaranteed
porpoise	aristocrat	leisurely
err	mediocre	untrue
lustrous	auspiciously	cloudy
sombrely	principle	tenacious
constituency	iniquity	probation
canvassed	manoeuvre	suspend
weirdly	macabre	culture
Norwich	incidental	submerge
delinquency	predominating	very
audible	corpulent	rather
credentials	expeditiously	permissive

26 These words can each act as more than one part of speech. Label
them accordingly, using the code-letters given in the last question.

press	vegetarian	grease
massage	support	square
medium	process	elaborate

lacquer	uniform	green
mortgage	coming	blame
flourish	coping	queue
essential	writing	lent
eccentric	graduate	slit
harbour	file	upright
parallel	fillet	sketch

27 Identify the following words as one of the following parts of speech:

PRO (pronoun), PRE (preposition), CON (conjunction).

into	he	where
beside	hers	you
them	otherwise	it
theirs	ourselves	around
although	after	lest
while	under	therefore
through	whence	during
off	but	ours
without	themselves	whom
these	still	which
that	when	between
she	towards	provided
than	over	with

28 Give nouns corresponding to the following verbs. If you know several nouns for any verb, give them all.

restrain	distil	frustrate
expedite	criticise	differentiate
create	insert	remember
connect	compare	antagonise
spend	decide	astonish
vex	succeed	breathe
begin	entangle	complete

29 Give verbs corresponding to the following nouns, and also corresponding adjectives. Arrange your answer in three columns.

horror	fright	condescension
solution	operator	economy
equality	indication	enthusiasm

203

illumination	admission	destruction
definition	marriage	secret
character	nomination	dissuasion
analysis	desperation	paralysis
competition	hypnotism	opposition
insinuation	number	synthesis
persuasion	satisfaction	variety

30 Form as many words as you can from each of the following words, arranging your work as shown in the example below:

call	take	fill	prove
know	find	point	use
tell	lay	tend	view
say	stall	send	sign
break	charge	cover	organise

Example, showing layout and method:

prove: approve (V), approval (N), approbation (N), approving (ADJ); disprove (V), disapproval (N), disapproving (ADJ); approvingly, (ADV), disapprovingly (ADV); improve (V), improvement (N), improving (ADJ); unimproved (ADJ), etc.

ABBREVIATIONS

Letters are widely used to show certain titles that would perhaps look too lengthy if written out in full, e.g.:

B.O.A.C. instead of "British Overseas Airways Corporation".
M.B.E. instead of "Member of the British Empire".

The next exercises include the most common abbreviations of this kind. See how many you know. If you are stumped by any, you will find the answers in any good dictionary.

Exercises

31 State the meanings of the following abbreviated forms:

B.A.	A.A.A.	A.A.	M.C.	Ltd. Co.
ad lib.	R.S.M.	a.m.	C.I.D.	cf.
B.Sc.	C.P.O.	I.T.A.	B.B.C.	B.M.A.
A.R.A.	A.D.C.	L.S.D.	M.B.	B.Ch.
D.S.O.	Coy.	Cantab.	C.B.E.	V.C.

32 State the meanings of the following abbreviated forms:

etc.	F.R.C.S.	G.P.	K.C.B.	Ll.B.
et seq.	I.O.W.	H.M.I.	K.G.	lb.
C.B.	F.R.S.	H.M.S.O.	L.B.W.	M.C.C.
B.D.	G.M.T.	i.e.	B.Mus.	M.D.
J.P.	G.O.C.	I.L.O.	M.A.	D.Phil.

33 State the meanings of the following abbreviated forms:

Messrs.	N.A.T.O.	p.p.	m.	T.T.
Ph.D.	N.F.S.	P.A.Y.E.	mm.	F.A.
M.C.	N.H.S.	Q.C.	M.	U.N.O.
M.M.	R.S.P.C.A.	R.C.	Mme.	U.N.E.S.C.O.
M.O.H.	N.S.P.C.C.	R.D.C.	Mlle.	U.S.S.R.
R.A.C.	C.D.	U.D.C.	R.S.V.P.	U.S.A.
M.P.	G.B.	C.C.	S.O.S.	V.H.F.
M.R.C.S.	O.B.E.	cc.	S.R.N.	viz.
M.R.C.P.	O.M.	cms.	R.N.	W.I.
M.R.C.V.S.	Oxon.	km.	R.M.	Y.H.A.

A FAULT TO AVOID

This section on vocabulary should help you to learn many new words. It is time, however, to remind you of some advice given in the first chapter of this book: you should not use long and complicated words in your everyday speech or writing just because they may seem impressive. Remember the three essentials for plain, workaday language: *clarity*, *simplicity*, and *conciseness*. Longer words do have their uses—they would not exist otherwise—but it is pointless to use them if you can express yourself equally effectively in simpler fashion. People who use long, high-sounding vocabulary without real need are guilty of a "writing-crime" which we call *verbosity*. (A similar "crime" is called *circumlocution*—using far more words than are necessary.) Here are some atrocities to show you what we mean (improved versions in brackets):

The cessation of house-building occasioned by the outbreak of hostilities operated over a period of five years.

(During the first five years of the war no houses were built.)

His garments suffered comparatively minor damage and are capable of effective reconditioning.

(His clothes were only slightly damaged and can easily be repaired.)

The unfortunate victims whose houses suffered inundation by the floods were evacuated to alternative accommodation.

(Those whose houses were flooded were moved elsewhere.)

Children of a tender age are unusually susceptible to infectious diseases, and if brought together in large numbers the risk of infections may attain serious proportions.

(There is a strong risk of infection amongst young children, especially where many of them congregate.)

Exercises

34 Express the following as briefly and clearly as possible:

(a) It is of first priority to determine an overall coal-production target.

(b) The personages here assembled comprised seven adults, three being of the masculine and four of the feminine gender.

(c) On the occasion of our successfully terminating our wanderings in close proximity to a suitable hostelry, we ventured inside with the intention of partaking of some refreshing repast.

(d) It is not without some distinct degree of hesitation that I venture to consult you with respect to the possibility of my being accorded in the not too distant future some recompense for the expenditure incurred by me on your behalf.

(e) There is irrefutable evidence in support of the claim as to the possible existence of bottlenecks in production, which, in the interests of improved efficiency, must receive immediate remedial attention.

(f) From the viewpoint of sanitary precautions it is considered to be a factor of urgent necessity that individual employees be equipped with personal handtowels to the limit of three per employee, gratuitously supplied.

(g) In assessing the minimum level of compensatory award to be made in individual cases, it might not be without relevance to establish the practice of completion of a straightforward questionnaire, to be required of all applicants prior to interview.

(*h*) You are respectfully required to furnish with your report a breakdown of houses now being erected in accordance with their several types.

(*i*) I am requested to draw your attention to the serious omission from the detailed plans previously submitted and now in my possession of ablution facilities, which, as you will doubtless be aware, are required pursuant to the Factories Act for the convenience and welfare of all employees.

(*j*) It is as a result of your regrettable omission to furnish the information repeatedly requested in my communications to you over the period of the last five months, that I am now reluctantly compelled to inform you that it is the decision of my committee no longer to entertain your application for refund of payments hitherto made by you.

35 Rewrite these needlessly involved sentences clearly and simply:

(*a*) This organisation's apparent longstanding neglect of your esteemed clients' oft-repeated request for renovation of the premises vacated by them is explicable in some measure by the fact that they claim non-liability in accordance with the terms of the agreement initially compounded between themselves and your client.

(*b*) She inserted into the appropriate receptacle a suitable measure of the dessicated fragrant leaf esteemed by connoisseurs as the justly renowned herb deriving from China and Ceylon.

(*c*) Consequent upon the application of an increased degree of persuasion, administered through the agency of his crowbar, the attendant charged with the distribution of the necessary equipment was at length enabled to secure access to the storage-chamber in which the items in question had been secreted.

(*d*) Notwithstanding the inescapable realisation of his regrettable omission on the score of politeness, for his rudeness had been amply perceived by all assembled there, he continued in his insistence on a mode of impertinent speech that could only further affront and dismay his audience.

(*e*) I feel it incumbent on myself to state without further hesitation that never yet in my natural existence have I perceived so close an affinity towards any member of the opposite or fairer sex as to wish to engage with her on a course of friendship leading ultimately to holy matrimony.

207

(*f*) There were discernible undoubted symptoms of an over-indulgence in intoxicating beverages, which must inevitably have rendered the consumer insensible and prostrate beneath the table at which he had hitherto been seated.

(*g*) The indefinitely continued association of my daughter, a young person of delicate and respectable upbringing, whom I have persistently shielded from the attentions of ineligible young reprobates like yourself, is a proposal which I refuse to contemplate with equanimity.

(*h*) She was definitely and overridingly convinced to the effect that the illumination afforded by the customary street-furniture in the proximity of her home was so insufficient as to withhold from her the privileges rightly hers in due measure as a ratepayer of the borough.

(*i*) The consequence of his skilful application of a prescribed medicament to the region of the afflicted portion of his anatomy was the rapid alleviation of discomfort and the full restoration of a sensation of well-being.

(*j*) The ultimate effect of consistent contact between the material enveloping his posterior and a considerable variety of abrasive surfaces, such as are commonly encountered in the course of boyhood recreation, was the development of a completely eroded portion of the aforesaid material, incurring for its owner reprehension from his indignant mother.

7 Picturesque Language

This section returns to the question of *style* in writing. It deals particularly with the ways in which writers achieve vivid and decorative effects in their work. Study first these opening lines from a modern detective story:

"It may be only blackmail," said the man in the taxi hopefully. The fog was like a saffron blanket soaked in ice-water. It had hung over London all day and at last was beginning to descend. The sky was yellow as a duster and the rest was a granular black, overprinted in grey and lightened by occasional slivers of bright fish colour as a policeman turned in his wet cape.

Already the traffic was at an irritable crawl. By dusk it would be stationary. To the west the Park dripped wretchedly and to the north the great railway terminus slammed and banged and exploded hollowly about its affairs. Between lay winding miles of butter-coloured stucco in every conceivable state of repair.

The fog had crept into the taxi where it crouched panting in a traffic jam. It oozed in ungenially, to smear sooty fingers over the two elegant young people who sat inside.

From *Tiger in the Smoke*, by Margery Allingham

You can feel that creeping, hateful fog, and the tension in the opening words. It is the kind of writing that makes you want to read on and see what happens next.

It is not always easy to see how a writer gets effects of this kind. Here there is a clever blend of colour, movement (or the lack of it), noises, and several other descriptive details, which together give a distinctly dismal impression of a London fog. The man's remark also makes a strong impression: "It may be only blackmail." Considering the sinister presence of the fog, and the book's mysterious title, we fear it might be something a good deal worse than blackmail—murder, perhaps? This is clever writing, subtly guiding the reader's thoughts and reactions in a definite direction.

FIGURES OF SPEECH

There are certain well-known methods used by writers to achieve vivid descriptive effects. We shall look first at the so-called "figures of speech", and the most useful are as follows:

Simile

To achieve a striking descriptive effect, something is said to be *as* or *like*
something else:

> The fog was like a saffron blanket soaked in ice-water.
> The sky was yellow as a duster.
> Cherry-blossom lay like driven snow upon the lawn.
> I have seen old ships sail like swans asleep.
> Now droops the milkwhite peacock like a ghost.

Notice that the comparison in each case is between things which are
actually quite different, but which share some feature of appearance or
association in which they are alike.

Metaphor

Another striking comparison between different things is achieved by
saying that something *is* something else:

> The moon was a ghostly galleon tossed upon cloudy seas.
> The road was a ribbon of moonlight over the purple moor.
> Life is Colour and Warmth and Light.
> Leaves, summer's coinage spent.

The following are also metaphors: although they do not actually
state that something *is* something else, they suggest, for vivid effect, that
something has a quality of appearance or action that really belongs to
something else:

> Here the snake across your path stretches *in his golden bath*.
> Still the *red, lurid wreckage* of the sunset *smoulders in smoky fire*.
> For all the haft twinkled with diamond *sparks*.

Personification

In this figure of speech *human* qualities are suggested as belonging to
non-human things:

> Slowly, silently now the Moon *walks the earth in her silver shoon*.
> From the dark woods that *breathe* of fallen showers.
> Whither, O splendid ship, thy white sails crowding, leaning across
> the *bosom of the urgent West*.
> Now *sleeps* the crimson petal, now the white.

210

Alliteration

A sequence of words beginning with the same sound:

> The fair breeze blew, the white foam flew, the furrow followed free.
> A bow-shot from her bower-eaves, he rode between the barley-
> sheaves.
> Where waters gushed and fruit-trees grew, and flowers put forth a
> fairer hue.

Very often this effect is strengthened by the chosen sound occurring not only at the beginnings of words, but also inside them or at the end:

> Pack, clouds, away! and welcome, day! . . .
> And all the men that fill the glen . . .
> Brown skeletons of leaves that lag my forest-brook along . . .

Assonance

This is the repetition of vowel-sounds in a sequence of words:

> And the bay was white with silent light.
> The ice did split with a thunder-fit.
> Over the cobbles he clattered and clashed in the dark inn-yard.

Alliteration and assonance can be cleverly blended. Poets get marvellous effects in this way; trace the intricate pattern of matching sounds in these few lines:

> The western wave was all aflame,
> The day was well nigh done!
> Almost upon the western wave
> Rested the broad bright Sun; . . .

Onomatopoeia

This is the strange name given to the effect achieved when words actually resemble a certain real sound. Whizz, hiss, babble, crash, bang, rattle, thump, chatter all have onomatopoeic quality. Examples from poetry are:

> The moan of doves in immemorial elms,
> And murmuring of innumerable bees . . .

> I heard the water lapping on the crag,
> And the long ripple washing in the reeds . . .

211

Three Queens with crowns of gold—and from them rose
A cry that shiver'd to the tingling stars,
And, as it were one voice, an agony
Of lamentation, like a wind that shrills
All night in a waste land, where no one comes . . .

Exercises

Write out the following quotations, and state the figures of speech which they contain:

1 Examples of simile, metaphor, and personification:

(a) A dusky barge, dark as a funeral scarf from stem to stern.
The other swiftly strode from ridge to ridge, clothed with his breath.
His own thought drove him, like a goad.
Smoothing the rugged brow of Night.
Forlorn! the very word is like a bell.
With beaded bubbles winking at the brim.
The luminous self-possession of ships on ocean.
I heard the South sing o'er the land.
I saw . . . the crimson brands of sunset fall.
He watched the liner's stem ploughing the foam.

(b) Watching the full-starred heavens that winter sees.
He sways his head from side to side, with movements like a snake.
The triumphant storm did flee . . . swift and proud.
Fair daffodils, we weep to see you haste away so soon.
An' smila weeth teetha so shiny like pearls.
Thy soul was like a star, and dwelt apart.
Earth-golden from the burning bowels of the earth.
He stood, and heard the steeple sprinkle the quarters on the morning town.
And on her hair a glory, like a saint.
Down the cold corridor of winter nights.

2 Examples of alliteration, assonance, and onomatopoeia:

(a) The sullen wind was soon awake.
Where name of slave and sultan scarce is known.
Lo! some we loved, the loveliest and best.

Fear no more the lightning-flash, nor the all-dreaded thunder-stone.

Of hammered gold and gold enamelling.

The leafy boughs on high hissed in the sun.

Alone he rides, alone, the fair and fatal king.

His soul was of the saints.

In sweetest season, when each flower and weed.

She walks in beauty, like the night of cloudless climes and starry skies.

(b) Who snorted like a buffalo.

There was a roaring in the wind all night.

The rain came heavily and fell in floods.

And singing still dost soar, and soaring ever singest.

All day the wind breathes low with mellower tone.

Roaring deeps and fiery sands, clanging fights . . . . and praying hands.

The arras, rich with horsemen, hawk, and hound.

And still she slept an azure-lidded sleep.

Till the slow sea rise and the sheer cliff crumble.

O Wild West Wind, thou breath of Autumn's being.

Note. A few of these examples may include more than one figure of speech!

3 Write 10 short sentences, each including a simile of your own making and aiming for vivid effect.

4 Use each of the following words in a metaphor:

(a) heart	(b) barrier	(c) painted
fruit	crystal	fountain
peak	root	echoing
shadow	star	flare
shell	crumbled	sparkle

5 Write picturesque sentences each containing examples of personification, and using the following words:

(a) nature	(b) river	(c) time
horror	gaiety	death
sleep	melancholy	thought
moon	silence	summer
breeze	gleam	winter

6 Write down 10 words that seem to you to have onomatopoeic quality, and use them in short sentences that show this quality, e.g.:

> *whizz:* The arrow whizzed through the air.

7 Search your poetry book, or any suitable book of prose, for five examples of each of the following:

alliteration	personification
metaphor	assonance
simile	onomatopoeia

8 There are many well-known metaphorical expressions. Explain clearly, without the use of other metaphors, what the following mean:

(a)	(b)
a fish out of water	a swan song
to eat humble pie	to throw up the sponge
picking a bone with someone	a skeleton at the feast
to let the cat out of the bag	a wet blanket
Hobson's choice	to send coals to Newcastle
crocodile tears	the last straw
mushroom growth	to put the clock back
to smell a rat	to get one's monkey up
to bury the hatchet	a Jack of all trades
to cross the Rubicon	to cry over spilt milk

9 Explain, in the simplest language, the meaning of the following metaphorical expressions:

(a)	(b)
to ride one's high horse	a self-made man
there are no flies on him	a storm in a teacup
to buy a pig in a poke	to paint the town red
to nip in the bud	a wolf in sheep's clothing
to pour oil on troubled waters	to pour cold water on

10 Use each of the following metaphorical expressions in a sentence, to show the meaning clearly, e.g.:

> *Hobson's choice:* We had Hobson's choice at the restaurant, for when we arrived there was only one main dish left—boiled fish.

(a)	(b)
pot luck	to grope in the dark
a snake in the grass	to set the Thames on fire
rose-coloured spectacles	to champ at the bit
a bird's-eye-view	to beard the lion in his den
the luck of the draw	to set the cat amongst the pigeons
to be on the carpet	an Indian summer
a mare's nest	a bull in a china-shop
a good samaritan	he could not see the wood for the trees
the gipsy's warning	
a Job's comforter	a chip off the old block

11 Briefly explain the meanings of the following expressions:

(a)	(b)
the heel of Achilles	baptism of fire
above-board	to beat about the bush
behind-hand	a bee in one's bonnet
a real Adonis	bats in the belfry
to build castles in the air	to bell the cat
pipe-dreams	to hit below the belt
in apple-pie order	his better half
tied to the apron-strings	to take the bit between one's teeth
to have an axe to grind	to bite the dust
to get one's back up	his bark is worse than his bite
to breed bad blood	to be in someone's black books
to keep the ball rolling	to blow hot and cold
a bad egg	a blue-stocking
to bandy words	once in a blue moon
off the cuff	in the same boat

12 Use the following expressions in sentences which clearly show their meaning:

(a)	(b)
a bolt from the blue	a cock and bull story
a bookworm	to give the cold shoulder
one's bread and butter	to come off with flying colours
to break the ice	to send to Coventry
to make a clean breast of	crocodile tears

(a)

to make bricks without straw
to bring down the house
to knit one's brows
to kick the bucket
to take the bull by the horns

(b)

as the crow flies
to cut a dash
Davy Jones' locker
a dead letter
a dog in a manger

(c)

to raise Cain
to burn the candle at both ends
to put the cart before the horse
a catspaw
to be in clover
to cut one's coat according to the
    cloth
to save one's face
to pull strings
a nine days' wonder
to put one's foot in it

(d)

in the doldrums
to draw the line at
Dutch courage
at the eleventh hour
at the end of one's tether
to make both ends meet
to see eye to eye
the fairer sex
a flash in the pan
to flog a dead horse

(e)

to play second fiddle
a feather in one's cap
to take French leave
to split hairs
a needle in a hay-stack
more haste less speed
strike while the iron's hot
check by jowl
to turn over a new leaf
to show the white feather

(f)

to play to the gallery
to have at one's finger-tips
the apple of one's eye
looking a gift-horse in the mouth
to live from hand to mouth
too many irons in the fire
a Jezebel
to rest on one's laurels
a white lie
to let sleeping dogs lie

(g)

to read between the lines
much of a muchness
in a nutshell
any port in a storm
pin-money
in for a penny, in for a pound
to make a silk purse out of a
    sow's ear

(h)

to leave in the lurch
to cast pearls before swine
to rob Peter to pay Paul
a hard nut to crack
to mind one's P's and Q's
a red herring
a quixotic person
caught red-handed

(g)   (h)
to be in Queer Street   to know the ropes
to ride roughshod over   red-tape
a red-letter day

Can you think of any more expressions like these?

13 Write effective similes, using the following beginnings:

(a) He rode his bicycle like . . .
The old aunt sat there eyeing her like . . .
The morning sun rose high, as . . .
His eyes were hooded, sinister, as . . .
His round, pale face was like . . .

(b) The wealth of colour in my garden was like . . .
The immense tree stood there, like . . .
The gloomy scene beneath the water was like . . .
As she spoke, the thunder rolled in the distance, like . . .
The eagle circled lazily above, as . . .

(c) His look was fierce and menacing, as . . .
They felt the cold envelop them like . . .
I saw the aircraft hurtling earthwards like . . .
Into the waves he plunged, as . . .
The tendrils of creeper clutched at his legs like . . .

14 These attempts at writing figures of speech are not really successful.
Can you explain why? Can you improve them?

(a) His pale, sick face was a brown study.
Hatred and terror sauntered through the land.
The arrow sang its sinister song as it shot through the air.
The elephant moved with cat-like tread.
The old frog sniffed the air.

(b) Her screams embedded themselves in the rock.
His footsteps shattered the silence of the forest.
Courage oozed from his fingertips as he faced the foe.
She stood there looking at him like a blind creature.
Delight gnaws at my heart.

(c) She lifted her face towards him, like an upturned dish.
I sat on my agony, trying to stifle it.
He's getting up my nose with all his fancy talk.

217

Frances fought against her fate, frantic fingers fumbling through the forest of fear.

He stared piercingly at his enemy, then struck him blindly in the face.

Let these horrors be a lesson to you: always consider the *effect* of the figures of speech that you write. They can sometimes be ridiculous rather than effective, e.g.:

He stood there, knitting a pair of black eyebrows!

SOUND-QUALITIES

Quite apart from figures of speech, ordinary words themselves may often possess distinctive sounds which a writer can use for effect. You have seen this at work in onomatopoeia, where word-sounds suggest actual sounds (whizz, scream, gurgle, etc.), but there is more to it than that. Put simply, short sounds in a sequence of words can suggest speed or briskness; longer sounds may give the effect of slowness, sleepiness, or mystery.

Giving the effect of speed:

> This is the night mail crossing the border,
> Bringing the cheque and the postal order,
> Letters for the rich, letters for the poor,
> The shop at the corner and the girl next door.
> > (an express train speeding along)

> About, about, in reel and rout,
> The death-fires danced at night.
> > (leaping flames and shimmering lights)

> The Sun's rim dips; the stars rush out:
> At one stride comes the dark.
> > (sudden nightfall)

> Wings linked. Necks a-strain,
> A rush and a wild crying . . .
> > (wild duck flying overhead)

Giving the effect of slowness, lack of movement, mystery:

> Day after day, day after day,
> We stuck, nor breath nor motion;
> As idle as a painted ship
> Upon a painted ocean . . .
> > (a ship becalmed)

They groaned, they stirred, they all uprose,
Nor spake, nor moved their eyes . . .
                    (dead men slowly arising, to man the ship)

Dark is the ground; a slumber seems to steal
O'er vale, and mountain, and the starless sky . . .
                    (landscape in the stillness of dusk)

Never did sun more beautifully steep
In his first splendour, valley, rock, or hill . . .
                    (the slow progress of sunrise)

Every good writer makes use of this kind of word-music. The long poem, *The Ancient Mariner*, by Coleridge, is packed with it. You can also suggest increasing or decreasing speed, as in this description of a train leaving the station:

After the first powerful plain manifesto
The black statement of pistons, without more fuss
But gliding like a queen, she leaves the station.
                                    (the start)

Beyond the town there lies the open country
Where, gathering speed, she acquires mystery.
                                    (moving faster)

It is now she begins to sing—at first quite low
Then loud, and at last with a jazzy madness—
The song of her whistle screaming at curves . . .
                                    (increasing to full speed)

From *The Express*, by Stephen Spender

Exercises

15 Write sentences, choosing your words carefully, so that their sounds contribute to the pace or atmosphere. Use these themes:

(a) waves breaking on a sea-shore, then receding.
   an unlit room in the gathering dusk.
   a space-rocket leaving the launching-pad and gathering speed.
   a lighthouse beam sweeping the sea.
   a train entering the station and coming to rest.
   a racing car roaring round the track, then crashing.
   a horse and cart jogging down the street.
   the last moments of a mile race on sports day.
   a person gradually realising the danger that threatens.
   sea-birds wheeling above a cliff edge.

219

(*b*) wind rising and increasing in intensity.
a speedboat chasing about off-shore.
an artist sketching.
clothes on the line, blown in the breeze.
a sailing-ship, gradually becalmed.
a snake, startled, moving away to cover.
a lion stalking, then springing on its prey.
a person's face, as he slowly realises the point of a joke.
yourself, slipping on a banana-skin.
a cat lapping up milk.

(*c*) a goldfish swimming round its globe.
daffodils nodding amidst the grass.
a dragonfly, hovering, then darting off.
a hovercraft at full speed.
the bow-wave from a speeding ship.
a dog's tail wagging with pleasure.
a glider coming in to land.
the sun going down below the horizon.
a tray of crockery dropped downstairs.
a factory chimney toppling sideways to the ground.

Effects to be avoided

Exercise 14 warns you to be careful when devising figures of speech; you must not overdo them or provide comparisons that are ridiculous Here are some more warnings:

(*a*) *Never mix your metaphors:* I smell a rat! I see it floating in the air! But fear not; I shall explore every avenue until I find that snake in the grass, when I shall nip him in the bud!

A vivid statement, if you like, but the result is nonsense. By all means *sustain* your metaphor (or simile) if you like—make it fairly lengthy, if it is a good one, but keep the comparison clear; don't compare first with one thing and then with another. Here are some examples of good "sustained" comparisons:

A library is, as it were, a rich granary of knowledge. Countless scholars have stored here the harvest of their labours, and all this golden grain is for our nourishment . . .

Rustum answered not, but hurl'd his spear;
Down from the shoulder, down it came,
As on some partridge in the corn a hawk

> That long has tower'd in the airy clouds
> Drops like a plummet: Sohrab saw it come,
> And sprang aside.

(*b*) *Avoid clichés:* A cliché is a word or phrase that has been so often used that its effect is too familiar to impress. We can only wince at these:

> in this day and age
> by fair means or foul
> far be it from me to
> speaking personally, I
> conspicuous by its absence
> a guardian of the law

You may be in some doubt, however, as to whether a phrase is going to seem "fly-blown" or not; sometimes well-known phrases like most of those in Exercises 8–12 are the best way of expressing your point. The best advice is not to use too many of them; do not litter your writing or speech with them, hoping they will sound expressive. If you try to be fresh and original in your choice of language, you will avoid writing too many clichés.

(*c*) *Avoid "over-enthusiastic" language:* Unfortunately we are surrounded nowadays by advertisements that use words of "high tension" effect, trying to shock or charm us into buying various products. A ninepenny bar of soap is "fabulous"; a tin of corned beef is "flavour-rich in succulent juices"; a film depicting some sordid little kitchen-sink drama in Wigan is a "breathtakingly daring challenge to our times"; a standard threepenny razor-blade can bring us "keen-edged morning freshness, smoothing life's path the whole day through".

You must try to see through this frantic struggle to sell you things by using high-tension language. And please do not sprinkle your own speech and writing with the same over-ripe phrases. Such words as "terribly", "awfully", "incredibly", "fabulous", "gorgeous", "scintillating", "breathtakingly", "superb" may have a use, but do not apply them unless they are really needed. Don't scatter such words around like confetti; confetti is appropriate to a wedding—a *special* occasion—and even there you would only use a small packet, not a tea-chestful!

(*d*) *Avoid slang in unsuitable places:* Slang, the picturesque language of speech, can be very entertaining, but you must be careful where you use it, and written work is rarely the proper place. You would not, presumably, say "Gor-blimey!" at the Vicar's tea-party; the effect would

221

be similar to picking up a plate of jelly and flinging it through the window. In your written work, then, avoid using slang expressions like "smashing", "bloke", "chap", "bike", "cuppa", "to get the sack", "lousy", "I went up the club", "we played around", "he pushed off", "they told us off", "my mate", "I copped it", "shut up", "see you", "bye-bye", "dirt cheap", etc.

(e) *Avoid puns, unless they are good ones:* A pun is a play on words which have similar sounds but different meanings:

> He played the piano solo—so low, you couldn't hear it!
>
> They went and told the sexton, and
>   The sexton toll'd the bell.
>
> Can I press you to a little jelly?

The effect of most puns is agonising; you should only pun if you can devise a really clever one.

PROVERBS

These are little sayings which have a grain of wisdom about them. Here are some you should know:

Exercises

Explain clearly the meaning of each of the following proverbs:

16 A bird in the hand is worth two in the bush.
   A drowning man will clutch at a straw.
   A fool and his money are soon parted.
   A friend in need is a friend indeed.
   A man is as old as he feels.
   A man's house is his castle.
   A miss is as good as a mile.
   Out of the frying pan, into the fire.
   A rolling stone gathers no moss.
   A stitch in time saves nine.

17 Absence makes the heart grow fonder.
   Actions speak louder than words.
   All that glisters is not gold.
   In the country of the blind the one-eyed man is king.

All's fair in love and war.
As you sow, so shall you reap.
Beggars cannot be choosers.
Better late than never.
Birds of a feather flock together.
Blood is thicker than water.

18 Charity begins at home (but should not end there).
Discretion is the better part of valour.
Do not put all your eggs in one basket.
Do not count your chickens before they are hatched.
Do not tell tales out of school.
Enough is as good as a feast.
Every cloud has a silver lining.
Everything comes to him who waits.
Familiarity breeds contempt.
Fine feathers make fine birds.

19 First come first served.
Forewarned is forearmed.
Give the devil his due.
Good wine needs no bush
Great minds think alike.
He knows most who speaks least.
He laughs best who laughs last.
He runs with the hare and hunts with the hounds.
If the cap fits, wear it.
It is a long lane that has no turning.

20 It is an ill wind that blows nobody good.
It never rains but it pours.
It takes two to make a quarrel.
Least said, soonest mended.
Let the cobbler stick to his last.
Look before you leap.
Make hay while the sun shines.
Manners maketh man.
Many hands make light work.
Necessity is the mother of invention.

How many more proverbs do you know?

8 Punctuation

We cannot do without punctuation marks in writing. They help to show how the words are intended to be spoken:

> you silly idiot get off my head will you if you dont ill bash you when i get up from here you see if i dont
>
> You silly idiot! Get off my head, will you? If you don't, I'll bash you —when I get up from here. You see if I don't!

Obviously, the second, punctuated version is easier to read, for it suggests where the speaker would pause or emphasise his words to get the necessary venom into his threat.

Sometimes punctuation is vital in showing the meaning intended by a writer:

> Woman without her man is a savage.
> Woman! Without her, man is a savage.
>
> The snowball was thrown by Perkins who is Head Boy for a joke.
> The snowball was thrown by Perkins, who is Head Boy, for a joke.

In each of these pairs of sentences you can see how the punctuation affects the whole meaning.

If your punctuating is weak, the chances are that you have neglected it for years. You must now repair that neglect, by studying the rules and examples given here; do plenty of the exercises also, and consciously try to apply the rules in all your written work.

THE RULES OF PUNCTUATION

Full stop

1 Most commonly it divides sentence from sentence:

> I am going dancing tonight. The dance begins at seven. Would you like to come with me?

(Note that the full stop is replaced by a question mark at the end of a question. Similarly, an exclamation mark ends an exclamation.)

224

2   Use a full stop also at the end of any abbreviated word:

R.A.F.	Hon. Sec.	Dr. J. C. Smith, F.R.C.S.	
P. 19	Nos. 1–5	Ex. 6	Ajax Mfg. Co.

Semicolon

This is useful in longer sentences if you want to present several ideas which, though separate, might properly belong in one sentence:

> You could wait for him here; on the other hand I could wait in your place; this would save you valuable time.
>
> I have not read any of his novels; I know his plays, though.

Do not be afraid to use semicolons. You could often use a full stop instead, but if the ideas really belong in the same sentence, a semicolon provides a useful pause, not quite so final as a full stop.

Colon

This introduces a quotation, a list of items, or a statement given as an example or enlargement of what has just been mentioned:

> The poem begins: "Earth has not anything to show more fair."
> For camping you need: a tent, groundsheet, sleeping bag, and cooking equipment.
> His house became what one might expect after years of neglect: a battered, decrepit wreck.

It may also introduce quoted speech, though a comma is more usual nowadays:

> He said to me: "Go home, will you?"
> He said to me, "Go home, will you?"

It will help you to think of the colon as having the meaning of "namely" or "to state in detail".

Question mark

Any word, group of words, or sentence forming a question must be followed by this mark:

> How?
> "Will you come too?" he asked.
> Can you see how it is done?

225

Note. Such sentences as "He asked me how it was done" are what we call questions stated *indirectly*, and they should not have a question mark.

Exclamation mark

Any word, group of words, or sentence intended to be spoken with special force, as an exclamation, must be followed by this mark:

> Stop!
> "Run for it!" she screamed.
> They will never take us alive!

Note. It is not done to use several exclamation marks or question marks at once: !!!!   ????   One is enough.

Brackets

These are sometimes used, especially in notes, to enclose additional information:

> The first stage in the process (see Fig. 1) is:

Use brackets sparingly. If brackets are needed inside brackets, use square ones inside the round ones:

> (—— [——] ——)

Dash

This is useful to suggest an abrupt break, especially in conversation, or to show faltering speech:

> "Let me tell you about—Oh! There's the telephone. Excuse me for a moment."
>
> "Yes—well—I would—only you see—it's not easy."

Hyphen

1   It separates parts of compound words:

> mother-in-law; dressing-table; sergeant-major

This use is growing less common, however; often you can do without such hyphens.

2   It divides a word if there is no room to complete it at the end of a line:

> .... be-
> cause ....

Note that the hyphen comes at the end of the line, not at the beginning of the next line. Also, you may only divide words at the end of a syllable: "beca-use" would be quite wrong.

The next three items are the trickiest. Study them with special care.

Comma

Wherever the sense demands that the reader or speaker should make a slight pause, a comma should be used. This is the whole purpose of the comma; if you apply this rule intelligently, you will not go far astray. Using the comma is, unlike most other punctuation, a matter of taste rather than rule, but here to help you are samples of all the common uses:

1 To separate items in a list:

We bought some shoes, gloves, a jersey, handkerchiefs, and a scarf.

2 Similarly, to separate adjectives or adverbs when several are used:

The children were noisy, mischievous, inquisitive, unruly, and altogether something of a nuisance.

The snow fell silently, densely, almost unnoticed, in an even whiteness which soon covered the whole landscape.

3 To separate parts of dates and addresses:

23rd July, 1962.   Monday, 15th August, 1874.

James Roberts Esq.,
Woodstock Manor,
Ancoats Road,
Wolverton,
Surrey.

4 In pairs, to enclose words used "in apposition"—words which follow a noun to tell you more about it:

This vase, a fine specimen of its kind, is now my property.
Randolph Spruce, Chairman of our Company, has just returned.
The dodo, a curious bird, is now extinct.

5 In pairs, to enclose words or phrases like: "however", "well", "by the way", "to speak plainly":

He admitted, however, that he was wrong.
You told me, by the way, that you still had it.

(Note also: However, he admitted that he was wrong.)

6 To separate or enclose names of people being spoken to:

Please, Mother, will you help me?
Try to do it now, Joan.
Thank you, Sir, for your advice.
David, will you please hurry?

7 To separate words spoken as direct speech from the rest of a sentence:

My brother said, "That is just as it should be."
"That is just as it should be," said my brother.
"That," said my brother, "is just as it should be."

Note the positioning. These are samples of the three punctuation patterns for sentences including direct speech. See the notes below on the use of inverted commas.

8 In letters, after Dear Sir, Dear Mr. Jones, etc., and after Yours faithfully, Yours sincerely, etc.

9 In all other cases, to separate parts of a sentence wherever *a slight pause* seems desirable. Study these examples:

If it is fine tomorrow, I should like to go cycling.
Although we tried hard to win the game, we lost by five runs.
My friend Avril, whom you met last week at my party, asked to be remembered to you.
When I saw how ill he looked, I decided not to tell him of our plans, but he asked me about them, saying how interested he was, and so I had no alternative.

In such cases as these, the modern way is to use as few commas as are needed to show the meaning clearly. Do not scatter your commas everywhere.

Inverted commas or quotation marks

These enclose all quotations or quoted speech-words written down exactly as spoken:

228

My sister said, "I cannot see how you can eat so much."
"If you can go," said Jane, "I shall be glad to join you."
The poem begins: "I wandered lonely as a cloud . . ."

Some modern printers prefer to use single marks: '——', but you are advised to use double: "——". If inverted commas are needed inside inverted commas, use single inside double: "—— '——' ——".

Peter said, "His reply was 'Certainly not!', as I had expected."

Note these three patterns for punctuating sentences containing direct speech. You must learn where the inverted commas, capital letters, commas, and all other marks must go:

1 John said, "That is all there is to be said."
2 "That is all there is to be said," said John.
3 "That," said John, "is all there is to be said."

Occasionally you may come across situations where you are not sure whether to place certain punctuation marks "outside" or "inside" the inverted commas. Here are samples:

We studied "Twelfth Night", "Macbeth", "Hamlet", and other plays.
Have you read "Treasure Island"?
"Have you seen the film of 'Hamlet'?" she asked.

Your guide here must be: do the marks belong to the piece in inverted commas, or to the sentence outside?

Apostrophe

1 One use is to show where certain letters have been missed out:

it's	(it is)	haven't	(have not)
can't	(cannot)	we'll	(we shall)
won't	(will not)	o'clock	(of the clock)

2 Use it also when you refer to letters or numbers in plural form: 2's, p's and q's; find all the Number 7's.

3 Its third use is to show possession by someone (or something) of some item or other:

This *man's* house.	The *dog's* basket.
My *friend's* new hat.	*Boys'* trousers.
Ladies' hairdresser.	*Motorists'* accessories.

In each of these samples, the italicised word can be thought of as "the possessor" of the articles that follow. The apostrophe must be added to the possessor, *not* to the thing possessed. Your problem is to know whether the apostrophe must go before or after the **s**. A simple rule can solve this doubt: *Always try to add* **'s** *to the word denoting the possessor. If the result then seems silly, remove the final* **s**. If you apply this rule you need never go wrong. Here are some examples:

Possessor	Thing possessed	Rule applied
a dog	bone	a dog's bone
women	hats	women's hats
wild animals	habits	wild animals'(s) habits*
my son	motorcycle	my son's motorcycle
the Indian people	wishes	the Indian people's wishes
these birds	nests	these birds'(s) nests*
men	overalls	men's overalls
that child	toys	that child's toys
our children	ages	our children's ages
the rivers	courses	the rivers'(s) courses*
his uncle	clothes	his uncle's clothes

(s) not needed

OTHER MATTERS OF PUNCTUATION

Where should capital letters be used?

1   To start the first word of every sentence:

He went out to find it. Two hours later he returned.

2   Always for the word "I":

I'm the king of the castle, I am.

3   To begin names of people, places, weekdays, special days, months:

Mr. George Wood	Blackpool	July	Boxing Day
His Majesty King Charles	America	Tuesday	Easter

4   To begin all main words in titles of books, essays, names of ships, businesses, institutions:

Gone with the Wind	The Heath Secondary School
My Favourite Music	Empress of the Seas
The Royal Society	Swiftsure Credit and Loan Co. Ltd.

230

5 For letters after people's names, or letters elsewhere standing for words (with some exceptions):

> John Gray, B.A., Ph.D.   R.N.   C.I.D.   B.B.C.
> *Exceptions:* e.g.   gms.   i.e.

6 Sparingly, for words that seem to merit special distinction:

> We must invite your Uncle and Aunt.
> There has been much activity at our School this year.

Beginning new paragraphs

Start a new paragraph about one inch in from the margin. All lines which follow start close to the margin:

Note also that when writing dialogue, using direct speech, you should start a new paragraph every time the speaker changes:

> "What are you doing?" asked Jean, looking up from her book. "Are you painting?"
> "Isn't it obvious what I'm doing?" I replied, as I daubed happily away at my sketch of a bonfire scene.
> "Well," she said, with a grin, "I could see it was paint you were using, but I couldn't decide whether you were painting the paper or the carpet all round it."

Exercises

Rewrite the following paragraphs, adding all necessary punctuation:

1 i call my new girl friend glub glub said horace glub glub exclaimed his brother charlie thats a very strange name is it her real one then in a way it is replied horace with a silly grin it should have been mavis but when she was christened the parson fell in the font.

2   having seen my friend safely on her way i hurried home to our house in devonshire avenue the laurels we call it though theres not a laurel bush in sight my father met me on the doorstep where have you been he said ive been waiting here for the last half hour why didnt you let yourself in i asked astonished because on the way up the path i dropped my key he snarled and it slid into the goldfish pond.

3   my brakes failed on the way down hill and careering helplessly to the bottom.i slid gracefully off the road over the bumpy grass verge and thumped into the slimy oozy ditch my bicycle buckled battered and falling apart draped round my neck a small boy was fishing in the water nearby he took one look at me and said cor thats what i call being on pleasure bent.

4   i went to my brothers wedding last week as you know he has married that nice girl who works in smarts the greengrocers well shes all right but he does not seem to get on so well with her relations i felt very sorry for him at the reception as he was making his bridegrooms speech for he dropped a large sized brick the noise of which echoed round the whole room he said and i am so pleased to see all my new relations here do tuck into the free food you have given us many lovely presents and i hope you will continue to do so in the future.

5   a lady went to open her refrigerator one day and she saw to her great surprise a tiny rabbit sitting on a packet of bacon on the top shelf what are you doing here she cried dont be silly came the squeaky reply dont you know the name of your wefwigewator of course i do said the lady its a westinghouse youre wight said the rabbit and im westing.

6   the bead bangled big chief wingle wangle had three lovely redskin squaws who slept in his wigwam one on a hide of moose one on a hide of reindeer and the third his favourite on a hide of hippopotamus eventually his wives presented him with lovely redskin babies a son from the squaw who slept on the reindeer hide a son from the one who slept on the moose hide but twin sons from the squaw who slept on the hippopotamus hide this all goes to show that the squaw on the hippopotamus hide of the bead bangled wingle wangle was equal to the sons of the squaws on the other two hides.

7   yes i have a pair of eyes replied sam and thats just it if they wos a pair o patent double million magnifyin gas microscopes of hextra power praps i might be able to see through a flight o stairs and a deal door but bein only eyes you see my wisions limited.

8   cos a coachmans a privileged indiwidual replied mr weller looking fixedly at his son cos a coachman may do vithout suspicion wot other men may not cos a coachman may be on the wery amicablest terms with eighty mile o females and yet nobody thinks that he ever means to marry any vun among them.

9   a man was riding in a bus one day when he noticed to his astonishment that a lady in front of him had a large banana sticking out of her ear excuse me madam he said politely going up to the lady but are you aware

that you have a large banana sticking out of your ear eh said the lady the man repeated his words growing more and more embarrassed eh said the lady you will have to speak louder you know cant you see i have a large banana sticking out of my ear.

10 what do you think of my latest painting said albert displaying what looked like a plain sheet of paper in a fancy frame oh lovely exclaimed sheila not wanting to seem ignorant what do you call it then its called cow in field eating grass was the proud reply but i dont see any grass no said albert the cows eaten it all but i cant see any cow either sheila cried youre right shes gone to look for some more grass.

11 *Apostrophe to show possession:* Write out these phrases, showing possession by each noun of the item which follows:

Possessor	Item possessed
three men	watches
a girl	handbag
my aunt	knitting
this flower	petals
our garage	doors
his brothers	cycles
your book	cover
Keats	poetry
Alex	friend
the rooms	colour schemes
this week	programme
children	games
these bottles	labels
his wife	sister
my car	spare wheel
women	hairstyles
the ships	anchorages
the carpet	pattern
the knives	edges
the swallows	nest

(Remember the rule: try to add *'s* to the possessor; if the result seems silly, remove the last *s*.)

12 Punctuate these sentences containing direct speech:

(*a*) whats that mark on your nose asked elsa

(*b*) that remark snorted the shopkeeper was rather silly wasnt it

(*c*) maureen whispered to him ill try to meet you here at seven thirty

233

(*d*) id like a pound of sugar said irene six large eggs and two lemons

(*e*) will you come asked joan we should love to have you with us

(*f*) the thief raised his fist snarling get out of my way will you

(*g*) the play is called the dumb wife of cheapside and its very funny said arthur do you know it

(*h*) only ten miles more cried the driver but the fogs closing in fast

(*i*) where exclaimed penny do you suppose i put my hat is it upstairs

(*j*) im hoping to buy a new suit said rex but im not sure if i can yet

13 Punctuate and set out these names and addresses as you would write them on envelopes:

(*a*) united bus co ltd 74 high street rowfold shropshire

(*b*) j smythe esq m b e the towers linton avenue highfield notts

(*c*) mr and mrs geo winkle spooky grange ramsbottom lancs

(*d*) the managing director weedy plant co nogrow nurseries wotton

(*e*) mrs o lovibunch meadowvista 1963 cable lane pine bluff texas

(*f*) lizzy tinribs c o mrs blodge 27 giants causeway blackpool

(*g*) sir james bunbury c b e hogg house nether wallop herts

(*h*) securit safe co ltd strongbox buildings bullion road leeds

(*i*) rev s n flinn the manse macgregor cove orkney

(*j*) messrs d f and c weevil bosky mill sugarloaf lane wilton

14 Write out these sentences, adding the necessary commas, semicolons, and other punctuation:

(*a*) after the heavy rain the sun reappeared by lunchtime all was dry once more

(*b*) we enjoyed having him to lunch after our meal we sat in the garden talking about old times

(*c*) some of the students were painting some demonstrated making pottery others staged a puppet show charging sixpence for admission the proceeds to go to charity

(*d*) we like devonshire cornwall is more spectacular but very crowded in summer we never go there then

(*e*) i enjoyed watching the serial play it is a little dull at times but the characters are interesting dont you think (*f*) our dog is a menace im sorry to say the neighbours dog is even worse and together they would frighten the hardiest postman

(*g*) if you fancy a swim now we just have time before tea otherwise we could go down to the beach this evening

(*h*) i can recommend the fish the roast beef is often good never order their soup though for whenever ive had it it has always tasted like well used washing up water

(*i*) after our journey through london with its fog and rain we wished we had stayed at home you can at least breathe real air where we live

(*j*) alison is getting married next week pat is engaged as for me im waiting for a millionaire to come my way but so far ive only had an offer from a bus conductor

15 Write out these sentences, punctuating each one in two different ways, to give it two quite different meanings:

(*a*) the manager said the shop assistant should be more polite

(*b*) he said my friend was a clumsy idiot

(*c*) i like english history and geography lessons

(*d*) let me introduce you to robert james

(*e*) peter your cousin is waiting for you

(*f*) this writer claims percy snitch the famous critic is insane

(*g*) fancy cakes for tea

(*h*) she thought richard was probably the guilty party

(*i*) i thought joe would like charlie here

(*j*) can you wait a minute while i wash harry

Rewrite the following paragraphs, adding all necessary punctuation:

16 the snow is everywhere the shrubs are weighed down by masses of it the terrace is knee deep in it the plaster apollo in the long walk is more than knee deep in it and is furnished with a surplice and wig like a half blown bishop the distant country looks like the very ghost of a landscape the white walled cottages seem part and parcel of the snow drifts around them drifts that take every variety of form and are swept by the wind into fairy wreaths and fantastic caves the old mill wheel is locked fast and gemmed with giant icicles.

Cuthbert Bede

17 wots the matter says the doctor wery ill says the patient wot have you been a eatin on says the doctor roast weal says the patient wots the last thing you devoured says the doctor crumpets says the patient thats i

235

says the doctor ill send you a box of pills directly and dont you never take no more of em he says no more o wot says the patient pills no crumpets says the doctor why says the patient starting up in bed ive eat four crumpets every night for fifteen year on principle.

Charles Dickens

18   weve known them and laughed at them these fussy little steamers all our lives we have called them the shilling sicks we have watched them load and unload their crowds of holiday passengers the gents full of high spirits and bottled beer the ladies eating pork pies the children sticky with peppermint rock sometimes they only went as far as the next seaside resort but the boldest of them might manage a channel crossing to let everybody have a glimpse of boulogne.

J. B. Priestley

19   lord nelson was at this time as he had been during the whole action walking the starboard side of the quarter deck sometimes much animated and at others heroically fine in his observations a shot through the mainmast knocked a few splinters about us he observed to me with a smile it is warm work and this day may be the last to any of us at a moment and then stopping short at the gangway he used an expression never to be erased from my memory and said with emotion but mark you i would not be elsewhere for thousands.

Lt.-Col. Stewart

20   bernard shaw once described his behaviour during moments of danger as follows in moments of crisis my nerves act in the most extraordinary way when disaster seems imminent my whole being is simultaneously braced to avoid it i size up the situation in a flash set my teeth contract my muscles take a firm grip of myself and without a tremor always do the wrong thing.

21   a lady from england staying with some friends in ireland thought to try her hand on the natives of limerick in the cause of temperance furnished with a list of names she proceeded to the poorer suburbs where she called on a mrs doherty good morning mrs doherty she said in a coaxing tone good morning maam replied the woman of the house taking her arms out of the washing tub what can i be doing for you im collecting for a drunkards home mrs doherty said the visitor you are maam replied the other then if you send round about ten oclock tonight you can collect doherty.

22   there was a gentleman here yesterday he said a stout gentleman by the name of topsawyer perhaps you knew him no i said i dont think in breeches and gaiters broad brimmed hat grey coat speckled choker said the waiter no i said bashfully i havent the pleasure he came in here said the waiter looking at the light through the tumbler ordered a glass of this ale would order it i told him not drank it and fell dead it was too old for him it oughtnt to be drawn thats the fact.

Charles Dickens

23   as it spoke i discerned obscurely a child's face looking through the window terror made me cruel and finding it useless to attempt shaking the creature off i pulled its wrist on to the broken pane and rubbed it to

and fro until the blood ran down and soaked the bedclothes still it
wailed let me in and maintained its tenacious grip almost maddening me
with fear how can i i said at length let me go if you want me to let you
in the fingers relaxed.

Emily Brontë

24 the house is very old indeed she went on and the story an unpleasant one
dates a long way back it has to do with a murder committed by a jealous
stableman who had some affair with a servant in the house one night he
managed to secrete himself in the cellar and when everyone was asleep
he crept upstairs to the servants quarters chased the 'girl down to the
next landing and before anyone could come to her rescue threw her
bodily over the banisters into the hall below.

Algernon Blackwood

25 the october leaves have fallen on the lake on bright calm days they lie
in thousands on the now darkening water mostly yellow flotillas of poplar
floating continuously down from great trees that themselves shake in the
windless air with the sound of falling water but on rainy days or days
after rain they seem to swim or to be driven away and nothing remains
to break the surface except the last of the olive yellow lily pads that in
high summer covered every inch of water like plates of emerald porcelain.

H. E. Bates

26 the crooked billet is a snug white washed brick pub with green shutters
and russet roof standing on a base of black flints nasturtium runs wild
up the hedge opposite and a white cow steps twice daily past a black
weather boarded barn within there is a grand open fireplace with ingle
seat bread oven and a good fireback and this is the home of mr silas w
saunders the pole lathe turner all day he works in the woods which wash
over the spurs cols and ridges of this area in seamless billows of foliage.

H. J. Massingham

27 there are all too many townsmen townsmen who have been known to
walk who are summer walkers spring walkers even autumn walkers who
know nothing of the joys of winter walking winter they think is cold and
wet cold it may be and why not pray for my part i like the cold which
brisks me up so that i can keep up with anybody on a cold day but wet
it most certainly is not at least not especially wet it rains far more i am
convinced in july and august than ever it does in december and january

C. E. M. Joad

28 beyond the foot of the falls the river is like a slipping floor of marble
green with veins of dirty white made by the scum that was foam it slides
very quietly and slowly down for a mile or two sullenly exhausted then
it turns to a dull sage green and hurries more swiftly smooth and ominous
as the walls of the ravine close in trouble stirs and the waters boil and
eddy these are the lower rapids a sight more terrifying than the falls
because less intelligible close in its bands of rock the river surges
tumultuously forward writhing and leaping as if inspired by a demon.

Rupert Brooke

237

9 Common errors

This chapter aims to expose the many errors we might make when speaking or writing English. Single out the common errors which you constantly make yourself, and guard against them.

Each exercise consists of ten faulty sentences. Rewrite them correctly, giving reasons for the changes you make. The numbers in brackets after each sentence are the reference numbers of the points involved. Look up these points in the numbered list of explanations which follows the exercises.

Exercises

Each sentence contains one or more faults. Rewrite the sentences correctly, and give a brief explanation of the changes you have made:

1 I know its the right one, for I recognise it's number. (4)
   We want everyone to enjoy themselves. (8)
   Due to our car breaking down, we were very late home. (15)
   She didn't see nobody in the garden, as it was dark. (13)
   I never did like these sort of chairs. (10)
   There is a wooden fence between each garden. (20)
   This cake is much more richer than our's. (23, 3)
   "Please can I have sixpence, Dad?" asked Fred. (27)
   Have you made it like I made mine? (31)
   We hope to one day richly repay your kindness. (35)

2 This thing is a sort of a tin-opener. (36)
   Was it your clothes and your money that was lying there? (33)
   This boy who I told you about is coming here tonight. (38)
   Your jacket is laying on the floor in a heap. (25)
   None of those colours are right for you. (30)
   Whose coming with us, do you now? (39, 1)
   Keep it safe, so as you will not loose it. (44, 1)
   Their not going with us now. (1)
   These drinks are for you and I. (6)
   We never have and never will lend money. (54)

238

3 I saw it, but I could not say where, however. (56)
   You might come tonight, if you can spare the time. (59)
   We saw 3 camels, 22 monkeys and 17 bears at the zoo. (57)
   George has eat the two last cakes. (25, 52)
   "He has mislead us," said my friend. (25)
   She promised me she will come, so you must not worry. (53, 43)
   You are much cleverer than what we are. (41)
   There are less cakes now than I put out. (22)
   He did it without us seeing him. (21)
   Then Mavis sung a lovely song four us. (25, 1)

4 You must practice your conjuring tricks. (1)
   Writing a letter today, the ink overturned. (17)
   "Have you got a pencil I could borrow?" he asked. (24)
   We find it hard to agree with your proposal. (19)
   Your style is much less clumsier than mine. (23)
   I have payed you for the suit, haven't I? (25)
   Go and see if you can lend a chisel from him. (49, 25)
   Is this the person that I saw you with? (45, 55)
   I was literally drenched with the rain. (47, 34)
   Laziness and carelessness was to blame for it. (33)

5 This one is the best of the two, but that is cheapest. (32)
   She never did what they blamed her for. (29)
   If we can afford it, we will come tonight. (2)
   Everyone should bring their own food. (8)
   "It isn't alright," he said, "as you well no." (5, 1)
   This cloth is different to that one. (11)
   You didn't ought to have eat it. (14, 48)
   Our sincere gratitude is owing to Sir Percy. (15)
   The management decides the policy and pay the workers. (16)
   They did enjoy theirselves; noone was disappointed. (8, 12)

6 We have laid in the sun all day. (25)
   My friend has born the cost of the outing. (25)
   We didn't used to live were you said. (28, 1)
   The four men were talking noisily to each other. (32)
   It is silly to obstinately refuse to pay him. (35)
   You know who I mean, don't you? (38)
   Whose taking you home tonight? (39)

Will you look in on us after? I hope sow. (40, 1)
This lady that I met yesterday is called Brown. (45)
That was the reason why we stayed at home. (37)

7 Neither the father nor the mother wish to see him. (33)
It was all together a lovely evening. (1)
We swum across the river against his advise. (25, 1)
The water has flown right threw our garden. (25, 1)
She is sowing a new dress to ware at the dance. (25, 1)
Seeing as you will not do it, I will not pay you. (42, 2)
Is this book your's or her's? (3)
Does no one want to finish their sandwiches? (12, 8)
He gave me much assistants while I was studying. (1)
I am completely disinterested in stamp-collecting. (1)

8 Between you and I, he wears dreadful cloths. (6, 1)
These apples are all rotten, everyone. (1)
Have you awokened him yet? (25)
When I saw what was below, I dare not jump. (25)
It was a luxuriantly furnished room. (1)
She suffers with bad pains in the stomach. (34)
He is one of those people who never likes anybody. (33)
My brother is a very unpracticable person. (1)
It is the principal of the matter that I dislike. (1)
My sister gave me some very nice stationary. (1)

9 Let us hope for some fine whether tomorrow. (1)
Have you been laying down for long? (25)
There was a good deal of thunder and lightening. (1)
The affect of the rain was to wash away the path. (1)
It is my friend who's essay won the competition. (39)
She was literally poisoned when she eat the pudding. (47, 48)
Will you go and see who it is at the door? (49)
Can you make out who it belongs to? (38, 55)
There is the lady whom we thought was a Indian. (38, 18)
First I hanged my coat up in the hall. (25)

10 He begun his work early that evening. (25)
He lent lazily against the fence. (25)
I have two brothers; Keith is the nicest of them. (32)
It's a sort of a thing for stopping draughts. (36)
He could not finish his work, due to the heavy snowfall. (15)

Have you a license for this motorcycle? (1)
Our college Principle is a very imminent person. (1)
These woman where wareing there best cloths. (1)
It is very quite hear, almost to quite too breath. (1)
Do you like these sort of films? (10)

11 Less people can afford to buy houses these days. (22)
I got up to get washed, then got dressed and got breakfast. (24)
The saying is: "As the crow flys." (25)
Can I see your passports, please? (27)
Are you the girl who we saw in those photographs? (38)
I haven't any money, so I cannot come with you. (43)
He is a notable criminal. (1)
Their coming with us too the carnival. (1)
I wonder weather he past the resent examinations. (1, 25)
Will you try to higher the fence around your garden? (25)

12 He is immgrating from this country next week. (1)
They shareid the sandwiches amongst the two of them. (20)
Have you lain the table for tea? (25)
The criminal has been hung for murder. (25)
I just cannot do it like you showed me. (31)
The reason he cannot do it is because it is impossible. (37)
May be I shall loose it if noone helps me watch it. (1)
Does anybody want to try their hand at this game of skill? (8)
We will meet you their at seven o'clock. (2, 1)
He has ladened his plate with food for a third time. (25)

Note: Ask your teacher to set regular tests on common errors. It is
easy to make up more exercises like these.

Notes on common errors in English

1 Confusing words of similar sound or similar spelling. There are
hundreds of these; make sure you know the difference between all those
listed in the vocabulary section of this book. Here are a few examples:

no	to	were	their	aloud
now	too	where	there	allowed
know	two	wear	they're	

2   *Shall/will.* These are often confused. Learn the following:

(*a*) To express simple *future* tense (i.e. what will happen in the future): I *shall*, we *shall*, but you, he, she, it, they *will* (be coming to the dance tonight).

(*b*) To express strong *determination*: I *will*, we *will*, but you, he, she, it, they *shall* (work hard to win the prize).

3   This article is *ours, yours, his, hers, its, theirs.* Note: *no* apostrophe is used. Only the word *one's* has an apostrophe, e.g.

One must look after *one's* possessions.

(But: Which are the right *ones*? No apostrophe here, because there is no idea of possession by someone.)

4   *Its* means *of it,* e.g. *Its* tail is long. (The tail *of it* is long.)
It's means *it is,* e.g. *It's* a long tail. (*It is* a long tail.)

5   *All right* ("alright" and "allright" do *not* exist).
Make sure you know the difference between *all together* and *altogether, all ready* and *already.*

6   *Between you and me; for Susie and him.*
It is quite wrong to write *I* and *he* in these situations.

7   *It's me; it's him.* Strictly speaking, these are wrong; you should say *It's I; it's she.* However, these forms are allowed nowadays in speech, though you should not write them.

8   *Everybody enjoyed themselves.* "Themselves" is quite wrong. The word everybody (or everyone) means *each single person,* and so you should say: Everybody enjoyed *himself (or herself).* As this seems a little clumsy, however, it is usual to say only one *or* the other: Everybody enjoyed himself. (Everybody enjoyed herself.) Alternatively, you could say: They all enjoyed themselves.

Be careful to avoid such monstrosities as: hisself, theirselves, which do not exist. Also, *oneself* is correct, but *one's self* is wrong.

9   *One should look after one's money.* It is quite wrong to say One should look after *their* money (or *his* money).

10   *This sort of play; this kind of book* (also: *these* sorts of plays; *these* kinds of books). It is wrong to mix these by using such phrases as: these sort of plays; this kind of books.

242

11   *Different from* is correct; different *to*, or different *than* is wrong.

12   *No-one* or *nobody* is correct; noone is wrong.

13   *I didn't do anything; I didn't see anybody.* The words *nothing* and *nobody* would be incorrect.

14   *He didn't ought to have done it.* This is very clumsy. Say: He should not have done it, or: He ought not to have done it.

15   *Due to; owing to.* These are often confused. Wherever you mean "because of " use *owing to*: *Owing to* the bad weather we could not go out. Due to means "should be given to" : Thanks are *due to* my friend.

16   *The committee decides.* Words like committee, management, audience, stand for a collection of people and one wonders whether to say: The committee decide*s*, or decide. It is best to follow the rule: *A* committee decide*s*; committee*s* decide.

17   *Being a lovely day, I went for a long walk.* This might suggest that the person speaking was a lovely day. It is better to say: *As it was a lovely day*, I went for a long walk.

18   *A* or *an?* The rule is that where the word following begins with a vowel or a silent h, use *an*:

   an animal   *an* hour   *an* enemy   (but note: *a* bad enemy)

19   *Agree to* or *agree with?* One agrees *with* a person but *to* a plan or proposal: I agree *with you* that we cannot agree *to his plan.*

20   *Between.* You should not really say: There is a space *between each house.* The word suggests between *two* things. Say: There is a space between each pair of houses.

   Similarly, you should not say: We divided the food *between* the three of us. Here you must say *amongst*.

21   *Without him knowing; without me seeing. Him* and *me* are not really correct here; you should say: without *his* knowing; without *my* seeing.

22   *Less* or *fewer?* Less refers to *quantity or amount*: e.g. less sugar, less water, less hope. Fewer refers to *number*: e.g. fewer eggs, fewer people, fewer houses. It is quite wrong to talk about "less people, less flowers".

23   *Cleverer, less noisy, than.* Never say: He is *more* cleverer than I; or: That is less nois*ier* than it used to be.

24 *Get; got.* Do not use these words too often. The real guide is to use this verb only when the idea of "to obtain" is involved: I got a new suit last week. Where can we get a meal?, etc. The words are not handsome, and to use them too often gives an ugly effect:

Getting up yesterday, I got into a difficult situation. I got out of bed to get my dressing-gown, but when I got on to the cold floor my feet got so cold very quickly and I turned to get my slippers instead. What a shock I got when my feet got entangled with . . .

25 Some verbs may also give trouble. Here are a few of them:

LIE, LAY

To lie is used when only the subject (the doer) is involved in the lying:

My uncle *lies* on the bed every afternoon.   (present tense)
We *lay* on the grass in the sunshine.   (past tense)
These stones *have lain* here for weeks.   (past tense)

To lay is used when the subject (the doer) lays *something else* down:

My father always *lays* his tools out on the bench
before he starts to work.   (present tense)
He *laid* the new linoleum on the kitchen floor.   (past tense)
Dora *has laid* her sewing on the arm of her chair.   (past tense)

Never confuse these verbs; remember:

I *lie*, I *lay*, I *have lain*.
I *lay the table*, I *laid the table*, I *have laid the table*.

Remember also, *to lie*, meaning *to tell lies*:

I *lie*, I *lied*, I have *lied*.

HANG

Confusion arises here between the past tenses, *hanged* or *hung*. The modern rule is simple, however: use I *hang*, I *hung*, I *have hung* (or it hangs, hung, has hung) for all purposes except when talking about executions: They *hang* the murderer, they *hanged* him, they *have hanged* him (or: He *was hanged, has been hanged*).

SING

I *sing*, I *sang*, I *have sung*. It is wrong to say: I *sung* a song. You should learn these other verbs also, where the parts are often confused:

I *ring*, I *rang*, I *have rung* the bell.
I *swim*, I *swam*, I *have swum* across the river.
He *begins*, he *began*, he *has begun* his work.
She *drinks*, she *drank*, she *has drunk* her cup of tea.
His tobacco *stinks*, *stank*, has always *stunk* of old socks.

Note these two verbs, however, which are rather different:

> It *spins*, *spun*, *has spun* round.
> The bee *stings*, *stung*, *has stung* me.

RISE, RAISE

Something *rises*, but we *raise* something. The parts of these verbs are:

> The river *rises*, *rose*, *has risen*.
> He *raises* his hat, he *raised* his hat, he *has raised* his hat.

Do not use "to higher" for "to raise". Although we have a verb "to lower" there is no verb "to higher".

LEAD

I *lead*, *led*, have *led* my horse into the field. Avoid the mistake of writing "lead" (like the metal) when you mean *led*.

PASSED, PAST

I *pass*, *passed*, *have passed* the town hall. The word "past" is not a verb; its use is as follows:

> We drove *past* his house.
> He ran *past* me, chasing his dog.

LOADED, LADEN

I *load*, *loaded*, *have loaded* the goods on the van. The word "laden" is an adjective: The van is heavily *laden*. Never use such words as *ladened*, *overladened*.

LEAN, LEND

These are sometimes confused. Learn the parts:

> He *leans*, *leaned* (or *leant*), *has leaned* (or *has leant*) here.
> I *lend*, *lent*, *have lent* him several books.

FLEE, FLY, FLOW

Learn the parts, and do not mix them:

> The thief *flees, fled, has fled* from the police.
> The bird *flies, flew, has flown* into that tree.
> Water *flows, flowed, has flowed* into the cellar.

Note also, I, you, we, they *fly*; he, she, or it *flies*.

LEARN, BURN

These are similar to the verb "to lean", in that you can say: I *learnt* it, or I *learned* it (*have learnt* or *learned*). Similarly: I *burnt* (*burned*) it; I *have burnt* (*have burned*) it.

LAY, PAY, SAY

The past forms are *laid, paid, said*. Never write: layed, payed, sayed.

BREAK

I *break, broke, have broken* it. "I have *broke* it" is a bad error. Never write "brocken" either.

WAKE, AWAKE; WAKEN, AWAKEN

These are very often confused. For everyday purposes use the verb "to wake" with "up":

> I *wake*, I *woke*, I *have waked* (or: *have woken**) up.
> I *wake him, woke him, have waked* (or: *have woken**) *him* up.
> * more usual

If you prefer, you can use "to awaken":

> I *awaken*, I *awakened*, I *have awakened*.
> I *awaken* him, I *awakened* him, I *have awakened* him.

DARE

> I *dare* not do it.   (present tense)
> I *dared* not do it.   (past tense)
> I *have* not *dared* do it. ⎫
> I *did* not *dare* do it. ⎭   (past tense)

It is wrong to write "I *dare* not do it" if you mean it in the *past tense*. Also avoid "durst", "durstn't".

BEAR

I *bear*, I *bore*, I *have borne* the sad burden. These are the right forms. Note, however: He was *born* in 1873.

246

BORROW, LEND

You *lend* something to somebody; you *borrow* something from somebody. It is wrong to say: May I *lend* your rubber?, if you mean *borrow*. (Remember also that the word "loan" is a noun: a *loan* of ten shillings. Do not use it as a verb.)

SOW, SEW

"To sow" refers to seeds; "to sew" refers to the craft of sewing. Learn the parts:

> The farmer *sows, sowed, has sown* the seeds.
> My wife *sews, sewed, has sewn* the dress beautifully.

Note also the nouns: *sowing* (of seed), *sewing* (of garments).

26 *Should, would.* It is hard to give rules for the use of these two. One guide is, however, to use *should* if the idea of "ought to" is present:

> You really *should* write to your Mother more often.
> I know I *should*, but I don't feel like it.

For the rest, it does not really matter nowadays whether you use *should* or *would*:

> I *should* do it if I were you.
> I *would* do it if I were you.

Instinct will be your best guide. After all, it is clear that *would* is needed in the following sentence:

> It *would* be very cold indoors if we had no fire in winter.

Similarly, *should* is plainly needed in this one:

> Ten pounds *should* be enough to cover the damage (i.e. it *ought to* be enough).

27 *Can, may.* "Can" has the idea of: "is able to"; "may" has the idea of: "is allowed to". Thus, if you say: "Can I borrow your pen, please?" do not be surprised if the reply is: "You can, but you may not." Similarly, *"Can* I go out?" should be: *"May* I go out?"

28 *I didn't used to.* This is wrong. Say: "I used not to. . . ."

29 *I never did it.* Do not say this if all you mean is: "*I did not* do it."

30 *None of these men are clever.* "None" means "not one" and so you should say: "None of these men *is* clever."

247

31 *Like, as.* It is wrong to say: "Do it *like* I do." The correct form is: "Do it *as* I do." The word "like" should introduce a noun or pronoun only, not a full clause with a verb:

> Do it *like Charlie, but not as I do it.*
> Make it look *like* a real castle.

32 *Better, best.* Remember: *better* of two, *best* of more than two.

> This is the *better* of these two houses.
> This is the *best* of all these houses.

This rule also applies to *worse, worst,* and to any other adjective or adverb used in the same way: e.g. bigger, biggest; faster, fastest; nicer, nicest, etc.

Similarly learn that "each other" refers to two persons, whereas "one another" must be used when more than two are involved.

33 *Verb with either, or, etc.* Always be careful to see that you use verbs in singular or plural form to match the subject:

> Either John or Mary *wants* to read it; I am not sure which.
> Neither he nor she *wishes* to come.
> A table and a chair *were* standing in the entrance hall.
> A table or a chair *was* standing in the entrance hall.
> A table with a chair *was* standing in the entrance hall.
> Hard work and study *were* responsible for our success.
> The reason for our success *was* hard work and study.
> He is one who *reads* badly.
> He is one of those who *read* badly.

34 *Prepositions wrongly used.* "different *from*" has already been mentioned. Now study these other examples:

I was disgusted *at* him.	Should be . . . *with* him.
He suffers *with* his feet.	„ „ . . . *from* bad feet.
I prefer coffee *rather than* tea.	„ „ . . . *to* tea.
He was killed *with* a car.	„ „ . . . *by* a car.
You play better football *to him.*	„ „ . . . *than* he (does).

35 *Split infinitive.* This is the name given to the following practice:

> I hope *to* properly *repair* it tomorrow morning.

It is better to avoid putting words in between the word *to* and the verb which goes with it. The sentence should read:

> I hope *to repair* it properly tomorrow.

36 *Thing, sort of, kind of.* Avoid vague expressions like these. Think of the exact words needed to convey what you wish to say.

37 *The reason why is because.* If you use the word "reason", there is no need to use "why" or "because". Say: The reason is *that* . . .

38 *Who, whom.* These words introduce a statement that tells you some more about a person already mentioned:

> This is the person/*who tried to sell us a new car last week.*
> This is the girl/*whom I want you to photograph.*

In deciding whether to write *who* or *whom*, look first at the verb in this extra statement being made. If its subject is the person already named, write *who*; if its subject is somebody else, however, write *whom*:

> This is the person who tried . . . (*the person tried;* write *who*, therefore.)
> This is the girl whom I want . . . (*I want;* not the girl; write *whom*)

Here are more examples:

> The lady *who* called here yesterday is here again.
> > (*Who,* because *the lady* called.)
> Where is the boy *whom* I asked to call at my office?
> > (*Whom,* because *I* asked, not the boy.)
> Was it the girl *whom* you introduced me to at the dance?
> > (*Whom,* because *you* introduced, not the girl.)

Now look at these trick examples:

> This is the man *who* the police thought had been at the crime.
> I met that girl *who* I believed had come from London.

The word *who* is correct in each of these. Can you say why? It might be helpful to put brackets round the phrases (the police thought) and (I believed).

39 *Whose, who's. Whose* means *of whom; who's* means *who is:*

> *Who's* that girl *whose* hair hangs down in ringlets?

40 *After, afterwards.* It is wrong to say: I'll see you *after.* You must say: I'll see you afterwards. The word *after* must be followed by words which clearly show "after *what*". For instance: I'll see you *after the dance.*

41 *Than what.* It is wrong to say: He is bigger than *what* I am. Just say: He is bigger than I (am).

42 *Seeing as.* Do not use this ugly expression: Seeing as I was cold, I stayed at home. Just say: As I was cold . . .

43 *So, and so.* Do not write: I was cold, *so* I stayed at home. It is better to use *and so* for joining your statements.

44 *So as, so that.* Do not confuse these. Study these examples:

> We stayed at home *so as* to keep warm.
> We stayed at home *so that* we could keep warm.

You can see that *so as* must be followed by a verb with *to; so that* is followed by a verb with subject.

45 *Who, whom, or that?* It is not good style to refer to a person as *that.* Instead of: "A man *that* I know . . ." say: "A man *whom* I know . . ." Use the word *that* to refer to *things,* not people.

46 *Position of only.* Use care in positioning this little word; you can alter the whole meaning of your sentence:

> Only we saw the film that evening.
> We only saw the film that evening.
> We saw only the film that evening.
> We saw the film only that evening.

47 *Literally.* This word is much used to emphasise what a person is saying: I was literally astonished. She literally shouted at me. Do not use it; use "absolutely" or "simply" instead.

48 *Ate, eaten.* Another verb that might confuse you. Learn the parts: I *eat,* I *ate,* I *have eaten* my dinner.

49 *Try to, try and.* It is better to say: I shall try *to* see it. Similarly, "Come *to* see me" is better than "Come *and* see me".

50 *Nouns ending in -y after a consonant.* These form their plural in *-ies.* It is a common error just to add *-s*; e.g. body, bod*ies, not* bodys. Note, however, with names: Mary (Marys): Three Queen Marys . . .

51 *Let you and me.* It is wrong to say: Let you and *I* go out.

52 *The three first.* He won the three first races. This should read: He won the first three races.

53 *Needless change of tense.* Beware of this, especially in your essay-writing. It is a common but curious fault for pupils to start their essays using *past* tense for the main basis, but to slip without any due reason into *present* tense, then back to past tense, and so on. Be *consistent* in your use of tenses. Note also such faulty sentences as:

He *said* he *is* coming. (Should be: He *said* he *was* coming.)
I *should be* obliged if you *will*. (Should read: . . . . if you *would*.)

54 *I never have and never will tell lies.* This should read:

I never have *told* and never will *tell* lies.

55 *Ending sentence with a preposition.* You may do this occasionally:

This is the kind of nonsense I cannot put up *with*.

To rearrange this would give a ridiculous effect:

This is the kind of nonsense up with which I cannot put.

Try, however, to avoid ending with a preposition too often.

56 *But, however.* Never use both of these; one or other is enough:

But I did not see him.
I did not see him, however.

Also, try to avoid starting a sentence with the word *but*. It is rather ugly if done often.

57 *Numbers in writing.* You should avoid littering your written English with numerals. If you have to mention numbers, observe these accepted rules:

(*a*) Days of month and years: numerals allowed.

(*b*) Numbers over one hundred: numerals allowed.

(*c*) Numbers below one hundred: write them as words.

(*d*) Statistics, prices (especially in business letters), also page or chapter references: numerals allowed.

58 *And who, and which.* You may only use these if the word "who" or "which" has already been used once in the sentence:

Right: This is the man *who* came last week, *and who* gave us such a good talk.

Wrong: This is the man we met last week, *and who* gave us such a good talk.

59 *May, might.* These are very commonly confused. You can remember the simple rule, however: Use *may*, if the idea is *present* or *future*; *might*, if it is *past*.

I *may* come tomorrow, if you can do with me.   (future)

He *may* be working on it even now.   (present)

You *might* have told me before.   (past)

60 *Common faults in handwriting:* The important rule about your handwriting is that *it must be clear*. Slipshod habits in handwriting cause only confusion to your reader, and if he is marking your examination papers, you will lose marks for anything that is unclear. Study all these common faults and make sure you are not guilty of them:

loops on *t* and *d*	uncrossed *t*
d written like *cl*	undotted *i* (or *j*)
k written like *h*	fancy *r*
a like *o*; *o* like *a*	sign for *and*
unclosed *a*, like *u*	unclosed *g*
words written in parts	untidy alterations

10   To Help You in Your Reading

This chapter can help you read wisely and with profit. It shows you what to look for in literature, how to judge quality, and how to write about what you read. Up-to-date reading lists are included, and exercises in appreciation.

WHY READ BOOKS?

Most young people lead busy lives: lessons, clubs, sport, homework, hobbies, friends, television, all clamour for attention and it is not easy to plan one's affairs so that all receive their share of time. Unfortunately, amidst all these hectic activities, reading is often neglected. Unless you get the reading habit fairly early in life, you might not become a real reader at all and this would be a sad loss to you, for three reasons:

1   There is much pleasure to be had from books: the world is a place of rich variety, containing more adventure and lively experience than any person can ever savour at first hand. Through books, you can experience all this richness—by your own fireside.

2   Apart from pleasure in reading, you can find wisdom and understanding also. Good writers are intelligent and sensitive people, alive to the problems of behaviour and human experience that face us all. A person who shuts himself off from this is going to remain poor.

3   You can improve your English by reading well-written books. A person who reads wisely and often is constantly absorbing samples of English properly and effectively used. Any teacher can tell you that pupils who are poor at English are poor because they do not read enough or because they read only rubbish.

What to read?

There are so many books nowadays that you may not know what to choose. Keen readers have many ways of "hunting": they browse in library and bookshop, asking for the best authors and titles to suit their special interests; they read book-reviews; they compare notes with friends and lend and borrow recommended titles. You can do all this, but probably your school librarian has already made the task easy for you by providing reading-lists to suit various tastes. The reading-list is your best plan; ask your teachers and librarian to help you, for they can suggest enough authors and titles to give you pleasure for years ahead. You can order any choice at the public library.

For those who like to own books, chances have never been easier: paper-backed editions are now in abundance and include all that is best in writing. At least one British firm specialises in paper-backed books of special appeal to young people, and book-clubs can be set up in schools enabling you to order recommended titles.

There is one problem, however. You need experience to choose your reading wisely—some yardstick by which to measure a book's qualities, both when choosing and later when reading your choice. Many books are badly written and may disappoint you, even though at first they may seem promising enough. It is not that bad writing is necessarily harmful; most "comics", "bloods", and pulp-magazine tales have a minor thrill or two to offer; it is a pity, though, that some people waste so much time reading these and never look at books that could give so much more pleasure. It is like living on "mouse-trap" cheese when you could have roast chicken every day. Here are some hints on what to look for in good writing; as most of us are keen on stories we shall start with those.

How to "size up" the promise of a story

You are browsing round the bookshelves, looking for a good "yarn". What features should you glance at, to help you choose well?

The title. Not a good guide on its own! You cannot be sure that *The Secret of Loch Shiel* will involve a secret worth pursuing for two hundred pages.

The picture on the cover. This also may deceive; it forms, with the title, the "fancy wrapper", which may possibly conceal inferior goods. A gorgeous blonde cringing before the sinister shadow on the wall might be nothing more than poor Mavis about to be given notice by her landlord.

The publisher's "blurb". It might give a fair idea of what the book is about—plot, setting, and general atmosphere may be summed up for you. You cannot always trust the glowing promises of delight, however: "... a gripping saga of one man's brave struggle against appalling odds; to delight the young in heart ..."

The first page or two. Here is a good chance to gauge quality. Any good writer seeks to grip his reader's attention at the start. Some need a page or two to set the story moving; others can do it in a first short sentence:

> Certain houses, like certain persons, manage somehow to proclaim at once their capacity for evil. . . .
>
> *The Empty House*, by Algernon Blackwood

Beginnings and endings of chapters. Like the beginning of a story, the beginning of each chapter should make a reasonable impact. The writer has a chance at these points to take a new grip on his reader's interest. Similarly, the end of a chapter allows him to leave the reader in suspense, wondering what will happen next:

> "You expect serious trouble?"
> "I expect a small war," said Mr. Campion frankly.
>
> *Mystery Mile*, by Margery Allingham

Descriptions of people, scenes, and action. These should seem fresh, interesting, unusual. One grows tired of finding the same old ideas:

> "The sinister shadow moved along the wall, menacing, evil."
>
> "She was clad in a gorgeous, low-cut evening gown, of some clinging material that well accentuated the proportions of her lovely form."
>
> "Macdonald used his mighty arms like a flail, felling the oncoming savages with lusty blows."

A good writer tries to avoid these old effects and find something new:

> . . . There were two hundred and eighty steps up to Cabrillo Street. They were drifted over with windblown sand and the handrail was as cold and wet as a toad's belly.
>
> When I reached the top the sparkle had gone from the water and a seagull with a broken trailing leg was twisting against the offshore breeze. . . .
>
> There was a cornflower in the lapel of his white coat and his pale blue eyes looked faded out by comparison.
>
> *Farewell, My Lovely*, by Raymond Chandler

Once you have glanced at all these features of a book, and it can all be done in a minute or so, you can usually judge whether you want to read it. Some words of warning: Never look at the end; do not be put off by length if the contents look good; do not be too cautious or prejudiced in your choice: just because you do not like stories about horses, it does not mean you cannot enjoy *any* of this type—you might be missing a real treat.

Exercises

(All these can be done numerous times, with different books.)

1 Apply the "browsing test" to any novel you may choose, and write a concise report to assess its promise under these headings:

 (*a*) Title, jacket-picture (if any), publisher's comments.

 (*b*) Opening pages.

 (*c*) Chapter beginnings and endings.

 (*d*) Description of people, scenes, and action.

2 Collect, from "comic", "blood", or woman's magazine story, some fairly brief samples of description (people, scene, or action) that seem to you rather poorly done. Write them down and under each one criticise the faults briefly.

3 Collect some descriptions of people, scene, or action that seem to you well done. Write them down and under each one say why you think it good.

4 Choose some chapter beginnings and endings that seem really effective. Write them down and under each one say what effect it had upon you.

5 Write a short essay about the qualities of the opening pages in a book that you have really enjoyed.

6 Deliberately take from the library shelves a novel with a title that would not normally attract you, apply the "browsing test" (see Exercise 1), and write a concise report, assessing the book's promise.

7 Make a list of titles that would really attract you (novels or short stories only). Under each one state briefly why you would be inclined to investigate the book further, having read the title.

Points to consider while reading a story

So far we have only considered points to glance at when choosing a story. The business of *appreciating* it, during and after reading, is a more lengthy matter. These are the aspects you should consider:

1 *The basic idea.* This can be summed up in a few words:

 Brown on Resolution, by C. S. Forester: A lone seaman, perched on a rock overlooking the anchorage of an enemy warship, holds the mighty ship and its entire crew at bay.

Ask yourself if the basic idea is worth writing about. Is it an original or a well-worn theme? Is it meaty enough to suit a long novel, or only slender, suitable for a short story?

2 *The Plot.* This is the name given to the *development* of the idea throughout the story. It is the planned sequence of events and situations, with an effective start and moving on to reach eventually its highest level of excitement (the "climax"), followed by the conclusion of the story. The same is found in a play.

Ask yourself these questions about plot:

(*a*) What is the sequence of events, in brief?

(*b*) What is the climax of the story?

(*c*) Is the plot clearly unfolded, one step leading clearly to the next, or is it muddled and hard to follow, disjointed, too complicated, too far-fetched?

(*d*) Is the interest well sustained, by tension and suspense? Are you kept wondering "What happens next?" or does the pace slacken or the next steps seem obvious? Are chapter beginnings and endings well used to help sustain interest?

(*e*) Is the ending satisfying?

3 *The characters.* In poor writing, the method is usually to describe characters first—their appearance and qualities, and then let them loose on the story:

A lean, lithe stranger, covered in dust, rode slowly into Pampas Gulch. He looked tired, but there was a hint of power about the set of his sun-bronzed jaw. of meanness about the six-gun he wore strapped down on his right thigh. With deft fingers he tied his skewbald mare to the hitching post outside the Diamond Ring saloon, and strode over the boardwalk to the saloon door.

You can always recognise these stock characters; there are so many of them, and they are nearly always described with the same words: the little shopgirl, clutching her coat about her slender but shapely form as she runs for her daily bus in the High Street; the sinister spy, with guttural accent, leather raincoat, Luger automatic, slouch hat, and duelling scar . . . so many more. Don't you get tired of them? They are all like flat, cardboard figures in a toy theatre, always looking the same, always reacting as you expect ("she gave a musical little laugh . . .", "he snarled, baring yellow-stained teeth . . .").

257

A good writer will make his characters much more lifelike. He will not just describe them first and then send them into action. Instead, the reader gathers information about them as the tale progresses: they reveal themselves in what they say or in the way they react to events; we learn about their secret thoughts and fears; they may end up changed by their experiences—just as real human beings are; we also learn about them from what other characters say. A fine example of this sort of character-drawing is C. S. Forester's Horatio Hornblower, a naval officer of Nelson's day. Forester has written many books about him, showing him at various stages in his career, from Midshipman to Admiral. Conan Doyle's famous detective, Sherlock Holmes, is another, as is his devoted friend, Dr. Watson. So lifelike are these two that some people even think they really lived.

Ask yourself these questions about characters:

(*a*) Do they seem flat, stock characters, described in familiar, well-worn terms?

(*b*) Are they lifelike characters, and if so, what are their qualities?

(*c*) In what ways are the characters revealed? (By direct description, by their own words, or the words of others speaking about them, by their secret thoughts being described, by their actions and reactions to events?)

(*d*) Are the characters changed in any way by their experiences?

4   *Description of scene and event.* Look for vivid and unusual touches here; a good writer will not let the progress of events be held up too long while he describes scenes; nor will he risk losing pace by filling his action sequences with unnecessary detail; above all he will avoid using well-worn words and old familiar touches:

> The front doors were unlocked. There was a roofed porch. The garden hummed with flowers. There was a white picket fence and a gate. The house was on a corner. It was a cool, moist night. No moon. . . .

This is real economy of description, from a tough American crime writer, Raymond Chandler. In a few words his detective describes what he saw, and then the action continues. Now for a different example:

> In a flash they were clear of the building; a deep-toned "twang" resounded from their left and something whizzed to thud into wood behind them. Over his shoulder Juhel saw a swinging first-floor shutter in the building

beside the mouth of the alley; then he was hauled past the low wall of the choristers' playground and flung into the black shadow of a buttress of the cathedral apse.

Joris of the Rock, by Leslie Barringer

Ask yourself these questions when judging description:

(a) Is it dull and commonplace, or unusual and striking?

(b) Is it unnecessarily lengthy, holding up progress?

5 *The general style.* Aspects of style have already been mentioned in earlier points, particularly the choice of words for description—are they dull and commonplace, or strikingly used? Are too many words used? It is not easy to sum up what constitutes a particular writer's style, but you may ask yourself these questions:

(a) Is there a careful choice and arrangement of words, for vivid and pleasing effect? (Especially in description.)

(b) Is the dialogue natural, or forced and unreal, not as real people would speak?

(c) Are mood and atmosphere well conveyed: tension, anger, sleepiness, sadness, storm, fear, joy, hate, etc.?

(d) If there is humour, does it make you laugh, or does it fail?

(e) Is there slang, bad grammar, unnecessary wordiness, "sloppy" emotion?

(f) Does the writer make use of the *sound* of words to help convey atmosphere? (See the chapter on "Picturesque Language": alliteration, assonance, onomatopoeia, sound-qualities.)

Exercises

(All can be done numerous times, with different books.)

1 State the basic idea of any novel, and outline the sequence of events, the climax, and the conclusion.

2 Do the same for any short story.

3 Choose from any story a character that seems to you to be flat or badly presented, and explain why you think so.

4 Show, with plenty of examples, how dialogue (conversation between people) can help to reveal a character's qualities to the reader.

5 Collect some brief but vivid descriptions of the appearance of characters.

6 Collect some good descriptions of various types of scene.

7 Collect some good examples of vivid action-writing.

8 Choose any story by Dickens and explain how he presents some of his characters. (A clue: he relies on fairly lengthy description, holding up the action meanwhile. They are vivid enough, though; he presents strange, picturesque individuals and makes them speak in a picturesque way.)

9 Write character-sketches of chosen people from any novel or short story, covering both appearance and personal qualities.

10 Collect some examples of dialogue that seems to you unnatural or forced, and state why you think so.

11 Describe a really funny incident from a story you have read.

12 Collect some examples of writing with strong atmosphere: tension, beauty, fear, sadness, brooding hatred, fierce action, tender love, etc.

13 Collect some good examples of figures of speech in prose: alliteration, assonance, onomatopoeia, simile, metaphor.

14 Show how a character may be revealed in ways other than direct description—by what he says and what others say about him, by his secret thoughts, by his actions and reactions to events.

15 Criticise a plot which seems to you unsatisfactory, and suggest improvements.

PLAYS AND FILMS

What to look for in a play, or film

A play or film has some features in common with a written story:

1 *Basic idea and Plot.* Consider these as for the story, asking yourself these questions:

    (a) Is it a good idea for a play?

    (b) Is it suitable for a long play or only a short one?

    (c) Does the sequence of events and situations unfold clearly or is it muddled, disjointed, hard to believe?

(*d*) Do the acts begin and end on an effective note?

(*e*) Is interest sustained throughout, or does it sag in places?

(*f*) Do the events lead to a good dramatic climax—a high point of tension?

(*g*) Is the ending satisfactory?

2 *Scene or Setting.* A story-writer must describe background scenes in words, but the theatre has actual scenery and lighting effects to help create atmosphere. Films and television plays can range fairly widely; a stage-production is more limited. Whatever scenery and lighting may be chosen, however, the aim will be, as in written descriptions, to provide a suitable background and atmosphere for the events that will take place.

When you see a play or film, consider these points:

(*a*) Is the setting too elaborate or fussy, distracting attention from the actors?

(*b*) Does it help to create the right atmosphere? If so, how? If not, why not?

(*c*) How do the lighting effects help the atmosphere?

(*d*) How can the grouping or positioning of characters help to convey atmosphere?

3 *Characters.* In a play or film the characters are seen by the audience. Physical appearance, costumes, make-up, movements, gestures, and facial expressions are all important means by which actors portray the characters they are playing. When you see actors at work, study all these aspects closely, in particular the skill with which actors can convey quite subtle feelings by their expressions and movements. In a written story all this must be conveyed in words.

Of course actors also use words. The lines they speak we call dialogue, but the dialogue in a play has to do much more than that in a written story. It serves three main purposes:

(*a*) It helps to reveal characters to the audience—their qualities and thoughts, feelings, moods, and motives. What the characters say about themselves and one another achieves this:

Buttons: I know I'm only a simple fellow, Cinders; penniless and all that, but I love you and . . .
Cinderella: Oh, Buttons, you're a dear, sweet lad; I'm so fond of you, but—well, I don't love you. . . .

261

(*b*) It has to present the main problems of the play and discuss them:

Cinderella: Oh, how I should love to go to the Ball. What *shall* I do? I have only these rags to wear, and no coach, and worst of all, no dashing young man to take me. Alack-a-day!

(*c*) It has to help further the action of the play, paving the way for events to come, or reporting events that have taken place elsewhere:

Baron de Broke: They do say the Prince has sent his herald all over the land, searching for the lass whose foot exactly fits the glass slipper. Now, you ugly daughters of mine: if only you didn't have all those bulging bunions. . . .

(The examples are hardly Shakespeare, but they show what is meant.)

It is not easy to write good dialogue; it must sound natural, and must always suit the character and mood of the speaker; words must not be used carelessly, for wordy speeches only tire the listener and hold up the action. You should study some dialogue from a good play and see how well it fulfils all the needs outlined here. To appreciate dialogue at its best, of course, you have to hear it spoken by fine actors. Most young people tend to be put off by Shakespeare, having in mind the dreary lessons spent trying to read the cold printed page. If your teacher could introduce you to one of the modern recordings of, say, *Macbeth*, you would find it a revelation: everything comes to life, and you experience something of the real Shakespeare. Another play on record which is a sheer delight to hear is *The Importance of Being Earnest*, by Oscar Wilde.

Exercises

(These are adaptable to many different plays.)

1 Collect examples of dialogue which reveal the main problems facing the characters in the play.

2 Collect examples of dialogue in which characters reveal their own qualities, or the qualities of others.

3 Collect examples of dialogue which hints at events to come.

4 Outline the plot briefly, arranging the events in order of scene and act.

5 Write character-sketches of chosen figures in the play, basing your judgments on what they say about themselves, what others say about them, and on how they act or react to events.

6 Is the ending of the play justified, bearing in mind the characters of the people involved?

7 Outline the climax of the play, explaining how the characters of the people concerned have helped to bring it about.

8 Collect examples of the ends of scenes which help to leave the audience in suspense as to what happens next.

9 What do you consider to be the most effective scene in the play, and why?

10 Collect examples of dialogue which strongly convey particular moods: sorrow, fear, pity, anger, etc. Comment on their effectiveness.

APPROACH TO POETRY

A good novel or play can bring you real enjoyment, and so can poetry, if you are led to it in the right way. Most of the greatest pleasures in life only come gradually, as you develop your skill and appreciation, and poetry is one of them. The real need is that you should not shut your mind from the start, dismissing poetry as the idle ravings of work-shy idiots; this is a fool's point of view. Good writers are exceptionally sensitive people, taking for their themes some part of the great variety of human experience, and expressing, often with wonderful effect, thoughts and feelings that we ordinary ones sense only dimly—or not at all. Nobody with any feelings at all would want to shut all this out of his life.

Apart from their sensitivity, writers are master-craftsmen in language, and in poetry this skill is at its most concentrated. You have only to read snatches of fine poetry to find a host of impressions conveyed in a few brief, simple words with an effect of magic that you could hardly capture in years of writing prose. That is the magic of poetry—it seems so brief, so simple, but it says so much. You can easily prove this to yourself: take any anthology of poems and browse here and there. Whatever your interest, your mood, you will find something to match it. Here are a few samples, out of thousands:

OLD SHIPS

Who knows how oft with squat and noisy gun,
Questing brown slaves or Syrian oranges,
The pirate Genoese
Hell-raked them till they rolled

Blood, water, fruit, and corpses up the hold.
But now through friendly seas they softly run,
Painted the mid-sea blue or shore-sea green,
Still patterned with the vine and grapes in gold.

From *The Old Ships*, by James Elroy Flecker

OLD AGE

Fear no more the heat o' the sun
Nor the furious winter's rages;
Thou thy worldly task hast done,
Home art gone and ta'en thy wages:
Golden lads and girls all must,
As chimney-sweepers, come to dust.

From *Fidele*, by William Shakespeare

EVENING IN THE CITY

The winter evening settles down
With smells of steaks in passageways.
Six o'clock.
The burnt-out ends of smoky days.
And now a gusty shower wraps
The grimy scraps
Of withered leaves about your feet
And newspapers from vacant lots.

From *Prelude*, by Thomas Stearns Eliot

ACTION

But in the gloom they fought, with bloodshot eyes
And labouring breath; first Rustum struck the shield
Which Sohrab held stiff out: the steel-spik'd spear
Rent the tough plates, but failed to reach the skin,
And Rustum pluck'd it back with angry groan.
Then Sohrab with his sword smote Rustum's helm,
Nor clove its steel quite through; but all the crest
He shore away . . .

From *Sohrab and Rustum*, by Matthew Arnold

MYSTERY

'Why does your brand sae drop wi' blude,
Edward, Edward?
Why does your brand sae drop wi' blude,
And why sae sad gang ye, O?

From *Edward, Edward*, an anonymous ballad

(*brand:* sword)

264

EARLY MORNING STILLNESS

This City now doth like a garment wear
The beauty of the morning; silent, bare,
Ships, towers, domes, theatres, and temples lie
Open unto the fields, and to the sky;
All bright and glittering in the smokeless air.

From *Upon Westminster Bridge*, by William Wordsworth

NATURE

Leaves, summer's coinage spent, golden are all together whirled,
sent spinning, dipping, slipping, shuffled by heavy handed wind,
shifted sideways, sifted, lifted, and in swarms made to fly,
spent sunflies, gorgeous tatters, airdrift, pinions cf trees.

From *Lapwing*, by Rex Warner

You may not like these samples, for nobody would expect you to like all poetry; your own individual taste is what matters, as with food, or choosing books, or clothes, or friends. At least, however, these short extracts should help you realise that there is something for everybody. As for what pleases *you*, as an individual, only you can decide. Read some poems and make your own personal selection. You will not be disappointed with everything you find.

What to look for in a poem

You can enjoy poetry without knowing how it is put together. These notes may increase your appreciation, however, and help you if you have to write about poems. All you need to know about the "technicalities" is explained here.

What should you look for in a poem? Here is a list of items:

1   What is the poem about?

2   How cleverly does the poet use words to convey what he is trying to tell us?

3   How does the *sound* of his word-patterns (as distinct from the meaning) help the poem to make an impression on us?

Only three points. There is a fair amount to look at under each heading, however. Let us take each in turn:

What is the poem about? Read the poem carefully, several times, and then try to state briefly what it is about. A little practice is needed here, but your teacher can help you develop your skill. Here is a sample statement (read the poem yourself also).

265

The Donkey, by G. K. Chesterton

In this short poem the donkey admits he is ugly and wretched. In the last stanza, however, he tells of his moment of triumph, when he bore Jesus through the streets of Jerusalem, cheered by the crowd. The poem suggests that all creatures, however ugly or humble, have their worth in the sight of God.

These are the main types of poem you will encounter:

Narrative poems are those in which a story is told.

Descriptive poems give a vivid impression of a scene—they "paint a picture" in words.

Reflective poems express the writer's serious thoughts on some matter he thinks important.

Lyrical poems are those in which the writer's mood or emotions are conveyed.

Often you will find some of these main approaches mingled: a narrative poem will contain much description, of scene and action; a descriptive poem will contain sometimes an underlying serious thought, or it might convey a mood of sadness or joy, and so on.

Your statement of what the poem is about should consider all this. If it is a narrative poem, give a short outline of the story; if it is descriptive, state what is being described; if the poem is reflective or lyrical, state the idea or mood being conveyed. If the poem is a blend of several approaches, point out what is being presented in each part.

Here are two more sample statements:

Leisure, by W. H. Davies

At the beginning and end of this short poem, Mr. Davies says:

> What is this life if, full of care,
> We have no time to stand and stare?

He is asking us to find time in our busy lives to look at all the beauty in the world around us. Some of the lovely things we should notice are mentioned in the other lines of the poem.

Sohrab and Rustum, by Matthew Arnold

This long narrative poem tells of a veteran Persian warrior, Rustum, who by tragic circumstance meets his own son, Sohrab, in single combat, before the assembled Persian and Tartar armies, and slays him. Only after he has mortally wounded Sohrab does Rustum find that it is his own son, for he had been told years before that his wife had borne him a daughter, and ever since then he had been away at the wars. His wife had deceived him, so that her child would not be torn away from her and trained as a warrior.

The poem contains some fine description, of the sandy plain beside the Oxus River, the dress of the warriors, the fight itself; and numerous lengthy similes help to convey all manner of descriptive effects.

How cleverly are words used to convey what the poet wants to say? A poet must use great care in choosing and arranging words to express his ideas—much more care than is demanded of any writer in prose. There is plenty of "elbow-room" in prose: another word, phrase, or paragraph —or one fewer—will hardly spoil the whole effect. A poem, however, is a highly concentrated piece of writing, with every word precisely chosen and placed, like a piece in a jig-saw puzzle, to help make up the finished pattern.

You must look, therefore, for really effective use of words and word-patterns in the poems you read; they are not too hard to find, for the poet intends them to be noticed. Here are some random examples:

> It was the Rainbow gave thee birth,
> And left thee all her lovely hues;
>> From *The Kingfisher*, by W. H. Davies

> Wings linked. Necks a-strain,
> A rush and a wild crying.
>> From *The Wild Duck*, by John Masefield

> And her bright striped frost-face will never watch any more,
> out of the shadow of the cave in the blood-orange rock,
>> From *Mountain Lion*, by D. H. Lawrence

> a saddle-cloth of broider'd green
> Crusted with gold, and on the ground were worked
> All beasts of chase, all beasts which hunters know:
>> From *Sohrab and Rustum*, by Matthew Arnold

> The splendour falls on castle walls
> And snowy summits old in story:
> The long light shakes across the lakes,
> And the wild cataract leaps in glory.
>> From *The Bugle*, by Alfred, Lord Tennyson

Sometimes you will find that only a line or so, or a phrase from a poem seems to echo through your mind—brief snatches, similar to those above; sometimes a whole poem may delight you for its clever use of words. Either way, there is some enjoyment.

It may be in narrative poetry that you find this skilful use of words, describing a scene or a tense moment; it may be a lovely piece of nature description, a brief but witty poem; perhaps an idea presented will make you think "Yes, how true that is!" Perhaps the mood of a poem might match your own mood, quite by chance, and some line or two may fix itself in your memory:

> So, we'll go no more a-roving
> So late into the night,
> Though the heart be still as loving,
> And the moon be still as bright. . . .
>
> From *So, we'll go no more a-roving*, by Lord Byron

Wherever you find it, this is a large part of poetry's pleasure—to encounter things cleverly and unforgettably expressed.

You will remember from the chapter entitled "Picturesque Language" that certain figures of speech, *simile, metaphor*, and *personification*, help writers to get vivid effects. Always look for examples of these in the poems you read, and decide whether they really help. Comment freely in written work on parts of a poem that you think show a clever use of words.

How has the poet used the sound-qualities of words to help him achieve his effects? Little needs to be said here, for it has all been explained in the chapter "Picturesque Language". You need to understand *alliteration, assonance, onomatopoeia*, and the idea of *"word-music"* (see notes on "Sound-Qualities: another aid to vivid writing"). Of course poets do not use words only for their meanings; you have only to hear poetry beautifully read to realise that its sounds are of great importance. Often they are skilfully used to help convey a mood or an atmosphere. Look at this shift of focus from the frisking, slick-swimming seal-pack to the slow-moving, ponderous ice-floes:

> . . . And thrusting on with threshing tail,
> With twist and twirl and sudden leap
> Through crackling ice and salty deep,
> Diving and doubling with my kind
> Until at last we left behind
> Those big white blundering bulks of death,
> And lay at length with panting breath
> Upon a far untravelled floe,
> Beneath a gentle drift of snow—
>
> From *The Ice-Cart*, by Wilfrid Gibson

Just as you examine a poem for its vivid use of language, examine it also for the sound-effects of its words, and see how cleverly the poet has made the sounds reinforce the effect he aims at.

We must now look at the other sound-effects in poetry, those produced by *rhythm*, *metre*, and *rhyme*. It is not hard to understand these.

Rhythm and Metre. To understand what makes poetry different from prose, you must first know what is meant by "rhythm" and "metre". Regular beats on a drum produce the simplest kind of rhythm:

> bong   bong   bong   bong   bong

A more complex kind of rhythm would be made if you introduced say two light taps between each pair of heavy beats:

> *bong* di di *bong* di di *bong* di di *bong* di di *bong*

Many other patterns of light and heavy beats are of course possible:

> di di *bong bong bong* di di *bong bong bong* di di *bong bong bong*
> *bong* di di *bong* di di *bong bong* di di
> di *bong* di *bong* di di *bong bong*

You could invent hundreds of these patterns; pattern-making from stressed and unstressed beats is the basis of all rhythm in music.

The same is true of language: our words may be stressed or unstressed when we speak them; longer words may have one part stressed and the other parts unstressed. Here are some samples; you only have to read them aloud to realise this fact:

> Last night I went to the pictures.

> As for myself, I was disappointed to hear it.

> Arthur was conspicuous without his trousers.

Clever writers of prose can make good use of this feature of language; they can choose and organise their words to give definite rhythmical effects: galloping hoofbeats, trains moving off and gathering speed, the lazy motion of a flowing river—all these and many more effects can be suggested. To the poet these chances are even more valuable. Here are some striking examples:

> We're foot—slog—slog—slog—sloggin' over Africa—
> Foot—foot—foot-foot—sloggin' over Africa—
> (Boots—boots—boots—boots—movin' up and down again!)
> There's no discharge in the war!

From *Boots*, by Rudyard Kipling

> The wind was a torrent of darkness among the gusty trees,
> The moon was a ghostly galleon tossed upon cloudy seas,
> The road was a ribbon of moonlight over the purple moor,
> And the highwayman came riding—
>   Riding—riding—
> The highwayman came riding, up to the old inn-door . . .

From The Highwayman, by Alfred Noyes

> Before the Roman came to Rye or out to Severn strode,
> The rolling English drunkard made the rolling English road.
> A reeling road, a rolling road, that rambles round the shire,
> And after him the parson ran, the sexton and the squire . . .

From The Rolling English Road, by G. K. Chesterton

Whenever, in poetry, the words are arranged into a definite scheme of rhythm, we refer to that pattern as *metre*. There are many different metres used in poetry; you do not need to know them all, but you should be able to recognise the pattern in a given poem, for it suggests how the poem should be read:

> Ĭ shóot thĕ Hĭppŏpótămŭs
> With bullets made of platinum,
> Because if I use leaden ones
> His hide is sure to flatten 'em.

From The Hippopotamus, by Hilaire Belloc

Here, as you can see from the markings over the first line, the pattern is "di *bong* di *bong* di *bong* di *bong*". The signs used are the proper ones to use when you are showing which parts are unstressed (˘) and which are stressed (´). All the other lines follow the same pattern. We would call this pattern the *metre* of this particular poem: ˘ ´ ˘ ´ ˘ ´ ˘ ´

Sometimes the metre may vary from line to line, unlike the example given above. Sometimes there may be quite a complicated metrical pattern, extending over several lines, or a whole verse, perhaps repeated in the next series of lines or in the next verse. The poet is free to arrange his metre as he wishes, to help him get certain effects. All you need do, to find out what the metrical pattern is, is write out the poem and mark each line as above, dividing the syllables into stressed and unstressed, until you see what scheme the poet has followed. Some poets, especially modern ones, may not use metre at all; they may only use momentary rhythm here and there, or they may avoid any suggestion of a regular rhythm.

270

Points to ask yourself when considering the rhythm or metre of a poem:

1 Does the rhythm or metre help the poem? Is it cleverly used to suggest types of movement being described, or the mood of the poem —calmness, sadness, joy, etc.?

2 Does it seem to you unsuitable for the poem? Is it jerky when the mood is gentle and quiet; is it monotonous when the mood is lively and exciting?

3 If the metrical scheme includes some shorter lines amongst the longer ones, does this help the poem especially?

4 If there is no regular rhythm—no metre—can you think why the poet has chosen to do without it? Is there any special reason why he should avoid it?

Rhyme. We all associate rhyming with poetry. It is the sound-effect made by placing a word at the end of a line which sounds similar to that at the end of another line:

> The naked earth is warm with Spring,   *a*
> And with green grass and bursting trees   *b*
> Leans to the sun's gaze glorying,   *a*
> And quivers in the sunny breeze;   *b*
>
> From *Into Battle*, by Julian Grenfell

(*a-a* are rhyming lines, as are *b-b*. This labelling of lines with letters *a-b-c* etc. is useful, if you wish to find out the rhyming scheme of the poem. Try it on some poems for yourself; you will see that many rhyming schemes are possible.)

Sometimes poets use what we call "internal rhyme": a word inside a line rhyming with the word at the end of that same line:

> What loud up*roar* bursts from that *door*! . . .

Poems need not necessarily contain rhyme; they may rely on other sound-effects instead. Shakespeare's famous "blank verse" is a celebrated example. It has no rhyme, but wonderful effects are possible:

> This royal throne of kings, this scept'red isle,
> This earth of majesty, this seat of Mars,
> This other Eden, demi-paradise,
> This fortress built by Nature for herself
> Against infection and the hand of war;
> This happy breed of men, this little world;

This precious stone set in the silver sea,
Which serves it in the office of a wall,
Or as a moat defensive to a house,
Against the envy of less happier lands;
This blessed plot, this earth, this realm, this England.

From *Richard the Second*, Act Two, Scene One

Summing up

This has been a fairly long explanation of what you should look for in poetry. Let us now sum up the main points. You can use this numbered list when preparing your step-by-step appreciations of individual poems:

1 State briefly what the poem is about, mentioning whether it is narrative, descriptive, reflective, lyrical, or a blend of any of these approaches.

2 Discuss the poem in more detail, stressing parts that seem especially important or striking, from the point of view of meaning and use of language. (Clever use of words, simile, metaphor, personification; dramatic effects, clever description, forcefulness of feeling, value of ideas presented.)

3 Consider the sound-qualities of the poem: alliteration, assonance, onomatopoeia, use of long and short sounds, rhythm, metre, rhyme (or lack of these). How cleverly does the poet interweave these effects to reinforce the impact of various parts of his poem?

Exercises

Your teacher will set you regular exercises, using selected poems, and training you to look at all the aspects mentioned above. Eventually you will learn to write a complete appreciation, covering all the qualities of a given poem. Try, for a start, some of the poems in the comprehension section of this book.

FOR YOUR ENJOYMENT

You will find plenty of entertaining reading among these lists; all the books mentioned have been enjoyed and recommended by people of your own age. All can be ordered at your public library and most are available cheaply in paperback editions. The sections do not pretend to include all the good books of any one type; the aim is only to suggest some of the most enjoyable. Your teacher or librarian will suggest others, and when you find authors that please you particularly, you can read other books by them.

Adventure

King Solomon's Mines	H. Rider Haggard
Alan Quatermain	H. Rider Haggard
She	H. Rider Haggard
Lost Horizon	James Hilton
The War of the Worlds	H. G. Wells
The Invisible Man	H. G. Wells
☾ *The Lost World*	Sir Arthur Conan Doyle
Prester John	John Buchan
The Power House	John Buchan
John Macnab	John Buchan
Round the World in Eighty Days	Jules Verne
20,000 Leagues Under the Sea	Jules Verne
Tschiffely's Ride	A. S. Tschiffely
The African Queen	C. S. Forester
The Blue Ice	Hammond Innes
The White South	Hammond Innes
Campbell's Kingdom	Hammond Innes
Cone of Silence	David Beaty
The Proving Flight	David Beaty
The Prisoner of Zenda	Anthony Hope
Rupert of Hentzau	Anthony Hope
Beau Geste	P. C. Wren
The Four Feathers	A. E. W. Mason

Animals

Seal Morning	Rowena Farre
Ring of Bright Water	Gavin Maxwell
Just Elephants	William Bazé
The Bafut Beagles	Gerald Durrell
The Overloaded Ark	Gerald Durrell
The Drunken Forest	Gerald Durrell
Born Free	Joy Adamson
Zoo Quest for a Dragon	David Attenborough
Thurber's Dogs	James Thurber
Tarka the Otter	Henry Williamson
The Story of San Michele	Axel Munthe
Carcajou	Rutherford Montgomery
Jock of the Bushveld	Sir Percy Fitzpatrick
Cranes Flying South	N. Karazin
National Velvet	Enid Bagnold
Bandoola	J. H. Williams
The Spotted Deer	J. H. Williams
Man Meets Dog	Konrad Lorenz
White Fang	Jack London
☾ *Leopard in My Lap*	Michaela Denis

273

Crime and detection

The Thirty-Nine Steps	John Buchan
Greenmantle	John Buchan
Huntingtower	John Buchan
The Island of Sheep	John Buchan
✗ *The Complete Sherlock Holmes Short Stories*	Sir Arthur Conan Doyle
The Hound of the Baskervilles	Sir Arthur Conan Doyle
The Sign of Four	Sir Arthur Conan Doyle
The Father Brown Stories	G. K. Chesterton
Traitor's Purse	Margery Allingham
Tiger in the Smoke	Margery Allingham
Look to the Lady	Margery Allingham
Mystery Mile	Margery Allingham
The Beckoning Lady	Margery Allingham
Mr. Campion (and other stories)	Margery Allingham
Artists in Crime	Ngaio Marsh
A Man Lay Dead	Ngaio Marsh
Death in Ecstasy	Ngaio Marsh
Death and the Dancing Footman	Ngaio Marsh
The Mystery of the Blue Train	Agatha Christie
The Murder of Roger Ackroyd	Agatha Christie
The Moving Toyshop	Edmund Crispin
Trent's Last Case	E. C. Bentley
Inspector French's Greatest Case	Freeman Wills Croft
The Thin Man	Dashiell Hammett
The Four Just Men	Edgar Wallace
The Man from the Sea	Michael Innes
Bulldog Drummond	Sapper (H. C. McNeill)
Black Gang	Sapper (H. C. McNeill)
The Woman in White	Wilkie Collins
High Wind in Jamaica	Richard Hughes

Exploration and endeavour

⌀ *The Silent World*	J. Y. Cousteau
Under the Red Sea	Hans Hass
South	Sir Ernest Shackleton
The Crossing of Antarctica	Vivian Fuchs and Sir Edmund Hillary
High Adventure	Sir Edmund Hillary
The Ascent of Everest	Sir John Hunt
The Kon-Tiki Expedition	Thor Heyerdahl
Columbus Sails	C. Walter Hodges
Mr. Oram's Story	Aubrey De Selincourt
The Kanchengjunga Adventure	Frank Smythe
News from Tartary	Peter Fleming
Brazilian Adventure	Peter Fleming

Exploration and endeavour

The Voyage of the Beagle	Charles Darwin
Scott's Last Expedition	pub. Murray
The Long Walk	Slavomir Rawicz
No Picnic on Mount Kenya	Felice Benuzzi

Especially for girls

Vanity Fair	W. M. Thackeray
Jane Eyre	Charlotte Brontë
Wuthering Heights	Emily Brontë
Northanger Abbey	Jane Austen
Pride and Prejudice	Jane Austen
Return to Jalna	Mazo De La Roche
Whiteoaks	Mazo De La Roche
The Houses in Between	Howard Spring
Regency Buck	Georgette Heyer
The Talisman Ring	Georgette Heyer
Mariana	Monica Dickens
One Pair of Hands	Monica Dickens
One Pair of Feet	Monica Dickens
The Happy Prisoner	Monica Dickens
The Egg and I	Betty MacDonald
The Plague and I	Betty MacDonald
The Lonely Plough	Constance Holme
✗ *Beautiful End*	Constance Holme
Crump Folk Going Home	Constance Holme
The Splendid Fairing	Constance Holme
Trumpet in the Dust	Constance Holme
South Riding	Winifred Holtby
Daddy Long Legs	Jean Webster
The Radium Woman	Eleanor Doorly
The Small Woman	Allan Burgess
Kathleen Ferrier	W. Ferrier and N. Cardus
The Old Wives' Tale	Arnold Bennett
Lark Rise to Candleford	Flora Thompson
The Secret Garden	F. Hodgson Burnett
Green Dolphin Country	Elizabeth Goudge
Life with Father	Clarence Day
Beau Brocade	Baroness Orczy
⟫*Fifteen*	Beverley Cleary
A Town Like Alice	Nevil Shute
A Girl of the Limberlost	Gene Stratton Porter
Freckles	Gene Stratton Porter
The Diary of Anne Frank	Anne Frank
Tess of the D'Urbervilles	Thomas Hardy

275

Historical

The Three Musketeers	Alexander Dumas
The Count of Monte Cristo	Alexander Dumas
A Tale of Two Cities	Charles Dickens
The Scarlet Pimpernel	Baroness Orczy
Eldorado	Baroness Orczy
Sweet Witch	Richard Llewellyn
Jim Davis	John Masefield
Under the Red Robe	Stanley J. Weyman
Frenchman's Creek	Daphne du Maurier
Jamaica Inn	Daphne du Maurier
Rodney Stone	Sir Arthur Conan Doyle
The Corinthian	Georgette Heyer
Powder and Patch	Georgette Heyer
Scaramouche	Rafael Sabatini
Captain Blood	Rafael Sabatini
Death to the French	C. S. Forester
The Gun	C. S. Forester

Humour

Guys and Dolls (and other stories)	Damon Runyon
Three Men in a Boat	Jerome K. Jerome
Three Men on the Bummel	Jerome K. Jerome
The Thurber Carnival	James Thurber
Uncle Silas Stories	H. E. Bates
Whisky Galore	Compton Mackenzie
Topper Takes a Trip	Thorne Smith
The Little World of Don Camillo	Giovanni Guareschi
The Honey Siege	Gil Buhet
Very Good Jeeves	P. G. Wodehouse
Carry On Jeeves	P. G. Wodehouse
My Man Jeeves	P. G. Wodehouse
Laughing Gas	P. G. Wodehouse
Summer Lightning	P. G. Wodehouse

Miscellaneous fiction

Animal Farm	George Orwell
The Bridge of San Luis Rey	Thornton Wilder
Kipps	H. G. Wells
The History of Mr. Polly	H. G. Wells
The Card	Arnold Bennett
The Man Who was Thursday	G. K. Chesterton
The Crowthers of Bankdam	Thomas Armstrong
Fame is the Spur	Howard Spring
How Green was my Valley	Richard Llewellyn
The Good Companions	J. B. Priestley

Miscellaneous fiction

The House Under the Water	Francis Brett Young
The Old Man and the Sea	Ernest Hemingway
A Kid for Two Farthings	Wolf Mankowitz
The Trumpet Major	Thomas Hardy
The Flight of the Heron	D. K. Broster
A Man of Property	John Galsworthy
The Horse's Mouth	Joyce Cary

Miscellaneous non-fiction

Silver Ley	Adrian Bell
Corduroy	Adrian Bell
The Cherry Tree	Adrian Bell
Memoirs of a Foxhunting Man	Siegfried Sassoon
Autobiography	Neville Cardus
Second Innings	Neville Cardus
Sweet Thames Run Softly	Robert Gibbings
Coming Down the Wye	Robert Gibbings
Small Calendars	J. B. H. Peel
The Compleat Angler	Izaak Walton
The Natural History of Selborne	Gilbert White

Science fiction

The First Men in the Moon	H. G. Wells
The Time Machine	H. G. Wells
The Golden Apples of the Sun (and other stories)	Ray Bradbury
The Day of the Tryffids	John Wyndham
The Kraken Wakes	John Wyndham
Aspects of Science Fiction	ed. G. D. Doherty
Out of the Silent Planet	C. S. Lewis

Seafaring

Mr. Midshipman Hornblower	C. S. Forester
Lieutenant Hornblower	C. S. Forester
A Ship of the Line	C. S. Forester
Flying Colours	C. S. Forester
The Commodore	C. S. Forester
The Happy Return	C. S. Forester
The Ship	C. S. Forester
The Cruel Sea	Nicholas Monsarrat
H.M.S. Marlborough Will Enter Harbour	Nicholas Monsarrat
H.M.S. Ulysses	Alistair Maclean
Typhoon	Joseph Conrad
Youth	Joseph Conrad

Seafaring

End of the Tether	Joseph Conrad
The Brassbounder	D. W. Bone
South Latitude	F. D. Ommanney
A Gipsy of the Horn	Rex Clements
Midshipman Quinn	Showell Styles
Quinn of the Fury	Showell Styles
The Last Grain Race	P. H. Newby
Moby Dick (Abridged edition)	Herman Melville
Nautilus 90 North	Cdr. W. R. Anderson

Supernatural

Tales of Mystery and Imagination	Edgar Allan Poe
Ghost Stories of an Antiquary	M. R. James
Selected Tales	Aigernon Blackwood
The Turn of the Screw	Henry James
The Picture of Dorian Gray	Oscar Wilde
More Ghost Stories	M. R. James
Lord Halifax's Ghost Book	Lord Halifax
The First Ghost Book	Lady Cynthia Asquith

War

Brown on Resolution	C. S. Forester
The General	C. S. Forester
The Wooden Horse	Eric Williams
Reach for the Sky	Paul Brickhill
Flames in the Sky	Pierre Clostermann
Appointment with Venus	Gerard Tickell
The Bridge on the River Kwai	Pierre Boule
One of Our Submarines	Edward Young
The Jungle is Neutral	F. Spencer Chapman
The Last Enemy	Richard Hillary
The Small Back Room	Nigel Balchin
The Guns of Navarone	Alistair Maclean

Western

Montana Rides	Evan Evans
The Song of the Whip	Evan Evans
The Big Range	Jack Schaeffer
The Pioneers	Jack Schaeffer
Riders of the Plains	Max Brand
The Coming of Cassidy	Clarence E. Mulford
Hopalong Cassidy	Clarence E. Mulford
Code of the West	Zane Grey
Fighting Caravans	Zane Grey
Arizona Ames	Zane Grey